Dedication

This work is dedicated with affection and esteem to my beloved friend, Dr. W.A. Criswell, Pastor, First Baptist Church, Dallas, Texas. He has been my spiritual "dad" in the ministry, an advisor, counselor, and helper in time of need. He is the greatest expositor of the Word of God in my generation. He planted in my heart the need for real, down to earth, Bible Study in the Church. To me he is the effervescent man of God, with a heart overflowing with the love of our Lord Jesus Christ.

He is truly a "Character of the Bible."

A.B.S.

GREAT CHARACTERS OF THE BIBLE

A BIBLE STUDY FOR THE LAY PUPIL AND THE LAY TEACHER

Alan B. Stringfellow, Lit. D.

ISBN 1-56322-046-6 paperback

HENSLEY
PUBLISHING
6116 E. 32nd St.
Tulsa, OK 74134

What This Study Will Do For You

You are about to begin an exciting journey through the Bible, involving real people. You will find a no more fascinating and rewarding experience than to trace in the lines of real men and women the fusion of God's divine providence with the human personality. You will study characters whose biographies have been preserved by divine inspiration in the Word of God. "All these things happened to them for examples: and they are written for our learning . . ." (I Corinthians 10:11).

You will learn, through the study of the sixty-one characters, God's methods in selecting and training people for His sovereign purpose. In these characters, you will see the victories, defeats, joys and sorrows of your own life. God enters into the affairs of men, taking their failures and using them as a refining fire to bring about His ultimate purpose.

God made man with a free will and man is always free to act, but never to act so as to frustrate His ultimate plan.

God's method has always been the use of people in achieving His purpose. You will see this vividly in this study of Bible characters. He does not always select the most brilliant, the most successful; but always He selects persons who are sensitive to His will and purpose and who have capacity for great faith.

As you study these people during this year, remember that you should never attribute to them superhuman qualities. They were people, not spiritual giants, as we often portray them in Bible stories. They were "people of like passions," ordinary people, who became extraordinary by the power and direction of God.

So, this study will teach you:

- How God uses ordinary people just like you
- How He chooses the weak at times instead of the strong
- How He sometimes has to break people to get their attention
- How God directs lives to bring about His ultimate will
- How the Adamic nature, the natural man, is depicted in the Bible. (Nothing is left out. The Bible tells the complete story, both bad and good.)
- How God always keeps His promises to people
- How the plan of God for our redemption is the main emphasis. (The Lord promised a "Seed" and He used people, selected a nation, a tribe, a family to give to us His Son, the Lord Jesus.)
- How everything in the Bible concerning people is relevant and of spiritual value
- How to become acquainted with some of God's people in a more intimate way
- How God deals with our imperfections and limitations
- How the entire Word of God is to us, for us, and for our learning (On almost every page of the Bible you find people. God speaks through them to us, because we understand other people.)
- How the will of God is the most important thing in life.

So you are about to see God's plan of redemption unfold, from Genesis to Revelation. In Bible times, the plan involved people. His plan still involves people: all the ones who know His Son are to reach the ones who do not yet know Christ.

Every character in this study is a Bible Story in itself. And since everyone likes a story, you'll find this material excellent for families. With all the family studying together (5th grade and up), you have a ready made setting for training children. Just make sure that you always include the Bible facts when you retell these wonderful stories.

Introduction For Students and Teachers

To receive maximum knowledge and inspiration during the next 52 weeks, heed the following suggestions. They are designed to help you become a disciplined disciple of God's Word.

"MUSTS" FOR THE STUDENT

— Attend every class session for 52 weeks.

— Read the assigned portion at the end of each lesson.

— Review your notes from the previous week's study.

— Mark your Bible with key references from one Scripture to another.

— Take notes in class.

— Search the Scripture and mark references in class. Write in the Scriptures in this notebook where lines are provided.

— Promise the Lord at least two or three hours each week for reading the assigned Scripture for the lesson and doing your homework.

Why these "musts?" Because we have expected too little from our Bible students the past several years. The time has come for Christians who mean business for the Lord to devote themselves to the study of His Word and to learning the basic principles that we all should know. Promise yourself and promise God you will live up to these "musts."

"MUSTS" FOR THE TEACHER

First you must prepare yourself spiritually by reading —

— I Corinthians 2:12-14

— Ephesians 1:17-18

— John 14:26

— John 16:12-16

These Scriptures will assure you as the teacher that the Holy Spirit will guide you and teach you as you study His Word and impart it to your pupils.

If you are in a church, the program is best taught to teachers by the pastor, minister of education, Sunday School superintendent or a specially selected teacher. This should be done on a weekday evening prior to the coming Lord's Day.

Part of the discipline of this course of study is that you attend each evening session each week without exception.

You must read the entire assignment for the next lesson, found at the close of each lesson study. The author has suggested that you read the chapters to be taught the following week; he has also listed key verses for pupils if they are unable to read a chapter in its entirety.

You must take notes and search out Scripture references. You must also be prepared to answer questions, add to or take away from the questions as you feel is necessary for your age group.

What's more, you must —

— Stay with the subject of each lesson.

— Not be afraid of being too elementary for your pupils.

— Stay on the major points, not minor ones.

— Keep the lesson teaching as simple as possible with all age groups.

— Not change the lesson outline. You may add illustrations and ideas, but do not change the major points of the outline.

PUBLISHER'S STUDY NOTE

It is important to note the author's premise in developing this course of study; namely, that *the Bible is the divinely inspired Word of God.* Nothing can take it's place.

Thus, *Great Characters of the Bible* should be read neither *in place of* the Bible nor as a study *about* the Bible. Rather you should use it as a guide that takes you *into* the Bible and involves you in the study of God's Word, resulting in your understanding it better and appreciating it more.

You will also note that the text of this manual appears in outline rather than exposition. This permits quick coverage of the controlling thoughts of the book under study along with the key verses, the central message and the major themes.

— Use your own personality and let the Holy Spirit use you as you teach.

— Expect your pupils to do their part.

You should teach at least 55 minutes every lesson. Even if you have to revamp your class schedule to teach for 55 minutes, it can be done. The assembly periods can be made shorter. It isn't necessary to have a devotional before going to Bible Study. One song and a prayer is sufficient for the assembly period. Class absentees and other business should be handled at class meetings. Make your Bible study period an hour of concentrated Bible study.

May God bless you, pupil or teacher, as you begin your study in *Great Characters of the Bible*. Let the Holy Spirit teach you both.

Because your manual is in this form, you will get maximum benefit if your study is under the direction of a teacher. The teacher in turn should be prepared by attending weekly teachers' meetings taught bay the pastor or other capable assistant.

Another major advantage of the outline form is that it allows the teacher far more latitude than does straight exposition.

In a few instances, you may find that the text differs slightly with your own theological beliefs. Please do not allow these occasions to over-shadow the overall value of this excellent course. Instead, use these differences as a point around which to further refine your own theology. This adds still more value to the program, for it enables you to see denominational differences.

In your study and discussion, always be guided by the Holy Spirit, and you will profit immensely from this work, despite differences in interpretation.

The publisher feels that *Great Characters of the Bible* is the inspired work of a devoted man of God.

FOREWORD

Great Characters of the Bible deals with many characters of Scripture — going back to Adam and proceeding through the Bible once again to Paul and the beloved Disciple, John.

This study deals with the lives of real men and women, showing their human frailties and personalities and God's divine providence in their lives.

As you study through this book, you will gain helpful insights into the principles for effective Christian living and service today. In the experiences of God's characters, we can see ourselves — in victories and defeats. In their lives, recorded for us by the Holy Spirit in His Word, we can learn God's eternal sovereign plan and purpose for us.

We must not attribute superhuman qualities nor an abundance of sanctity to these characters in Scripture. All of them were people with the Adamic nature — "men of like passion" — in most cases; they were ordinary people who became *extraordinary* by the power and sovereign will of God.

Dr. F. B. Meyer of Britain once said, "to recruit a dwindling congregation, to sustain interest in a crowded congregation, to awaken new devotion to the Bible, and to touch the many chords of human life there is nothing to be compared with the retelling of the stories of the Bible heroes and saints."

Dr. C. E. Macartney says, "the great advantage of preaching (teaching) Bible characters is the fact that you summon these characters and allow them to preach (teach) for you."

The Bible tells the whole story of God's dealing with His creatures. Once He chooses a man or woman, He allows both the good and the bad of their characters to be recorded in His Holy Word.

Similarly, He accepts us as we are, good and bad, on the basis of our faith in His son, our Blessed Lord.

I wrote these studies with the pupil in mind. "Pupils" are those of any age who can read and enjoy the story, from approximately 9 years up through the oldest adult.

I have used resources available in the writing and teaching of these lessons. Among them are the distinguished works of Herbert Lockyer, *All The Men of The Bible* and *All The Women of The Bible;* Edith Deen's, *All of the Women of the Bible;* the sermons and tapes of Dr. W. A. Criswell which I have preserved from his ministry; and finally the radio Bible study notes of Dr. J. Vernon McGee.

Plato once said about borrowing thoughts: "Bees cull their several sweets from this flower and that blossom, here and there where they can find them, but they make the honey which is purely their own. So he who borrows from others and blends together what shall be absolutely his own, he is not obliged to discover whence he had his materials, but only to produce what he has done with them."

The task of gathering this material, putting it into a down-to-earth teachable form, trying and proving it by teaching it to lay teachers and pupils, has been an exciting adventure for me. Credit is hereby given to the above — anything else in this study has been taken from a background of years of teaching, preaching and writing.

Above all else, the Word of God has been the main source of these lessons.

Alan B. Stringfellow, Lit. D.

INDEX

About Photocopying This Book

Lesson 1
"Adam"

NOTES

(Where lines are provided, look up Scripture and fill in the entire Scripture or the main Truth of the passage.)

1. **THE MEANING OF THE NAME:**

   Adam means "of the ground — red earth."

2. **BASIC SCRIPTURES:**

   Genesis 1:26-31; 2:7; 2:15-20; 3:1 to 5:5; Romans 3:12-13; I Corinthians 15:22; 15:45-49; I Thessalonians 5:23

3. **FAMILY BACKGROUND:**

   Adam was the first human son of God (Luke 3:38). He was made by God out of the materials of the universe, and life was granted by God. He had no family background since he was the first man.

4. **WHAT THE OLD TESTAMENT SAYS ABOUT ADAM:**

   (1) He was created by the Trinity (Genesis 1:26).

   "And God said, Let *us* make man in *our* image, after *our* likeness . . ."
   The "us" and "our" are plural — God the Father, God the Son and God the Holy Spirit.

   (2) He was created in the "image" and "likeness" of God.

   "Image" means "representation" of God. "Likeness" means the "character" or "model" of God.

   Look up Ephesians 4:24 _____

   _____

   Also Colossians 3:10 _____

   _____

   (3) He was formed out of the dust, and God breathed into Adam and he became a living soul (Genesis 2:7).

   Jesus confirmed this in Matthew 19:4 _____

   _____

   _____

   (4) Adam was created as a trinity (both image and likeness), having a body, spirit and soul (Genesis 2:7).

   Look up I Thessalonians 5:23 _____

   _____

   Here Paul says we, too, are body, spirit and soul.

   (5) God made the earth for man, and then man for the earth (Genesis 2:8 and 15)

   Adam was the crown of God's creation.

   (6) God had told Adam to be fruitful and multiply, and subdue the earth and all things on the earth (Genesis 1:28-30).

   So God took from the side of Adam—Woman—and gave her to Adam (Genesis 2:21-25).

   Adam did not name the Woman until after the fall. Then he called her name Eve, meaning "the mother of all living" (Genesis 3:20). *This name shows the faith of Adam.*

(7) In Genesis 2:15-17, God placed a *limit* on man.

Man was to be obedient to God or he would die.

What was the tree named which man was not to eat? _____

_____

When all around was life, God spoke of death.

(8) The temptation and fall is found in Genesis 3:1-7.

When Eve saw that the "tree was good for food, pleasant to the eyes, made one wise, she gave also to her husband and he did eat" (verse 6).

Then they realized that they were naked and they began to cover their sin (verse 7).

(9) God immediately sought them, and it has been that way since (Genesis 3:8-13).

(10) Adam, with his wife, received the promise of the Savior (Genesis 3:15).

This verse, translated into laymen's terms, could read:

> *"And there will be intense hatred between Satan (thy seed) and Christ (her seed). Eventually Christ will crush the head of Satan, and Satan will only bruise the heel of Christ."*

THIS IS THE FIRST DIRECT PROPHECY OF CHRIST.
(We shall consider this again in Lesson 2.)

(11) Because of the fall (sin), Adam is told of the curse upon the earth (Genesis 3:17), and the pronouncement of death (verse 19).

(12) God covered their sin (Genesis 3:21).

Notice that "God made coats of skin." From the beginning *"something had to die to cover sin."*

(13) Adam had two sons, Cain and Abel.

In Genesis 4 you find recorded the extreme sinfulness of sin — the first murder. *Cain was sent from the presence of the Lord. He knew his wife and she conceived.*

Cain's wife is always asked about in casual conversation. Where did she come from? You find that answer in Genesis 5:4.

(14) Adam died at 930 years of age (Genesis 5:5).

5. **WHAT THE NEW TESTAMENT TEACHES US ABOUT ADAM:**

(1) In Luke 3:23-38, the genealogy of Christ is traced back to Adam.

(2) Sin entered the world by one man, Adam.

Romans 5:12 _____

_____

(3) The First and Second Adams.

The first Adam was made a living soul (I Corinthians 15:45).

Look up Genesis 2:7 _____

_____

Now read I Corinthians 15:46-47. The first man, Adam, was earthy. The Second Adam was and is the Lord from Heaven.

Read Romans 5:15-21. Here we find that even though all of us are sinners, there is an abundance of grace for all who will receive the Second Adam, *our Lord Jesus Christ.*

Read I Corinthians 15:21-22 and write the meaning of these words to you personally:

_____

Remember, the first Adam was **made** a living soul by the breath of God (Genesis 2:7). While the Last Adam, Jesus, was a **life giving spirit.** He was and is the fountain of life and He gives that life to others (John 1:4; John 5:24).

Look up John 10:10 _____

_____

In the first Adam all die — but in Christ (the Second Adam) all are made alive.

Look up, again, I Corinthians 15:45 and write in the verse:

_____

_____

6. **THE LESSON YOU SHOULD LEARN FROM ADAM:**

The Principle of the Second before the First.

Early in the study of characters in the Bible, we need to understand a principle in God's Word. It is the "Principle of the Second before the First." In I Corinthians 1:26-27, we see that God chooses the "nothings" for His purpose. Only thus is the self praise of the "natural" man destroyed. For this reason, it is a pervading characteristic of the whole course of redemption that God keeps on choosing the younger before the elder, sets the smaller in priority to the greater, and chooses the second before the first. For example:

- not Cain, but Abel and his substitute Seth;
- not Japheth, but Shem (Genesis 10:21);
- not Ishmael, but Isaac (Genesis 17:19);
- not Esau, but Jacob (Genesis 25:23);
- not Manasseh, but Ephraim (Genesis 48:14);
- not Aaron, but Moses (Exodus 7:7);
- not Eliab, but David (I Samuel 16:6-13);
- not the first king, Saul, but the second, David (I Samuel 15:28);
- not the Old Covenant, but the New (Hebrews 8:13);
- not the first Adam, but the Second Adam
  (I Corinthians 15:45).

Thus, God continually "takes away the first that He may establish the second" (Hebrews 10:9). He chooses for Himself the weak of the world so as to put to shame the strong (I Corinthians 1:27). He calls the last and makes it first and the first becomes the last (Matthew 19:30). All of this comes to pass so that "no flesh shall glory before Him," but that, "he who glories, let him glory in the Lord" (I Corinthians 1:29-31).

As we proceed through the Bible characters, may this principle help you understand the mind and workings of God among us.

CAN YOU REMEMBER?

1. What does Adam mean?
2. How was Adam created?
3. Who created Adam?
4. What made him different — a soul?
5. How did sin enter the world?
6. Who is the Second Adam?
7. What "principle" did you learn today?

YOUR NEXT ASSIGNMENT:

1. Read Genesis 2 through 5:5; I Corinthians 11:3-12; I Timothy 2:15 & Ephesians 5:21-33.
2. Review and restudy the lesson on Adam.
3. Mark your Bible where new truths were learned.
4. Pray for the Holy Spirit to teach you every truth you need.

Lesson 2
"Eve"

(Where lines are provided, look up the Scripture and fill in the entire *Scripture or the main Truth of the passage.)*

1. **THE MEANING OF THE NAME:**

   There are three names applied to Adam's wife:

   > **"Woman"** — She shall be called "Isha" because she was taken out of "Ish." ("Woman" taken out of "man.")

   > **"Adam"** — Both Eve and her husband are called Adam. (Genesis 1:27 and 5:2 - note: "he called *their* name Adam.")

   > **"Eve"** — Eve was the name given her after the fall (Genesis 3:20). Adam named her "Eve," "the mother of all living — life giving — the mother of all who have life." Thus her life is in *all* of us.

   Why didn't Adam let her remain known as "Mrs. Adam?" Because he gave her a name which expresses the prophetic life of the seed of the woman through which eternal life was to come.

2. **BASIC SCRIPTURES:**

   Genesis 2 through Genesis 5:5; I Corinthians 11:3-12; I Timothy 2:15; Ephesians 5:21-33.

3. **FAMILY BACKGROUND:**

   Eve was the first woman to live upon the earth. She was a product of divine creation. The first female to be *born* was the daughter of Eve (Genesis 5:4). Remember, Eve was not "born" but was created out of Adam. In Genesis 2:21-22, you read how God made woman.

   The word "rib" is used in verse 21 in the King James Version, but no other place in the Bible is that word ever translated "rib." Everywhere else in the Bible, the word used is "side," such as the "side of the tabernacle," "the side of the Ark," or the "side of the altar." The translation here in Genesis 2:21 should also be "side." *God took out of the side of Adam and created Eve.*

   When Adam saw her, he gave to us her background in Genesis 2:23.

   _____

   _____

   _____

4. **WHAT THE OLD TESTAMENT SAYS ABOUT EVE:**

   (1) As we have seen, she was *the first woman*.
   God had said for them "to multiply" (Genesis 1:28).

   (2) She was the *first wife* (Genesis 2:18).
   Now, write in that all important verse:

   Genesis 2:24 _____

   _____

   _____

   (3) She was a "helpmeet" — by the *side* of, not *above* man and not *below* man.
   Since God, in His creation, created them male and female, they were ONE FLESH.

This Biblical view should make us realize that their two hearts beat as one for each other. Marriage should still mean "they shall be one flesh." Marriage, then, is not merely a civil contract, *but a divine institution.*

(4)   **Eve was *created without sin* — coming from the hand of God.**

Being the first woman, Eve had no inherited sin — she was pure and holy.

However, she became the world's *first sinner,* and introduced sin to her children; thus, all since Eve have been "shapen in iniquity; and in sin did my mother conceive me" (Psalms 51:5).

(5)   **Eve was the first one satan attacked on earth.**

Satan began his rebellion on earth by starting his attack upon Eve — by casting doubt, suspicion. (Remember that the serpent, in Eden, was a beautiful creature, but it became a writhing reptile *as a result of the fall.* This creature was *used* by Satan to cause the fall of man.)

Note the way Satan works:

Genesis 3:1   "Yea, hath God said" — casting doubt.
Genesis 3:2-3   "Neither shall ye touch it" — added to the Word.
Genesis 3:4   "Ye shall not surely die" — the first lie.
Genesis 3:5   "Ye shall be as gods, knowing good and evil" — the appeal to pride.

Now Satan strikes!

Genesis 3:6   ● "she saw the tree was *good for food*"
               ● "pleasant to the eyes"
               ● "a tree to be desired to make one wise"
               ● "SHE TOOK - AND GAVE TO HER HUS-BAND WITH HER; AND HE DID EAT."

In this one verse we see the fall of man and also the way Satan *still* tempts us.

Notice: ● "food" — lust of the flesh.
        ● "pleasant to the eyes" — lust of the eyes.
        ● "make one wise" — pride of life.

Look at I John 2:16 _____

_____

_____

(6)   **Eve made the first clothes.**

After the fall, they *saw* that they were naked. Fig leaves were the material used to cover their bodies. In Genesis 2:25, "they were not ashamed — they were both naked;" but here in Genesis 3:7 they *saw* their transgression in partaking of "the tree of knowledge of good and evil." God told them not to do it in Genesis 2:17.

After they covered themselves with fig leaves, they began making excuses — trying to cover their act with words:

Notice: ● "they heard the voice — walking — and they hid themselves" (Genesis 3:8).
        ● "Adam — where art thou?" (God seeking the lost) (Genesis 3:9).
        ● "I was afraid — and I hid" (Genesis 3:10).

Write in Genesis 3:11 _____

_____

Now notice how Adam blames Eve and she in turn blames the serpent — (verses 12 and 13). Underline these two verses.

From this point in Scripture, Adam, the federal head of the human race, *is responsible for Adamic sin.*

6

(7) Eve was the first to receive the divine prophecy of Christ.

(Also studied in lesson 1)

Genesis 3:15 is the first prophecy of Christ. This Scripture could be paraphrased so a young child might understand as follows:

"And I (God) will put hatred between Satan and Christ (woman's seed). In the end Christ will crush the head of Satan, and Satan will only bruise the heel of Christ."

(8) Eve was the first mother (Genesis 4:1-2).

God had said in Genesis 3:16 that "in sorrow thou shalt bring forth children."

She had two sons, Cain and Abel. Eve was the *first mother to lose both sons* in one day. Abel died at the hands of Cain. Cain became a fugitive and vagabond — away from his family.

5. **WHAT THE NEW TESTAMENT SAYS ABOUT EVE:**

   (1) Jesus used the same words that God had given to the first man and woman.

   Look up Matthew 19:4-5 _____

   _____

   _____

   (Thus Jesus confirms the Genesis narrative.)

   (2) Paul compares the church and Eve.

   Look at II Corinthians 11:2-3 _____

   _____

   _____

   (3) Paul uses the same words as the Lord God did in Genesis 2:24 and as Jesus did in Matthew 19:4-5.

   Paul compares this man and wife relationship to illustrate the love of Christ for His bride, the church.

   Write in Ephesians 5:31 _____

   _____

   _____

   and Ephesians 5:25 _____

   _____

6. **THE LESSONS YOU SHOULD LEARN FROM EVE:**

   (1) Satan is *real,* subtle in his approach.
   (2) We should love the one God has given to us to love as we love ourselves.
   (3) The love of Christ for His church.
   (4) Eve was a real person with real emotions. Neither she nor her husband are myths, but real people — with real children — who suffered real heartache.

CAN YOU REMEMBER?

1. What does "Eve" mean?
2. What other names are applied to Eve?
3. How was Eve created?
4. Was she born?
5. Eve was tempted in three ways. Can you name them?

YOUR NEXT ASSIGNMENT:

1. Read Genesis 4 and 5: Luke 3:38; Hebrews 11:4.
2. Review and restudy the lesson on Eve.
3. Mark your Bible and make marginal references where one Scripture shines light on another.
4. Read all you can on these men: Cain, Abel and Seth. We shall study all three in our next lesson.

Lesson 3
"Cain, Abel and Seth"
The First Children
Born In The World

(Where lines are provided, look up the Scripture and write the Scripture or its meaning in the space provided.)

1. **THE MEANING OF THE NAMES:**
   - Cain means "acquisition" or "possession."
   - Abel means "breath" or "vapor."
   - Seth means "substitute."

2. **BASIC SCRIPTURES:**
   Genesis 4 and 5; Luke 3:38; Hebrews 11:4; I John 3:11-15; Jude 11.

3. **FAMILY BACKGROUND:**
   After God created Adam and Eve, He said to them, "Be fruitful and multiply, and replenish the earth" (Genesis 1:28). "Thou shalt bring forth children" (Genesis 3:16).

   We must remember that Adam and Eve had no children until *after the fall* in the Garden of Eden. As parents, Adam and Eve had no birth, no childhood, no youth, but appeared as perfect fully developed adults. From those two, we have the population of the human race, beginning with Cain and Abel.

   Genesis is the book of "beginnings" *and this lesson shows the beginning of family life.*

   (We shall examine the three boys under both the Old and New Testament references to them.)

4. **WHAT THE OLD TESTAMENT SAYS ABOUT THESE THREE:**
   (1) Cain - the first child born to natural parents.
   Cain was born after the transgression, or fall, and was therefore "born in sin." The fallen nature is seen in this first child.

   Eve's statement in Genesis 4:1 — "I have gotten a man from the Lord" — intimates that even then, she thought Genesis 3:15 might be fulfilled in her firstborn.

   Genesis 4:2 tells us that "Cain was a tiller of the ground." His vocation was agriculture; he labored in the field.

   What did Cain bring to the Lord? Look up Genesis 4:3

   _____

   _____

   He was right in his desire to give an offering, but wrong in trying to give a product of *his own ingenuity and labor.*

   Genesis 4:5 tells us that God did not "respect" or accept, Cain's offering.

   Because his offering was not accepted, he became mad (wroth) and committed the first murder. So the first child became the first murderer and gave the earth its first grave (Genesis 4:8).

   Look up Genesis 4:9 _____

   _____

In Genesis 4:11-15, God set a mark on Cain. Exactly what it was, Scripture does not say. It was a mark that made Cain feel the judgment of God — yet, it was mixed with mercy. He dwelt in the land of Nod and was the father of the first civilization.

(2) **Abel - the second child of Adam and Eve was, by calling, a shepherd — a possessor of flocks.**

Genesis 4:4 _____

_____

The Lord accepted Abel's offering (verse 4).

We learn here that the offering brought by Abel showed the character of the offerer. It showed the surrender of the heart to God — by offering nothing which he had made, but *offering something which God had given him to care for – an offering of blood sacrifice*.

Because God accepted Abel's offering, Cain murdered him (verse 8).

Notice what God said in Genesis 4:10 _____

_____

_____

He was the first victim of jealousy and murder and, therefore, the *first one of the human race to die*.

(3) **Seth - God gave to Eve another son called "appointed" or Seth.**

Note what Eve says about Seth in Genesis 4:25 _____

_____

_____

Seth became the "appointed" one to take the place of Abel. The Godly line, through which the "Seed of the woman" was to come, was reestablished in Seth.

Follow the genealogy of Jesus in Luke 3:23-38. You will find Seth in verse 38. This shows the line of Christ back to Adam — all of them born "after his kind." Adam could be no myth — if so, then Jesus is a myth.

5. **WHAT THE NEW TESTAMENT SAYS ABOUT THESE:**

(1) **Cain - The New Testament has some valuable lessons for us in reference to Cain.**

Look up I John 3:11-12 _____

_____

_____

_____

"The way of Cain" is found in Jude 11. Here "the way of Cain" is associated with false teachers. The apostate (false) teachers are those who speak "of those things they know naturally" (verse 10). Cain was a "religious" but natural man who did not please God.

The sin of Cain was merely an echo of his parents' sin.

(2) **Abel - The blood of Abel is placed in Scripture with the shed blood of Christ, which is *better* than Abel's.**

Abel's blood cried out for vengeance, but the blood of Christ cries out for mercy, atonement, forgiveness.

Look up Hebrews 12:24 _____

_____

Jesus refers to "righteous Abel" in Matthew 23:35.

Note again I John 3:12 (written above). Abel is listed in the grand "hall of faith" of Hebrews. Look up Hebrews 11:4. He is the first mentioned in the great list of this chapter.

So Abel was "righteous," said Jesus, as did the author of Hebrews, and the beloved Apostle John. Why?

Because he offered God the best of his flock. He offered, by faith, a sacrifice of blood.

(3) **Seth - The only mention of Seth in the New Testament is found in Luke 3:38.**

He did become the substitute for "righteous Abel" and *is thus found in the line of our Lord.*

Eve accepted this child as a special gift from God.

It was from this seed that our **Substitute** came who died for our sins.

6. **THE LESSONS YOU SHOULD LEARN FROM CAIN, ABEL AND SETH:**
   (1) The first parents had the same joys and sorrows as parents today.
   (2) Family life was the first organized unit in society.
   (3) The Adamic nature is passed on to the children - "after his kind."
   (4) Our gifts to the Lord are not as important as *how* we give them.

CAN YOU REMEMBER?

1. What does "Cain" mean?
2. What does "Abel" mean?
3. What does "Seth" mean?
4. When were the first children born?
5. Why was God displeased with the offering of Cain?
6. Why was Abel's offering acceptable?
7. Did you not find the same sinful nature in these first children that you find in the world today? Explain.
8. Which one of the three are in the "hall of faith" in Hebrews 11?

YOUR NEXT ASSIGNMENT:

1. Read Genesis 5:21 through 10:1.
2. Review and restudy the lesson on "the first children."
3. Mark your Bible.
4. Read all you can on Noah and his sons — our next lesson.

Lesson 4
"Noah and His Sons"

(Where lines are provided, look up the Scripture and write the Scripture or its meaning in the space provided.)

1. **THE MEANING OF THE NAMES:**
    - **Noah** means "rest" or "comfort."
    - **Shem** means "renown."
    - **Ham** means "hot."
    - **Japheth** means "beauty" and "let him enlarge."

2. **BASIC SCRIPTURES:**

    Genesis 5:21 through 10:1; Hebrews 11:7; I Peter 3:20; II Peter 2:5; Matthew 24:37-39. Also note Isaiah 54:9; Ezekiel 14:14 and 20; I Chronicles 1.

3. **FAMILY BACKGROUND:**

    Nothing is known of the early life of Noah except that he was the son of Lamech (Genesis 5:28-29). Noah was 500 years old when Shem, Ham and Japheth were born (Genesis 5:32). Noah was from the line of Seth, the tenth man from Adam.

    He lived in a time when the wickedness of man was corrupt; there was universal apostasy and the mixing and marriage of the Godly with the ungodly.

    Noah appeared on the scene as God's man. *God always has His man for every situation and every age.*

4. **WHAT THE OLD TESTAMENT SAYS ABOUT NOAH AND HIS SONS:**

    (1) "Noah found grace in the eyes of the Lord" (Genesis 6:8).

    This is the first mention of "grace" in Scripture. Grace means "favor undeserved" but given by the Lord.

    (2) "Noah walked with God" (Genesis 6:9).

    He was a just and sincere man. Only two men are so described before the flood — Enoch and Noah. Both "walked with God."

    Noah lived just and righteously in spite of the surrounding sin.

    Note Genesis 6:5 _____

    _____

    Also Genesis 6:12 _____

    _____

    (3) God's judgment is plain and it is told to Noah in Genesis 6:13

    "God said to Noah, the end of all flesh is come before men; and the earth is filled with violence through them; and, behold, I will destroy them with the earth." God said He would destroy the wickedness *with* the earth. (The earth is 2/3 water.)

    (4) Noah was obedient to the letter in following God's instructions.

    Note in Genesis 6:14-22; 7:5 that he built the Ark according to God, and selected two of each living thing for the preservation of the species and placed them in the Ark (Genesis 6:19).

    In Genesis 7:2, Noah was told to take seven pairs of the *clean* beasts for *sacrifice,* food and reproduction.

13

(5) **Noah, his wife, his sons and their wives - eight in all - were shut in the Ark (Genesis 7:7 and 16).**

They were safe because they obeyed God.

(6) **Noah and his family were "remembered" by the Lord and the Ark was safe.**

The first thing Noah did after coming out of the Ark was to build the first recorded altar (Genesis 8:20 - notice "clean beasts"). Read and underline

_____

_____

(7) **God's Covenant with Noah (Genesis 8:21 to 9:17).**

(a) God would not curse the ground anymore (Genesis 8:21).

(b) Man was given what we know as "human government." He was made responsible for protecting the sanctity of human life (Genesis 9:1-6).

(c) The order of nature is confirmed (Genesis 8:22; Genesis 9:2).

(d) Meat is added to man's diet (Genesis 9:3-4).

(e) God would not destroy the earth and future generations by water. Note the word "covenant" seven times in verses 9 through 17. Look up Isaiah 54:9.

(f) A declaration is made concerning Ham's son, Canaan. Because of the sin of Ham, Canaan would be a servant to the children of the other two, Shem and Japheth (Genesis 9:25-26).

(g) "Blessed be the Lord God of Shem" (Genesis 9:26). *Jesus, after the flesh, descends from Shem.* "Japheth shall be enlarged" (Genesis 9:27). History has proven that all Europe, a great part of Asia, and America are examples of this enlargement (Note Genesis 9:27: "He (God) shall dwell in the tents of Shem." This is the correct reading).

(h) The token of all this is the "rainbow." I call the "rainbow" God's signature — His promise which He signs in color for us to gaze upon in the sky.

(8) **"Shem," the second oldest son of Noah, was born when Noah was 500 years old (Genesis 5:32).**

The name means "renown," and foreshadowed the greater name "above every name," Jesus. In Genesis 11:10 and on, the generations of Shem lead us to Abram. Matthew 1 takes us from Abraham to Jesus.

(9) **"Ham means "hot."**

The sin of Ham was the result of the sin of his father (Genesis 9:20-29). The result of the sin of Ham has *nothing to do with race or color.* Sure the generations of Ham went to the South and the hot countries, but the meaning here in Genesis 9 is far deeper than race or color. He was the younger son of the three (Genesis 9:24).

The truth of this Scripture is simply this: when we let the imagination of our lives run wild — look upon lewdness, read about lewd acts in a book, or when we rush to tell the fault of a brother to others — *then all of us are acting like Ham.* "There is a little Ham in all of us" — no pun intended.

(10) **"Japheth" means "beauty" and enlargement."**

He was the eldest son of Noah. This is a little known fact revealed in only one verse of Scripture. Read Genesis 10:21 and you read "Japheth, the elder." Japheth and Shem received the blessing of Noah. Japheth did enlarge to a mighty population as seen in the dispersion of the nations in Genesis 10. They spread north and west over the earth.

These three sons of Noah repeopled the world as they were told by

14

the Lord God in Genesis 9:1. In Genesis 10:1 we see the generations of the three sons.

(11) The Dispersion After the Flood (see diagram).

THE DISPERSION AFTER THE FLOOD

"And the sons of Noah, that went forth of the ark, were Shem, and Ham, and Japheth: and Ham is the father of Canaan. These are the three sons of Noah: *and of them was the whole earth overspread*" (Genesis 9:18-19).

"These are the families of the sons of Noah, after their generations, in their nations: *and by these were the nations divided in the earth after the flood*" (Genesis 10:30).

"When the Most High divided to the nations their inheritance, when he separated the sons of Adam, *he set the bounds of the people according to the number of the children of Israel*" (Deuteronomy 32:8).

"And (God) hath made of one blood (Adam) all nations of men for to dwell on all the face of the earth, and hath determined the times before appointed, and the bounds of their habitation" (Acts 17:26).

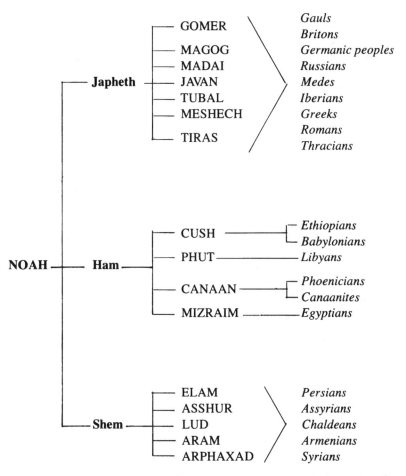

5. **WHAT THE NEW TESTAMENT SAYS ABOUT NOAH AND HIS SONS:**

   (1) Jesus compares the days of Noah and the flood to His coming again.

   Look up Matthew 24:37-39. Write in verse 37 _____

   _____

   _____

The reason for the judgment of the flood is found in Genesis 6:5 (compare with Matthew 24:37-39 above).

(2) Noah was saved by faith (Hebrews 11:7).

Write in the meaning of the verse _____

_____

(3) Peter refers to the flood twice.

In I Peter 3:20 and II Peter 2:5. Note that Noah is called "a preacher of righteousness."

(4) Shem is mentioned in Luke 3:36, in the genealogy of Mary.

6. **THE LESSONS YOU SHOULD LEARN FROM NOAH AND HIS SONS:**

(1) God always judges the wicked.

(2) God always blesses the righteous, those who believe, not just good people.

(3) Remember Noah as a righteous man, a builder of the Ark, a preacher of righteousness, elected, protected and delivered by God. As in all of his faults and failures, he was in God's covenant of safety. When one is overtaken in a fault "ye which are spiritual, restore such a one in the spirit of meekness; considering thyself, lest thou also be tempted" (Galations 6:1).

Shem and Japheth did just that.

(4) The Ark saved Noah and his family. The Ark is a perfect picture of Christ; we are sealed into His body if we believe (Ephesians 1:13-14).

(5) The Lord God always cares for His own. He will never leave us nor forsake us. We are in His Ark of safety, the Lord Jesus Christ.

(6) For your own knowledge about the genealogy from Adam to David, look up I Chronicles 1 and follow verses 1, 4, 17, 27, 28, 34; chapter 2:1, 3, 11, 12, 15.

CAN YOU REMEMBER?

1. The three sons of Noah and the meaning of their names?

_____

_____

_____

2. What does "grace" mean? Where is it first mentioned in Scripture?
3. Name three or four of the things mentioned in the covenant with Noah.
4. Why was judgment sent upon the earth in the form of a flood (Genesis 6:5-7)?
5. Why were two of every living beast and seven pairs of every clean beast placed in the Ark?

YOUR NEXT ASSIGNMENT:

1. Read Genesis 11:10 to Genesis 25:9; Isaiah 41:8; Isaiah 51:2; John 8:33; Acts 7:2-8; Romans 4:13-25; Galatians 3:6-29; Hebrews 11:8-13; James 2:21-23.
2. Review and restudy the lesson on Noah and his sons.
3. Mark your Bible where new truths were learned.
4. Pray for the Holy Spirit to teach you the rich truths of Abraham, one of the greatest characters in this study and the character for the next lesson.

Lesson 5
"Abraham"

(Where lines are provided, look up the Scripture and write the Scripture or its meaning in the space provided.)

1. **THE MEANING OF THE NAME:**
    Abram means "high father." In Genesis 17:5, God changed his name to Abraham, meaning "father of many nations."

2. **BASIC SCRIPTURES:**
    Genesis 11:10 to Genesis 25:9; Isaiah 41:8; Isaiah 51:2; John 8:33-39; Acts 7:2-8; Romans 4:13-25; Galatians 3:6-29; Hebrews 11:8-13; James 2:21-23.

3. **FAMILY BACKGROUND:**
    Abraham was born to Terah in the Ur of the Chaldees; therefore, he was a Chaldean. He was born in the line of Shem, and thus he is in the line of Christ (Genesis 11:10-26). Little is known of his parents. He was close to his family, it appears, from the record we have in Scripture. He married Sarai, his half-sister. When his brother Haran died, Abraham, Sarai, Lot (Abraham's nephew), and Terah, his father, migrated to Haran "and dwelt there" (Genesis 11:31). In Genesis 12:1, we read "Now the Lord *had* said . . ." past tense. Therefore, the move from Ur to Haran was God's divine call to Abraham.

    Abraham, born to the Adamic race, was called of God and became the *first Hebrew* (Genesis 14:13). He uttered no prophecy, wrote no book, gave no laws. In the sovereign will of God, Abraham was chosen, selected to be the heir of God's unconditional covenant.

4. **WHAT THE OLD TESTAMENT SAYS ABOUT ABRAHAM:**

    (1) His call (Genesis 12:1).

    God's call to Abraham was simple and clear.

    > " 'The Lord had said to Abraham,
    > Get thee out of thy country,
    > From thy kindred
    > From thy father's house,
    > Unto a land I will show thee.' "

    (2) God's covenant with Abraham (Genesis 12:2-3).

    Note the seven promises of God:
    - (a) "I will make thee a great nation" (verse 2)
    - (b) "I will bless thee" (verse 2)
    - (c) "I will make thy name great" (verse 2)
    - (d) "Thou shalt be a blessing" (verse 2)
    - (e) "I will bless them that bless thee" (verse 3)
    - (f) "I will curse them that curse thee" (verse 3)
    - (g) "In thee shall all the families of the earth be blessed" (verse 3)

    (3) Abraham's Obedience (Genesis 12:4-9).

    By faith, Abraham departed from Haran and went to the land of Canaan. In Abraham we see a life of faith, trusting in divine guidance, believing divine promises.

    In the land, Abraham built an altar unto the Lord who appeared to him. The Lord said, "Unto thy seed, will I give this land" (verse 7).

(4) Abraham in Egypt (Genesis 12:10-20).

Without any command from God, Abraham went down into Egypt because of the famine in the land of Canaan. Abraham faltered and failed in Egypt. He lied about Sarai, his wife, to Pharaoh, saying that she was his sister. Abraham had to learn that this new life with God meant separation from the things of the world.

(5) Divine Restoration (Genesis 13).

In this chapter, Abraham went up out of Egypt with all of the wealth and, of course, Lot with him. (Note verses 3 and 4.) He went back to where he had built an altar "at the first." God always restores us back to our position of forgiveness, if we only ask Him.

In verse 7, the strife between the herdsmen of Abraham and Lot caused them to separate. Lot took the rich plain of Jordan and pitched his tent toward Sodom, a wicked place (verses 12-13).

After Lot and Abraham separated, *God* chose for Abraham, while Lot *chose for himself* (verse 14). God deeded to Abraham, in one moment, all the land he could see, then to Abraham's Seed.

Write the promise in verse 15 _____

_____

(6) The First War and Lot Rescued (Genesis 14).

In Hebron, Abraham was at home when he received word of a war between four Eastern kings and five kings of Canaan. They captured the people of Sodom, and Lot was one of the captives. Abraham takes his 318 trained servants, surprises them by a night attack, and rescues Lot and his goods.

Then a strange thing takes place. That mysterious king and priest of God, Melchizedek, appears and blesses Abraham (read verses 18 and 20). Abraham then gives a tithe of all to this king and priest, Melchizedek. He sends back all the goods taken, keeping only the people. (Note verse 23.)

What a lesson in this chapter!

(7) A Spiritual Seed Promised (Genesis 15).

God's promise of a great nation to Abraham in chapter 12 is hard for him to believe. God simply says to "Look now toward heaven, and as the number of stars, so shall thy seed be" (Genesis 15:5).

Now write in verse 6 _____

_____

God reconfirms the covenant with Abraham (verses 18-21). Notice in Genesis 13:15 God said, "I *will* give thee." Now in Genesis 15:18 "Unto thy seed *have* I given."

(8) The Birth of Ishmael (Genesis 16).

Abraham makes the mistake of rushing into a relationship without inquiring of God. Hagar bears Ishmael, causing strife.

(9) Name Changed to Abraham (Genesis 17).

God renews the covenant when Abraham is 99 years old (verses 2-8). God gives Abram the name Abraham, "father of many nations" (verse 5).

The sign, or token, of the covenant was circumcision (verse 11). Sarai's name changed to Sarah, "princess" (verse 15). The Lord even names the "seed" to come, Isaac (verse 19).

(10) The Intercession of Abraham (Genesis 18 and 19).

Once before Abraham had saved Lot by *doing*. Now Abraham *prays* Lot out of Sodom.

Note Genesis 19:16 _____

_____

Also verse 22 _____

_____

Lot had two children by his own daughters. Lot's last step in backsliding produced the Moabites and Ammonites, enemies of Israel for the years to come.

(11) Birth of Isaac (Genesis 21).

When Abraham was 100 years old, Isaac was born. God keeps His promise "at the set time" (verse 2), twenty-five years after His promise (Genesis 12).

(12) The Test of Faith (Genesis 22).

Abraham's faith is equal to the test. God commands Abraham to offer Isaac, his only son, on Mt. Moriah.

Abraham obeys. Write in Abraham's words of faith to Isaac (verse 8).

_____

_____

Now notice verse 13: God provided His substitute. There are many lessons in this chapter.

(13) The Last Acts of Abraham (Genesis 23-25).

He chooses Machpelah, near Hebron, as the burying place for Sarah, chapter 23.

He chooses a bride for Isaac, chapter 24.

He marries Keturah and has sons by her, but all he had went to Isaac, chapter 25.

He dies at the age of 175, and is buried by Sarah in Machpelah.

5. **WHAT THE NEW TESTAMENT SAYS ABOUT ABRAHAM:**

(1) In John 8:33-39, Jesus says to the Pharisees (verse 39) _____

_____

_____

(2) In Acts 7:2-8, Stephen sheds light upon the call of Abraham.

The call came while Abraham was in Ur of the Chaldees before he went to Haran (verse 2). Stephen confirms all that God had said to Abraham. Note verse 8 especially.

(3) In Romans 4:13-25, Paul declared the promise to Abraham was not through the law but through faith (verse 13).

Write in Romans 4:20 and 22 _____

_____

Now verse 24, "But for us also, if we believe on Him that raised Jesus from the dead." Paul states that our justification is apart from the law.

(4) In Galatians 3:6-29, Paul says that no man is justified by the law but by faith, the same faith Abraham had.

Note and write in verse 14 _____

_____

Notice verse 16, "To Abraham and his seed were the promises made. He saith not, and to seeds, as of many; but as of one, and to thy seed, which is **Christ.**"

The law does not add to the Abrahamic Covenant (verses 17-19).

(5) Read and underline Hebrews 11:8-13 in your Bible.

(6) (James 2:21-24) James says that "by works, faith is made perfect" (verse 22).

Abraham is called "the friend of God" here in verse 23. Also in Isaiah 41:8 and II Chronicles 20:7.

6. **THE LESSONS YOU SHOULD LEARN FROM ABRAHAM:**
   (1) Live a life of complete faith in God.
   (2) Obey God regardless.
   (3) Be willing to give our lives for Him if necessary.
   (4) Go where He sends us, by faith.
   (5) Stay in God's will and "out of Egypt."
   (6) Believe God to keep all His promises even if it takes time.
   (7) Be a real, true "friend of God" because we believe in the "Seed," Jesus Christ.
   (8) Give to the Lord. Abraham paid tithes before the law was given.
   (9) Look forward to "that city whose builder and maker is God" (Hebrews 11:10), just like Abraham.

CAN YOU REMEMBER?

1. Did Abraham forsake his kinfolk at first?
2. Who was constantly causing him problems?
3. Can you name four parts of the Abrahamic Covenant?

   _____   _____

   _____   _____

4. What did God promise Abraham?
5. What good qualities did Abraham have?
6. According to Galatians, who was the Seed of Abraham?

YOUR NEXT ASSIGNMENT:

1. Read Genesis 14; Psalms 110; Hebrews 5:1-10; Hebrews 6:13-20; Hebrews 7:1-28.
2. Read all you can in Hebrews 4:14, on through Hebrews 10 on the subject of Christ, our High Priest, and the priesthood of the believer. Our next character will be Melchizedek.
3. Review your study of Abraham.
4. Mark your Bible where new truths are learned.

Lesson 6
"Melchizedek"

(Where lines are provided, look up the Scripture and write the Scripture or its meaning in the space provided.)

1. **THE MEANING OF THE NAME:**

   Melchizedek means "justice" or "righteousness." So he would be the "King of Righteousness and Justice and the King of Salem (peace)."

2. **BASIC SCRIPTURES:**

   Genesis 14:17-20; Psalm 110; Hebrews 5:1-10; Hebrews 6:13-20; Hebrews 7:1-28.

3. **FAMILY BACKGROUND:**

   There is no record of his parentage, no mention of his name in any genealogy. When studied closely in this lesson, you may say it was an "inspired omission."

4. **WHAT THE OLD TESTAMENT SAYS ABOUT MELCHIZEDEK:**

   (1) **Melchizedek is mentioned in only two portions of the Old Testament.**

   First, in Genesis 14:17-20.

   (2) **Note who he was: In verse 17 he is called the "King of Salem and priest of the most high God."**

   "King of Salem," which is Jerusalem. We know this from the name itself, meaning "peace," and also from Egyptian records which have been discovered.

   "Priest of the most high God" (Hebrew — El Elyon). El Elyon simply means "God the highest."

   The first revelation of this name indicates its distinctive meanings. Abraham, returning from his victory over the kings, is met by Melchizedek, King of Salem, the "priest of the most high God" (El Elyon — the highest) who blesses Abraham in the name of El Elyon, "possessor of heaven and earth." This revelation produced a remarkable impression on Abraham and he immediately gave "tithes of all" he had taken in battle. When the King of Sodom offered Abraham more goods, Abraham responded by saying, "I have lifted up mine hand unto the Lord (Jehovah), the most high God (El Elyon), the possessor of heaven and earth, etc." (verses 19-21).

   The same usage of "the most High" is found in Deuteronomy 32:8 when He "divided to the nations their inheritance when he separated the sons of Adam."

   So, this "most High" is used to identify this Melchizedek, a priest, with all authority from God.

   (3) **Note what he did.**

   "He brought forth bread and wine" which are symbols of the Lord's Supper and the death of Jesus. This speaks loud of the record of Paul in I Corinthians 11:23-29; "do this in remembrance of me . . . until He comes." Abraham was blessed, and he was to remember the goodness of God.

   (4) **David writes of Melchizedek in Psalms 110:1-4.**

   Note verse 1 (and I translate): "And God said to Jesus, sit thou on my right hand, until I make thine enemies thy footstool." So we have identified who is speaking to the other. He —"God"— continues on through verse 4: "The Lord (God, Jehovah) hath sworn and will not repent (change His mind). Thou art a priest forever after the order of Melchizedek."

All of this seems strange until we turn to the New Testament, and there the picture is completed.

5. **WHAT THE NEW TESTAMENT SAYS ABOUT MELCHIZE-DEK:**

 (1) **Hebrews 5:1-10, read and write in verse 6** _____

 _____

 Here Jesus, not of the tribe of Levi or Aaron, is called "a priest after the order (rank, arrangement, position) of Melchizedek."

 (2) **Copy Hebrews 6:20** _____

 _____

 (3) **Hebrews 7:1-10 presents a full portrait of Melchizedek, which underscores the depth and meaning of the book of Hebrews.**

 It tells us the full story of Melchizedek and the meaning of our own priesthood **if** we have Jesus as our High Priest.

 Note the review in Hebrews 7:1-2. Then in verse 3, notice that Melchizedek was "without father, without mother, without descent (genealogy), having neither beginning of days, nor end of life; but **made like unto the Son of God:** abideth a priest continually." So, Melchizedek *was made like the Son of God.*

 Jesus is the original, Melchizedek the copy.

 Melchizedek was only a *fragment* and is completely, totally fulfilled in Jesus Christ.

 So Christ was *without father on earth as to His humanity, and without mother as to His deity.* He was the only begotten of the Father and without pedigree as to His priesthood.

 Notice verse 4. "Consider how great this man was." Even Aaron and Levi paid tithes to this one through Abraham (verses 9 and 10).

 (4) **The need for an everlasting priest (Hebrews 7:11-28).**

 Read all of this at least twice.

 The Aaronic priesthood made nothing perfect in and through the law (verses 11-13).

 Jesus came from Judah which had nothing to do with the priesthood (verse 14).

 So there was a need for one made, *not after the law, but after the power of an endless life* (verses 15 and 16).

 Write verse 22 _____

 _____

 The Aaronic priests died, Jesus lives forever (verses 23 and 24).

 Jesus became a High Priest because of us. He can save *all* who come to God *by Him* because He makes intercession for us (verse 25).

 Jesus offered **one** sacrifice **once,** Himself. *Sacrifices are not needed daily any longer, because the Lord Jesus, sinless, undefiled, gave Himself once and for all* (verses 26-28).

 (5) **Because Jesus is our High Priest forever, we are priests with the privilege of praying to God through Him.**

 Read Hebrews 10:1-25.

 (6) **Melchizedek, then, is a type, picture, a shadow of Jesus because:**

 (a) He was a king-priest; so is Jesus.

(b) His name means "righteous;" so does Jesus' name.

(c) He was King of Salem; Jesus will be King in Jerusalem.

(d) He had no recorded beginning nor ending; Jesus was in the beginning and is everlasting.

(e) He was made a high priest by the most High God; Jesus completes the pattern.

(7) **Finally, Abraham gave tithes (10%) of all the goods to Melchizedek.**

This was *before* the law and the Levitical priesthood (Hebrews 7:1-10). **Tithing is not from the law. Abraham gave as an act of love, faith, and reverence.**

So in this New Testament passage of ten verses, six speak of tithing. Tithing came *before* the law, and if Jesus is the original and Melchizedek the copy, the lesson is clear and plain concerning stewardship.

Some students will jump over this part of the lesson, but it is essential that we learn and act upon *all of the Word of God.* Now read Luke 6:38 for what Jesus had to say about giving.

6. **THE LESSONS YOU SHOULD LEARN FROM MELCHIZEDEK:**

(1) There are types, symbols, shadows, pictures in the Old Testament which are fulfilled in the New Testament.

(2) Melchizedek was a type of Christ.

(3) Jesus is our High Priest forever.

(4) The respect and love of Abraham toward Melchizedek was of God.

(5) The giving of the tithe was before the law and is an act of love and obedience on our part.

(6) We should recognize that we are priests in that we can pray boldly to God through Jesus, our High Priest.

(7) He can save all who come to God by Him (Hebrews 7:25).

CAN YOU REMEMBER?

1. Who is Melchizedek?

2. What did he do?

3. Who did he represent?

4. What is an example of a type or picture in Scripture?

5. Is tithing a part of the law?

6. What is our title (as Christians), if Jesus is our High Priest?

YOUR NEXT ASSIGNMENT:

1. Read Genesis 21 through 27; Hebrews 11:17-20; and James 2:21-23. Also Genesis 17:19-21 and 18:10-15.

2. Isaac was one of the patriarchs and is our study for the next lesson. Read all you can find on him.

3. Review your study of Melchizedek.

4. Mark your Bible where new truths are learned.

Lesson 7
"Isaac"

(Where lines are provided, look up the Scripture and write the Scriptures or the main truth in the space provided.)

1. **THE MEANING OF THE NAME:**

   Isaac means "he laugheth" or the "laughing one."

2. **BASIC SCRIPTURES:**

   Genesis 17:19-21; Genesis 18:10-15; Genesis 21 through 27; Hebrews 11:17-20; James 2:21-23.

3. **FAMILY BACKGROUND:**

   Isaac was the son of Abraham and Sarah, born when his father was 100 years old and his mother was 91 (Genesis 17:17 and 21 and Genesis 21:5). When the promise was made that Sarah should bear him a son, Abraham laughed (Genesis 17:17-19). When Sarah heard the promise, she laughed (Genesis 18:10-15). When Isaac was born Sarah joyfully said that God had prepared laughter for her and her friends (Genesis 21:6).

   Isaac is one of the few cases in the Bible in which God selected a name for a child and announced it before he was born (Genesis 17:19). In the Old Testament, the Lord God named Isaac, Ishmael, Solomon, Josiah, Cyrus, and Isaiah's son, Maher-shalal-hash-baz. In the New Testament, John the Baptist and Jesus.

   We have no record of Isaac's early life apart from the record of his circumcision when he was eight days old (Genesis 21:4) and his weaning (Genesis 21:8).

4. **WHAT THE OLD TESTAMENT SAYS ABOUT ISAAC:**

   (1) The offering of Isaac by Abraham (Genesis 22).

   This was a test of faith for Abraham. Write in verse 2 _____

   _____

   _____

   Abraham obeyed God and Isaac went with his father to Mt. Moriah (in Jerusalem). Most people think Isaac was only a small boy, but Josephus says he was at least 25 years old. Other scholars think he was about 33 years of age.

   The lesson to remember is the testing of Abraham's faith. God had promised Abraham that from Isaac He would raise up a great nation; *now He commands Abraham to offer Isaac as a burnt-offering.* How God would reconcile this, Abraham did not know, nor was that his business. His business was to **obey** God and trust Him regardless.

   Isaac asked only one question: "where is the lamb for the burnt-offering?" (verse 7).

   Write in the answer from verse 8: _____

   _____

   Underline the words *"God will provide himself a Lamb."*

   So here we have a beautiful picture in the Old Testament of a New Testament reality. God gave His only Son (the Lamb) as a sacrifice for our sins.

Now, underline in your Bible verses 11 through 13. In all this we see:

- *Abraham, offering his only son.*
- *Isaac, obedient even unto death.*
- *A ram, a substitute.*

(2) There is an essential truth to be learned at this point, which has already been alluded to.

Now the details of that truth:

- *Isaac's birth is a foreshadowing of the birth of our Lord Jesus Christ.* Here are some of the similarities:
- Both Isaac and Jesus had been promised. Abraham was promised a son 25 years earlier and it happened. A Seed was promised in Genesis 3:15, and Paul clarifies the Seed in Galatians 3:16. Write in this verse _____

_____

_____

- The announcement of both births was unusual. So incredible were the announcements that Sarah and Abraham laughed. Mary even questioned the virgin birth of Jesus, in Luke 1:34: "How shall this be, seeing I know no man?"
- Both were named *before* birth. God told Abraham to call his name Isaac (Genesis 17:19). The angel told Joseph to name Him Jesus, "for He shall save His people from their sins" (Matthew 1:21).
- Both births occurred at God's appointed time (Genesis 21:2).

_____

_____

_____

Galatians 4:4 _____

_____

- Both births were miraculous. Abraham was 100 years old and Sarah 90 plus. No man had a part in the virgin birth of Jesus. Read Romans 4:19-25.

(3) A Bride for Isaac (Genesis 24).

Abraham sent a servant to find a bride for Isaac. The servant, guided by God (verse 27), came to Rebekah who was ready and willing to go as Isaac's bride (verse 58). As she and the servant neared Abraham's home, Isaac came to meet her.

Isaac took her into his mother's tent and she became his wife *and he loved her* (verse 67).

Isaac was comforted by Rebekah's love, remembering the death of Sarah, his mother.

(4) Isaac and His Two Sons (Genesis 25:19-34).

At 60 years of age (verse 26), Isaac became the father of Esau and Jacob.

Note and write in verse 23 _____

_____

The boys were born fighting. Esau and Jacob were grown men when the Scripture reveals the sale of the birthright.

Esau, the eldest, means "red." God said in verse 23 that "the elder shall serve the younger." Jacob means "supplanter" or "usurper."

Isaac loved Esau and Rebekah loved Jacob (verse 28).

In Esau we see a man of the world, living for the physical. Jacob was no saint, but he did have an inward desire for good (as we shall see in the next lesson).

The birthright did not mean much to Esau. It could have meant control and head of the family, but God had said "the elder shall serve the younger." All of the cheating and trickery by Jacob was not necessary. Esau was hungry, and gave up his birthright, which he did not really care for (verse 32). So Esau gave his birthright for a bowl of *red* pottage and his name was called "Edom" (verse 30). "He despised his birthright" (verse 34).

God knew all this before it happened.

(5) The Covenant Confirmed to Isaac (Genesis 26).

In verses 1 through 5, God instructs Isaac *not* to go to Egypt and confirms the promise of the covenant.

But Isaac, being a natural man, did the same thing as his father. At Gerar, south of Hebron, he misrepresented Rebekah as his sister (verse 9).

Isaac became a well-digger because of the struggle for water. He moved to Beer-sheba, and there God appeared and blessed him and repeated the promises of the covenant.

Note verse 24 and write in _____

_____

(6) The Stolen Blessing (Genesis 27).

Remember that our lesson is on Isaac. Here we see Isaac, his sight almost gone, on his deathbed, so to speak. His one desire is to eat. His favorite food was venison.

The story speaks for itself. Isaac knew that God had said the oldest would serve the younger son, but he bypassed that and told Esau to bring in some meat and he would bless Esau. Rebekah, hearing the instruction to Esau, decided to trick Isaac because her favorite was Jacob. They deceived Isaac and he in turn *blessed Jacob*. Esau was so mad he plotted to kill Jacob (verse 41). Jacob, following his mother's advice (verse 43), and with Isaac's blessing (Genesis 28:1), fled to Laban, the brother of Rebekah.

Esau went to Ishmael and married one of his daughters (Genesis 28:9).

In the end, Rebekah lost both sons, for she never saw Jacob again.

Isaac dies in Genesis 35:27-29. Isaac stands between two stately and impressive names, Abraham and Jacob. He is referred to in Scripture some 30 plus times in connection with Abraham and Jacob. Recall in you own mind the times you have read "Abraham, Isaac and Jacob" in Scripture.

5. WHAT THE NEW TESTAMENT SAYS ABOUT ISAAC:

(1) Indirect references are made in Romans 4:1-4; Romans 4:13-25; Galatians 3:6-18 (read these Scriptures and underline in your Bible).

Now write in Galatians 3:29 _____

_____

(2) Turn to Hebrews 11:17-20.

This confirms the faith of Abraham. He offered up "his only begotten son," knowing that God was able to raise Isaac from the dead; from whence also he received him in a figure" (verse 19). Now look at Hebrews 9:9. Isaac was a figure, a picture of Christ.

Are you confused? Don't be. Jesus confirmed this with His own words in John 8:56

_____

_____

Isn't that great? *The Scripture teaches us Scripture,* if we look and search His Word.

(3) Turn now to James 2:21-23.

James is simply saying here that faith and works go together. The test of Abraham's faith came when he actually did exactly what God had said (and that is works).

"By works was faith made perfect" (verse 22).

6 **THE LESSONS WE SHOULD LEARN FROM THIS STUDY:**

(1) What God promises, He always does, even if it takes 25 years (as in the case of the birth of Isaac).

(2) What God requires of us, we should do, knowing that His way and His will is the best for our lives.

(3) Faith is a *must* for a Christian. Abraham had so much faith that he offered his only son.

(4) Isaac teaches us in the Old Testament what was completed and fulfilled in the New Testament.

(5) Trickery and worldly schemes only bring heartache to any family.

CAN YOU REMEMBER?

1. When was Isaac named?

2. How old were his parents at his birth?

3. What does Isaac mean?

4. In what way is Isaac a picture, a foreshadow of Jesus Christ?

5. Did Abraham see the ultimate Seed, Jesus Christ, in his soul (Remember John 8:56)?

6. Isaac had human weaknesses and faults. Can you name three?

YOUR NEXT ASSIGNMENT:

1. Read Genesis 27 through 35; Genesis 46 through 49; Matthew 22:29-33; John 4:6-13; Acts 7:6-19; Romans 9:9-13; Hebrews 11:20-21.

2. Jacob is our next study and is one of the greatest names in Scripture. Study all you can about him.

3. Review your study on Isaac.

4. Mark your Bible where new truths are learned.

Lesson 8
"Jacob"

(Where lines are provided, look up the Scripture and write the Scripture or the main truth in the space provided.)

Before entering the study of this famous character, by now it should be very clear in your mind that the Bible is an unusual book. It paints the black as well as the white; the natural, Adamic man; as well as the spiritual man. We saw this in Adam, Noah, Noah's sons, Abraham, Isaac, and now we see the same in Jacob. So, the Bible speaks to us, just as *we are*, both carnal and spiritual.

1. **THE MEANING OF THE NAME:**

   Jacob means "supplanter" which means "taking the place of another."

2. **BASIC SCRIPTURES:**

   Genesis 27 through 35; Genesis 46 through 49; Matthew 22:29-33; John 4:6-14; Acts 7:6-19; Romans 9:9-13; Hebrews 11:20-21.

3. **FAMILY BACKGROUND:**

   Jacob was the second son of Isaac and Rebekah. He was the twin brother of Esau. Jacob was born only a short time after Esau and is, therefore, called the *younger* brother. In a prophetic revelation to Rebekah *before* the birth, the Lord God said to her: *"two nations are in thy womb, and the elder (Esau), shall serve the younger (Jacob)"* (Genesis 25:23). Why? Paul explains in Romans 9:11: "that the purpose of God, according to election might stand."

4. **WHAT THE OLD TESTAMENT SAYS ABOUT JACOB:**

   (1) **He gained the birthright from Esau (Genesis 25:27-34).**

   (We covered this in the last lesson.)

   (2) **He tricked his father into giving him the blessing and is thus called "the supplanter" meaning "taking the place of another" (Genesis 27).**

   Write in Genesis 27:36 _____

   _____

   Here we see one of the common weaknesses of the flesh: trying to help God. Rebekah and Jacob scheme together in order for Jacob to receive the blessing of Isaac. God had already promised this to Jacob in His statement, "the elder shall serve the younger."

   (3) **Jacob fled to Haran on the advice of his mother (verses 41-46).**

   Rebekah did not know that she would never see Jacob again. Jacob was afraid. He ran from Esau into another life of hard knocks and deception. The lesson here is the *unchanging law of sowing and reaping*.

   (4) **Jacob at Bethel (Genesis 28).**

   Jacob was blessed by Isaac and told to go to Laban and there choose a wife. He was not to marry a Canaanite girl (verses 1-5).

   Esau married a daughter of Ishmael. He already had two wives (Genesis 26:34 and 28:9).

   The lesson for us to learn from this incident is, "be not unequally yoked together with unbelievers" (II Corinthians 6:14).

   Jacob went toward Haran and stopped for a night's rest. With stones for a pillow, he dreamed of a ladder from heaven to the earth with angels ascending and descending. God confirmed to him the Abrahamic Covenant. **When God repeats, one should listen.** He has confirmed the Covenant over and over again to Abraham, Isaac, and now Jacob. When Jacob awoke, he said: *"Surely the Lord is in this place and I knew it not"* (verse 16).

The dream promised to Jacob was that his seed should be "as the dust of the earth." The dream was a picture of Jesus Christ let down from heaven. The angels of God ascend and descend, they come from the Lord Jesus, *giving us access to God through Him.* Jesus interpreted this for us in John 1:51 (write in this verse).

_____

_____

Jacob anointed the stone which had been his pillow, and he called the name of that place Bethel, meaning "this is the house of God." The place had been called Luz, meaning "separation."

Bethel becomes a significant place in Scripture.

Note verse 22. Jacob, in view of God's grace and blessing, promised to *give* a tithe. This verse indicates that the tithe was given to God at God's house. This was 250 years before the law. *(Abraham tithed 430 years before the law.)*

(5) Jacob's Years at Haran (Genesis 29).

Jacob began to reap what he had sown. He had deceived his father, Isaac, and was in turn deceived by Uncle Laban.

He meets Rachel in verses 10 through 12.

Laban enters the picture in verses 13 and 14. He required Jacob to serve seven years for Rachel (verse 18). Jacob loved Rachel and served gladly, then was given Leah by Laban, a dirty trick. Laban said "the oldest daughter should be married first, according to custom," (verses 21-26).

Jacob had to work another seven years for Rachel (verses 27 and 28). Jacob had to learn patience and humble subjection, something new for him, since he had been a trickster in years past. *"The week"* in verses 27 and 28, is seven more years. He had served fourteen years and had two wives. Rachel was barren while Leah could have children.

(6) The Children of Jacob (Genesis 29:32 through 30:24).

Born to Leah:

1. Reuben (Genesis 29:32)
2. Simeon (verse 33)
3. Levi (verse 34)
4. Judah (verse 35)
5. Issachar (Genesis 30:18)
6. Zebulun (verse 20)

Born to Bilhah, Rachel's maid:

7. Dan (Genesis 30:5)
8. Naphtali (verse 6)

Born to Zilpah, Leah's maid:

9. Gad (verse 11)
10. Asher (verse 13)

Born to Rachel:

11. Joseph (verse 24)
12. Benjamin, (not born until Genesis 35:18, when back in Canaan. Rachel died in childbirth).

From these twelve sons, comes the twelve tribes of Israel. Mark them in your Bible.

(7) Jacob Departs for Canaan (Genesis 31).

After much bargaining and arguing with Laban, Jacob did as the Lord told him and returned to the land He had promised Jacob (verse 3). So Jacob and his entire family and cattle leave and Laban overtakes him. Again, they argue and finally agree. This is where we find the famous Mizpah. Write in Genesis 31:49

_____

_____

After 20 years (verse 41) Jacob is finally on his way to Canaan.

(8) Jacob Becomes Israel, "A Prince of God" (Genesis 32).

From fear of his brother, Esau (or Edom), Jacob cried out to God for help. He sent his family across the brook called Jabbok and Jacob remained on the other side alone.

Now read Genesis 32:24-30.

Write in verse 28 _____

_____

Who wrestled with Jacob that night? Scripture says *Jacob wrestled with the mysterious visiter until Jacob was brought to a place of helplessness.*

There are many speculations about who that was. I believe the Scriptures teach that it was the pre-incarnate Christ (verse 30). Hosea 12:1-5 says, "The Lord in His name." Joshua saw Him in Joshua 5:13-15. Isaiah saw Him in Isaiah 6:5. Paul saw Him in Acts 9:1-6.

So, Jacob is now Israel.

Now you know where Israel and the twelve tribes came from. Remember this well.

Remember, too, the flesh was conquered in Jacob, not removed, only made to lean on the Lord God.

After this, Jacob was a changed man. In chapter 33, he was reconciled to his brother Esau. Esau even ran to meet Jacob and embraced him (verse 4).

(9) Sowing and Reaping (Genesis 34 through 36).

The principle lesson of chapter 34 is sowing and reaping. Jacob had stopped at Shalem. His sons Simeon and Levi killed the men because of their sister, Dinah (verse 25). Jacob could only think of himself. Notice the personal pronouns in verse 30 and underline.

He could do only one thing: "go back to Bethel," as God said (Genesis 35:1).

"Dwell there and make an altar there" (verse 1).

He had stopped short of Bethel, and idols defiled his household (verse 2). Note also Jacob said in verse 2: "be clean, change your garments." In verse 3, "let us arise and go up to Bethel." When they arrived at Bethel, Jacob built an altar and called the place El-Bethel, meaning "the God of the house of God" (verses 6 and 7).

After the Abrahamic Covenant was again confirmed to Jacob, (verses 9-13), he lost Rachel, his wife, in childbirth, when Benjamin was born (verses 16-20).

His twelve sons are listed in this chapter. Number them in your Bible (verses 22-26).

Isaac died and Esau and Jacob buried him (verses 27-29).

(10) Israel (Jacob), in Egypt (Genesis 46 through 50).

Here, the seed of Abraham left Canaan. They were not to return until Joshua led them in hundreds of years later. Jacob went in the permissive will of God to see his son, Joseph, in the land of Egypt.

Only 70 souls went down into Egypt (for explanation of the different count, see page 8 of "Through The Bible In One Year," Basic Course.)

31

Jacob blessed his twelve sons and he gave instructions (which were prophetic) to each one. Read especially Genesis 49:8-12, concerning Judah and write in verse 10 _____

_____

Jesus came from the tribe of Judah.

Jacob died in Egypt and was taken back to Canaan and buried in Machpelah with his father, Abraham.

5. **WHAT THE NEW TESTAMENT SAYS ABOUT JACOB:**

There are many references to Jacob, or Israel, but we shall take only a few:

(1) *(Matthew 22:29-33)* **Jesus answers the Sadducees in reference to the resurrection.**

He gives them answers from the Word. Write in verse 32 _____

_____

_____

(2) *(John 4:6-14)* **This is the story of the Samaritan woman at the well, Jacob's well.**

Read all the Scripture and write in verse 12 _____

_____

The practical and spiritual teaching is in verse 14.

(3) *(Acts 7:6-19)* **Stephen uses the leadership of God in the lives of Abraham, Isaac and Jacob in his message before the Sanhedrin.**

Note verses 8, 14, and 15.

(4) *(Romans 9:9-13)* **God's purpose, according to His "election" must stand; therefore the seed of Isaac, Jacob, was the sovereign will of God.**

Also read and underline Romans 11:26-29.

Note: "There shall come out of Zion a Deliverer (Redeemer)"
"And shall turn away ungodliness from Jacob (Israel)"
"For this is my covenant unto them"
"For the gifts and calling of God are without repentance (can never change)."

(5) *Hebrews 11:20-21,* **write in verse 21** _____

_____

6. **THE LESSONS YOU SHOULD LEARN FROM JACOB:**

(1) It never pays to be a cheater, trickster.
(2) Jacob paid over and over again for scheming.
(3) We should never try to help God by rushing ahead of His will for us.
(4) We should always remember the unchanging law of sowing and reaping.
(5) God never breaks a promise. He had promised the blessing to Jacob before he was born. God brought it to pass in His own time.
(6) Sometimes we need to "go back to Bethel."
(7) God has a unique plan for Israel, part having been fulfilled, part yet to be fulfilled.

CAN YOU REMEMBER?

1. What does Jacob mean? What is Jacob's other name?
2. When did God give the Abrahamic Covenant to Jacob?
3. Where is the Scripture about being unequally yoked?
4. What does Bethel mean?

5. How many sons did Jacob have? Why should we place emphasis on them?

6. Where did Jacob go for his last journey? How many went with him?

YOUR NEXT ASSIGNMENT:

1. Read Genesis 37 through 50; Acts 7:9-19; Hebrews 11:21-22.

2. Read all you can about Joseph, the man who was a foreshadow of Christ in so many ways.

3. Review your study on Jacob, "Israel."

4. Mark your Bible where new truths are learned.

Lesson 9
"Joseph"

(Where lines are provided, look up the Scripture and write it or its meaning in the space provided.)

1. **THE MEANING OF THE NAME:**
   Joseph means "may He (Jehovah) add" or "adding."

   See Genesis 30:24. _____

   _____

2. **BASIC SCRIPTURES:**
   Genesis 37-50; Acts 7:9-19, Hebrews 11:21-22.

3. **FAMILY BACKGROUND:**
   We come now to the fourth outstanding figure in the story line which began with Abraham. From here (Genesis 37), through the remainder of Genesis, the central figure is Joseph, even though we are still dealing with the family of Jacob. More chapters are devoted to Joseph than to Abraham or Isaac. Why should Joseph be given such prominence in Scripture?

   First, because he was a good example of a good and great life.

   Second, there is no one in Scripture who is more like Christ in his person and experiences than Joseph. The likeness is not accidental. The parallel is so evident; therefore, we shall mention some of these parallels in this lesson.

   Joseph was born in Haran before Jacob returned to Canaan. He was Jacob's favorite child because he was the son of his old age, and also Rachel's child.

4. **WHAT THE OLD TESTAMENT SAYS ABOUT JOSEPH:**
   (1) The Humiliation of Joseph (Genesis 37-40).

   Joseph was a shepherd boy ("feeding the flock") and he was loved by his father, Jacob (Israel) (Genesis 37:2-3). He was hated by his brothers because he was the favorite son. They were jealous of him. Jacob made him a coat of many colors, a mark of distinction, honor and separation (verses 3 and 4).

   In verses 4 through 11, three times we read of the hatred toward Joseph by his brothers (in verse 4, then again in verse 5, and again in verse 9).

   Joseph was a dreamer. From these dreams he could see the future when his brothers would bow down to him (verses 9 and 10). This was another reason they hated him. Jacob sent Joseph to look after the welfare of his brothers. When they saw him coming, they plotted against him.

   Though Reuben wanted to save him, *Judah sells him for twenty pieces of silver* to some Ishmaelites. Joseph was taken from the pit and sold. The boys took Joseph's coat and sprinkled it with blood and took it to Jacob who believed his beloved son dead. All of this is in Genesis 37:12-35.

   Note, now, where Joseph really was (verse 36). He was sold into Egypt. *Don't forget where Joseph was and how he got there.*

   (2) The Shame of Judah (Genesis 38).

   This chapter makes a break in the history of Joseph to tell a sordid story of Judah. It is important because our Lord came through the tribe of Judah. When you read this chapter, you see that Jesus came to the very depths when He condescended to be made in the form of sinful man.

Judah married a Canaanite (Genesis 38:2) and had three sons. His first, Er, married Tamar. Tamar lost her husband and tricked Judah into thinking she was a harlot (verse 15). Judah gave her a signet, bracelets and his staff. Tamar conceived and then used the gifts to prove that she was the one Judah had taken as a harlot. Now read verses 27 through 30 as to what happened.

Tamar had twins, Pharez and Zerah. So we have names that sound familiar. Turn to Matthew 1:2-3.

Write in verse 3 _____

_____

This is the line that led to Boaz, Ruth, Jesse, David and on to Jesus Christ.

Look up Ruth 4:18-22 for additional confirmation.

(3) **Joseph Tested by Adversity (Genesis 39-40).**

Joseph became a servant in Potiphar's house. He was prosperous, greatly pleased his master, and became a great blessing to others (Genesis 39:1-6).

Joseph was greatly tempted, yet did not sin (verses 7-12).

Joseph was falsely accused and cast into a prison (verses 16-20). But prison was different with him in it. Write in verse 21 _____

_____

_____

In chapter 40, Joseph in prison was a blessing to one prisoner and a condemnation to another (verses 5-22). In all of his adversity, Joseph spoke only of God. Note Genesis 39:9, and now Genesis 40:8. Notice also Genesis 40:23, the one who received the blessing forgot Jospeh.

(4) **Joseph's Exaltation by Pharaoh (Genesis 41).**

Pharaoh had a dream and Joseph was summoned to interpret. Again in verse 16, Joseph magnified God, not himself. God was working, He was the one to deliver Joseph out of prison.

He interpreted the dream, both good and bad. He gave explicit instructions to Pharaoh. Notice his statement about Joseph in verse 39: "a man in whom the Spirit of God is."

Joseph was made ruler over all the land of Egypt (verse 41). He received a Gentile bride (verse 45). He provided bread for all (verse 57).

(5) **Joseph's Exaltation by His Family (Genesis 42-45).**

The first visit by Joseph's brothers was caused by the famine in Canaan. It was hunger that made them go to Egypt (Genesis 43:1-5).

The brothers did not recognize Joseph, but he knew them (verses 6-16). They had not seen one another since they had sold Joseph at the age of seventeen. Now he was thirty years of age. Joseph demanded that Benjamin be brought the next time they came to Egypt.

In chapters 43 and 44, Jacob consented to Benjamin going on the second trip. Judah assured his father that Benjamin would return. As they returned homeward, they were humiliated when overtaken by a servant of Joseph. They were accused of stealing Joseph's silver cup. It was found on Benjamin and they were taken back to Joseph and there Judah pleaded their case.

In chapter 45, Joseph made himself known and wept aloud (notice verses 1 and 2). He revealed that God had sent him to Egypt for a definite purpose (Genesis 45:7)

This is one of the important verses in Genesis. Joseph showed marvelous grace in verse 4 and verses 14 and 15. His brothers left to tell of Joseph and even Pharaoh's favors.

(6)   Jacob's Blessings Upon the Twelve Tribes (Genesis 46-50).

In this section we see a little more of the last lesson. "Jacob, or Israel, took his journey to Beer-sheba and offered sacrifices unto God." (Genesis 46:1).

God spoke to Israel in verses 2 and 3. *This is the seventh and last recorded time that God spoke to Jacob:*

- The first time (Genesis 28:13)
- The second time (Genesis 31:3)
- The third time (Genesis 32:1)
- The fourth time (Genesis 32:24)
- The fifth time (Genesis 35:1)
- The sixth time (Genesis 35:9)
- The seventh time (Genesis 46:2)

God said to Israel, "I will go down with thee and I will surely bring you up again" (verse 4). They were going down, they thought, for a short time. Little did they realize that 70 souls would grow to a great multitude before Joshua would lead the exodus out of Egypt.

They were exalted in Egypt by Pharaoh and given the land of Rameses — the same as Goshen (Genesis 47:1-11). Jacob lived in Egypt 17 years. Before he died, Jacob had some things to say and blessings to give. Jacob repeated the covenant in Genesis 48:3-4. He then accepted Joseph's sons, Ephraim and Manasseh as his own. In verses 8-14, he blessed the second son over the first. *(Remember, the Principle of the Second Before the First, Lesson 1).* This is the **fifth** time in Genesis that this principle has applied.

In chapter 49, Jacob blesses his twelve sons and utters some prophetic statements concerning them. We shall not consider all of them, only one, Judah. Note in Genesis 49:8-12, Jacob utters a prophecy of the coming of Christ. *Jesus came through the line of Judah.*

Write in verse 10 _____

_____

The word "Shiloh" means Christ.

In chapter 50, Jacob is dead. Notice that the Egyptians mourned for three days. Very unusual, wouldn't you say? He was taken to Canaan and buried in Machpelah with his family.

Joseph died at the age of 110, promising his brothers that "God will bring you out of this land unto the land He swore to Abraham, Isaac and Jacob" (verse 24). So we come to the end of the life of Joseph and the book of Genesis.

5.   WHAT THE NEW TESTAMENT SAYS ABOUT JOSEPH:

(1)   (Acts 7:9-19) If you want a quick review of Israel, remember the sermons of Stephen, Peter and Paul.

Stephen says, first in verses 6 and 7, that God said "His seed should sojourn in a strange land four hundred years," (referring back to Genesis 15:13). Then in verse 9-19, Stephen retells the story of Joseph and Israel in Egypt. This is New Testament confirmation of all God had said and it came to pass.

(2)   (Hebrews 11:21-22) "By faith, Joseph made mention of the departing of the children of Israel."

In his death, Joseph reminded Israel of her land and inheritance.

Now, a new student of the Word will ask, "Why did we spend so much time on seemingly little things in the life of Joseph?" Remember that all Scripture is for our learning and example. So as we approach "The Lessons We Should Learn," this explanation is needed for a new student. *In Scripture there is no one more like Christ, in person and experience, than Joseph.* Yet nowhere in the New Testament is Joseph given to us as a type or picture of Jesus. The parallel cannot be accidental; it is of the Lord. We list only a few of the analogies.

6. **THE LESSONS YOU SHOULD LEARN FROM THIS STUDY:**

JOSEPH AS A PICTURE OF CHRIST

JOSEPH	JESUS
1. Was the well-beloved son of his father (Genesis 37:3).	1. Was the well-beloved Son of His Father (Matthew 3:17).
2. Lived in Hebron, the place of fellowship, with his father before he was sent to his brethren (Genesis 37:14).	2. Lived in Heaven, the place of fellowship, before coming to the earth (John 17:5).
3. His father sent him, but he was perfectly willing to go (Genesis 37:13)	3. His Father sent Him, but He was perfectly willing to go (John 3:16, Philippians 2:5-7).
4. Testified against his brothers' sin, and they hated him (Genesis 37:2).	4. Testifies against their sin, and men hated him (John 15:18).
5. Revealed to them the exalted position he would hold in the future, and they hated him the more (Genesis 37:5-8).	5. Revealed to man the exalted position He would hold in the future, and they hated Him the more (Matthew 24:30, 31).
6. His brethren plot against him (Genesis 37:19, 20).	6. His brethren, according to the flesh (the Jews), plot against Him (Luke 20:13, 14; Luke 19:46, 47).
7. Judah sells him for twenty pieces of silver (Genesis 37:26 and 28).	7. Judah sells Him for thirty pieces of silver (Matthew 26:15).
8. Was tempted and did not yield (Genesis 39).	8. Was tempted but did not yield (Matthew 4:1-11).
9. Accused wrongfully (Genesis 39:13-18).	9. Accused wrongfully (Matthew 26:59, 65).
10. Put in the Egyptian dungeon, the place of death, with two malefactors (Genesis 39:20).	10. Put on the cross, the place of death, with two malefactors (Mark 15:27, 28).
11. One of the malefactors died and the other lived (Genesis 40:21, 22).	11. One of the malefactors died and the other lived — spiritually (Luke 23:39-43).
12. Was raised from the place of death by the king of the land. (Genesis 41:14).	12. Was raised from the place of death by the King of the universe (Ephesians 1:19-20).
13. Was given all power in Egypt (Genesis 41:42-44).	13. Was given all power in heaven and earth (Matthew 18:28).
14. After his exaltation took Gentile bride to share his glory (Genesis 41:45).	14. After His exaltation takes Gentile bride (the church) to share His glory (Ephesians 5:23-32).

JOSEPH AS A PICTURE OF CHRIST

JOSEPH	JESUS
15. Acknowledged to be the saviour of the people and their ruler (Genesis 47:25).	15. Acknowledged to be Saviour and Ruler (Philippians 2:10, 11).
16. All must get their bread (physical life) through Joseph (Genesis 41:55, 57).	16. All must get spiritual life through Jesus Christ (Acts 4:12).
17. Gives all honour to the king, and delivers all things into his hands (Genesis 47:14-20).	17. Gives all honour to the King (God) and delivers all things into his hands (I Corinthians 15:24).
18. Knew the past history of his brethren (Genesis 42:33).	18. Knew what was in man (John 2:24, 25; Matthew 9:4).

We have listed 18. There are more. What a blessing it is to let the Scriptures speak to us and reveal, even in the first book of the Bible, the Lord Jesus.

CAN YOU REMEMBER?

1. Why was Joseph hated so much by his brothers?
2. Jacob gave to Joseph an article of clothing, most people remember this one thing about Joseph. What was it called?
3. Joseph was sold by whom, for how much?
4. In Egypt, what did Joseph become?
5. Why was Joseph in Egypt? Was it his will, or just because his brothers sold him?
6. How was Joseph able to gain control over Egypt?

YOUR NEXT ASSIGNMENT:

1. Read again Genesis 29:31-35; Genesis 38:11-30; Genesis 49:3-12; Numbers 24:16-19; Joshua 15:1-12; II Samuel 2:1-11; Matthew 1:1-17; Luke 3:23-38; Hebrews 8:7-13; Revelations 5:5.
2. The character for the next lesson is Judah, from whom came our Lord Jesus. Read all the above.
3. Mark your Bibles where new truths are learned.
4. Review the study of Joseph.

Lesson 10
"Judah"
(the fourth son of Jacob)

(Where lines are provided, look up the Scripture and write it or its meaning in the space provided.)

1. **THE MEANING OF THE NAME:**
   Judah means "praise." Look up Genesis 29:35 _____

   _____

2. **BASIC SCRIPTURES:**
   Genesis 29:31-35; Genesis 38:11-30; Genesis 49:3-12; Numbers 24:16-19; Joshua 15:1-12; II Samuel 2:1-11; Matthew 1:1-17; Luke 3:23-38; Hebrews 8:7-13; Revelation 5:5.

3. **FAMILY BACKGROUND:**

   Judah was the fourth son of Jacob by Leah (Genesis 29:35). His mother named him Judah, "praise," because of her gratitude to God for him. Later, in Scripture, a distinguished mother praised the Lord for a greater Son who came from the tribe of Judah. Look up Luke 1:46-47: _____

   _____

   Judah, being the fourth son, was selected by Jacob. Because of the sins of Reuben, Simeon and Levi, they were passed over and Judah was selected as the one who would bring forth our Lord Jesus, "the Lion of the tribe of Judah, the Root of David" (Revelation 5:5). Judah was the spokesman to Joseph in Genesis 44:18-34, one of the most eloquent speeches ever made. As a result, Joseph revealed himself as the brother. Judah was a strong leader. God works in mysterious ways, and He did in the selection of Judah.

4. **WHAT THE OLD TESTAMENT SAYS ABOUT JUDAH:**
   (1) His birth (Genesis 29:31-35).

   Judah was born in a mixed-up household. Jacob had two wives. He loved one of them, Rachel, who was barren at the time. Leah could bear children and Judah was her fourth son. Judah finally had eleven brothers born to Jacob by four different women. He must have learned patience in a family such as his.

   (2) Judah was sinful (Genesis 38:11-30).

   Even though we think that the great men of God were some sort of "sinless" creatures, the Bible reveals just the opposite.

   In this passage, Judah is a sinner. He committed adultery with Tamar, his dead son's wife. She played the role of a harlot, a temptation to Judah who fell into the trap. Tamar conceived and had twins, Pharez and Zarah. Judah's sin was the way of the Canaanites, and that was one reason God allowed them to go to Egypt. He sinned against God and his own daughter-in-law.

   We think we are in a sex revolution now! There is nothing new about that. For centuries the "natural" man has had sexual freedom. The Canaanites are gone; God judged them. That is a warning to any person. Judah was acting just like the Canaanites. Turn to Matthew 1:2-3

Here you find the names of Tamar, Pharez and Zarah, going on down to Boaz, Ruth and David. They were in the line of Christ.

(3) It was from the tribe of Judah that the Messiah, our Lord Jesus Christ would come (Genesis 49:3-12).

Read this Scripture twice. It is one of the greatest prophetic statements in all the Bible. Jacob told his sons what would happen to them. We shall consider only Judah.

Already we have been told that there would be a seed of the woman in Genesis 3:15. That seed was confirmed to Abraham, Isaac and Jacob. Here it is confirmed to Judah. It is out of the line of Judah that HE shall come.

Notice now Genesis 49:8—"Thou art he whom thy brothers shall praise, thy father's children shall bow down before thee." Judah means "praise." He was to be superior to the rest of the tribes. Judah's tribe led through the wilderness journey.

Now verse 9: "Judah is a lion's whelp." The lion is the king of beasts. Judah was to be strong, a leader. Judah's emblem was the lion.

Verse 10: "The scepter shall not depart from Judah, until Shiloh come." (Underline this verse in your Bible.)

The "scepter" was the symbol of authority and the highest form of a scepter was a crown. This was seen in the Old Testament in David. That crown shall be given to the King of Kings on the throne of David some day.

"Shiloh" means Christ our Savior. Jacob, dying, saw Christ's day, and it was his comfort and support during his death.

Now look at verse 24 of this same chapter. Write in this verse

Jacob was addressing Joseph, and in the last part of the verse he said, "Joseph's hands were made strong by the hands of the mighty God of Jacob (from thence is the Shepherd, the Stone of Israel)."

Jesus is Shiloh.

Jesus is the One to come holding the scepter. The scepter of the universe today is held in nail-pierced hands.

Jesus is the Shepherd and He is the Stone. Think of all these things in reference to His coming to the earth as Messiah:

- He is the Seed promised of woman (Genesis 3:15).
- He is Shiloh who brings rest (Genesis 49:10).
- He is the King who holds the scepter (Psalm 2:7).
- He is the Shepherd who gave His life for the sheep (us) (John 10:11).
- He is the Chief Shepherd who is coming again (I Peter 5:4).
- He is the Stone that the builders disallowed but is now become the Headstone of the corner (Matthew 22:42).
- He is the Star, the bright and morning Star for His church today (Revelation 22:16).

The line to produce the "Seed" went from Adam to Seth. From Seth it went through Noah to Shem, then to Abraham, Isaac, Jacob and now Judah.

Genesis 49:11, this prophecy was fulfilled when Jesus came riding into Jerusalem on a donkey offering Himself as the Messiah and King of Israel. He washed His garments in "wine" and that was His own blood which He shed for the world.

So, from Judah, our Savior came. From Judah the line of Christ proceeded through Obed, Ruth, Jesse, David and on to Joseph, the husband of Mary (Matthew 1:1-17).

42

(4) Now we are able to understand these important words in the Bible, since we have studied all three characters:

Hebrew—Abraham first called a Hebrew (Genesis 14:13). First one called a Hebrew came through Shem. See Lesson 4.

Israel—Jacob is named (Genesis 32:28).

Jew—One belonging to the tribe or Kingdom of Judah (II Kings 16:6; 25:25). Then the meaning was extended, and the word was applied to anyone of the Hebrew race returning from the captivity, and finally to anyone of the Hebrew race. Look up Esther 2:5 and Matthew 2:2.

Their language was and is Hebrew.

5. **WHAT THE NEW TESTAMENT SAYS ABOUT JUDAH:**

(1) In Matthew 1:1-17 and Luke 3:23-38, we have the two lines of Christ listed in detail.

In Matthew the lineage is through Joseph. In Luke through Mary. In Luke 3:23 we are told that Joseph was the son of Heli. In Matthew 1:16, we are told that Joseph was the son of Jacob. *He could not be the son of both.* **Joseph was the "son-in-law" of Heli.** Heli was the father of Mary. (Don't let these two Scriptures confuse you.) Judah is found in both genealogies (Matthew 1:2-3 and Luke 3:33-34).

(2) In Hebrews 8:7-13, the New Covenant is promised to Israel and Judah.

This refers back to Jeremiah 31:31-34. This New Covenant rests upon the sacrifice of Christ, and secures the eternal blessedness under the Abrahamic Covenant of all who believe (Galatians 3:13-16). Write in Galatians 3:14

_____

_____

(3) Now look up Revelation 5:5 _____

_____

Jesus is "the Lion of the tribe of Judah." To Him belongs the scepter, the emblem of royalty and authority.

(4) In Revelation 22:16, Jesus says: "I am the root and offspring of David, and the bright and morning star."

(5) In Romans 15:12, Paul quotes Isaiah 11:1 and 10.

Romans 15:12, says "there shall be a root of Jesse . . ." Notice Isaiah 11:1, "There shall come forth a *rod* out of the stem of Jesse and a Branch (Christ) shall grow out of his roots."

All of this confirms the fact that God, in His divine wisdom, selected Abraham, Isaac, Jacob and then Judah and out of Judah would come the Lord Jesus Christ. He is called many names and we have given only a few to make you search the Scriptures. In future studies we shall dig deeper into this subject.

6. **THE LESSONS YOU SHOULD LEARN FROM THIS LESSON:**

(1) That the Lord God works in His own way and selects those who should do a special work for Him. This was true of Judah.

(2) Judah, selected by Jacob, was a sinful man. God used him anyway. We are all sinners, carnal, yet the Lord can use us if we are His and have accepted Him. There is that constant struggle between the spiritual and the carnal.

(3) Through Judah came Christ. God was faithful to His promise to Abraham, Isaac, Jacob and Judah. The "Seed" of Genesis 3:15, and the "Seed" promised to Abraham, was in the loins of Judah and those after him.

(4) "Shiloh" is another name, among many, for Christ. The word means "rest," and Jesus Christ is our "rest" (Matthew 11:28).

(5) Jacob saw into the future the coming of the Messiah, Shiloh, Jesus, the Son of God.

(6) The Lord Jesus is "the Lion of the tribe of Judah." He is the "rod out of the stem of Jesse and a Branch." Jesse was the father of David.

CAN YOU REMEMBER?

1. What does Judah mean?
2. Why was he selected over his three younger brothers?
3. What is the meaning of "Shiloh?" Of a scepter?
4. What is Jesus called, identifying Him with Judah?
5. What was Judah's position among the other tribes in the wilderness?

YOUR NEXT ASSIGNMENT:

1. Read Exodus 1 through 24 (the entire book if you can). Also read Numbers 9 through 21; Deuteronomy 32 through 34; Acts 7:22-38; John 3:14-16; John 6:31-32; Hebrews 3:1-19; Hebrews 11:23-29.
2. Read all you can on Moses. He will be the character of our next study.
3. Review your study of Judah.
4. Mark your Bible where new truths are learned.

Lesson 11
"Moses"

GREAT
CHARACTERS
OF THE
BIBLE

NOTES

(Where lines are provided, look up the Scripture and write it or its meaning in the space provided.)

1. **THE MEANING OF THE NAME:**
   Moses means "to draw out" or "extraction." Look up Exodus 2:10 and write in the last sentence:

   _____

   _____

2. **BASIC SCRIPTURES:**
   Exodus 1 through 24; Numbers 9 through 21; Deuteronomy 32 through 34; Acts 7:22-46; John 3:14-16; John 6:31-35; Hebrews 3:1-19; Hebrews 11:23-29.

3. **FAMILY BACKGROUND:**
   In Exodus 2:1-2; we read, "And there went a man of the house of Levi, and took to wife a daughter of Levi. And the woman conceived and bare a *son*." The "son" was born under the sentence of death by the Pharaoh at that time. The child was placed in an ark and hidden because, "every son that is born ye shall cast into the river" (Exodus 1:22). The daughter of Pharaoh found the ark. The baby's sister, on the river bank, suggested Jochebed, the mother of the baby, as the nurse to rear the child and care for him (Exodus 2:7-8).

   The parents of Moses are not named until Exodus 6:20. He was born to Amram and Jochebed. Amram was from the Levitical tribe, the son of Kohath.

   Moses, raised in a princely fashion, became instructed in all the wisdom of the Egyptians, who were then the most influential people in the world. Being in the palace of Pharaoh for the first forty years of his life equipped Moses for what *God* had in mind, not the Pharaoh of Egypt. Even though he learned the court life, the pomp and ceremony of royalty, the arts and glory of Egypt, Moses knew and remembered his origin and believed the promises which had been made to the Hebrew people by the Lord God.

4. **WHAT THE OLD TESTAMENT SAYS ABOUT MOSES:**
   (1) Moses' Life is Divided into Three 40-Year Periods:
   - 40 years in the palace of Pharaoh (chapter 2)
   - 40 years in Midian on the backside of the desert (chapter 3)
   - 40 years as the deliverer of his people from Egyptian bondage (chapter 5 and on). Read Exodus 7:7.

   (2) After the first 40 years, Moses identified himself with Israel and he fled from Pharaoh (Exodus 2:15).
   The king (Pharaoh) of Egypt died and the children of Israel cried because of their bondage (Exodus 2:23). God heard their cry and remembered His covenant with Abraham, Isaac and Jacob (Exodus 2:24).

   (3) The Call of Moses (Exodus 3).
   During the period Moses spent in Midian, out on the backside of the desert, God called and commissioned him to lead Israel out of bondage.

First, his call (Exodus 3:2-10). God appeared to Moses in a burning bush and the bush was not consumed (verse 2). God always appeared in a cloud or in fire. Moses could not turn away from such a sight. Out of the midst of the bush, God called Moses by name (verse 4). Write in verse 5 _____

_____

Second, God commissioned Moses to be the leader and "bring forth my people the children of Israel out of Egypt" (verse 10).

(4) The Excuses of Moses (Exodus 3:11 through 4:13).

Moses was just like most of us. God called and Moses made excuses to Him that he couldn't do what God said. Note the four excuses:

First excuse—"Who am I, that I should go . . ." (Exodus 3:11)
The answer—"Certainly I will be with thee . . ."(verse 12)
Second excuse—"When they say to me, what is his name, what shall I say unto them?" (verse 13)

The answer—(verse 14) Write in: _____

_____

God is the great "I AM."
Third excuse—"They will not believe me . . ." (Exodus 4:1).
The answer—"What is in thy hand?" (verses 2-9) God used a rod and the sign of leprosy on the hand of Moses. God uses what we have. The less we have, the more evident is His power.
Fourth excuse—"Oh Lord, I am not eloquent. I am slow of speech and of a slow tongue." (verse 10)
The answer—"Who hath made man's mouth? Go and I will be with thy mouth, and teach thee what thou shalt say." (verses 11 and 12)

Still, Moses said to God, "Send someone else" (verse 13). God then selected Aaron, the brother of Moses, to speak for Moses. God would use the heart and head of Moses and the tongue of Aaron. *The lesson is, there are no excuses if God calls us to a work. He will provide all we need.*

(5) The Contest with Pharaoh (Exodus 5:1 through 12:51).

After the call of God, Moses and Aaron returned to Egypt (Exodus 4:19-31).

Then in Exodus 5:1 begins the difficult stage in the life of Moses. He and Aaron made the first appeal to Pharaoh for God: "let my people go." Pharaoh was the first agnostic, "Who is the Lord?" (verse 2). He only increases the work burden of the children of Israel (Exodus 5:2 and 4-9).

After the Lord assured Moses in chapter 6:1-8 that He would do all He had promised, He renews His commission to Moses. (Underline the seven "I wills" in 6:6-8).

In the contest, the Pharaoh becomes fierce (chapters 7 through 11). We shall list only the "plagues of God" and each of these plagues was against one of the Egyptian gods:

Nature of Plague	The Plague	The Egyptian God Defeated
	1. Water into blood (Exodus 7:19-25)	Osiris, Nile god;
Touches the comfort	2. Frogs (Exodus 8:1-15)	Heka, frog goddess;
of the people	3. Lice (Exodus 8:16-19)	Geb, earth god;
	4. Flies (Exodus 8:20-24)	Khepara, beetle god
Touches property	5. Death of cattle (Exodus 9:1-7)	Apis, cattle god
Touches their person	6. Boils (Exodus 9:8-12)	Typhon, physical god
	7. Hail (Exodus 9:22-35)	Isis, air goddess;
Renders them helpless	8. Locusts (Exodus 10:12-20)	Serapis, insect god;
	9. Darkness (Exodus 10:21-23)	Ra, sun god
Death and doom	10. Death (Exodus 11:4-7)	Against all false gods

The purpose of the plagues was to reveal the power and holiness of God (Exodus 9:16-17); to reveal God to Egypt (Exodus 7:5); judgment upon the gods of Egypt (Exodus 12:12); to honor Israel (Exodus 8:22-23); to give a testimony to future generations (Exodus 10:1-2).

Moses stood firm on all the announcements for God. He withstood every temptation of Pharaoh.

(6) The Passover (Exodus 12)

God provided a way of escape through the Passover. Read all of the chapter. Write in verse 13

_____

_____

Finally Pharaoh tells Moses to go (Exodus 12:29-32).

In the face of the judgment of death, God provided a way out for His people. The Passover has important words, "When I see the blood, I will pass over you."

Christ is our Passover (I Corinthians 5:7). _____

_____

(7) Moses led Israel across the Red Sea (chapters 13-14).

Look up and underline Exodus 13:21-22; 14:21-22; 14:29-31. (Notice that the Lord appeared in a cloud by day, and fire by night, to lead them.)

The song of the redeemed is in chapter 15. Note especially verse 26. (Underline in your Bible.)

(8) The Lord God provided manna and quail for 40 years (Exodus 16:4, 13, 35).

They were in the wilderness, wandering around.

The Lord instituted the Sabbath (Exodus 16:23; 26-30).

(9) The Smitten Rock (Exodus 17:1-7).

Moses struck the rock in obedience—(later he strikes the rock in disobedience) (Numbers 20:7-13). Look up I Corinthians 10:4, and write in:

_____

_____

(10) To Moses, the Law was Given (Exodus 19-24).

   (a) **Commandments**—governing moral life (chapters 19 and 20). Jesus includes all of these in Matthew 22:37-39.

   (b) **Judgments**—governing social life (chapters 21-22).

   (c) **Ordinances**—governing religious life (chapter 24). The law was given, and did not take away the Abrahamic Covenant. Look up Galatians 3:17-18

_____

_____

Look up Galatians 3:19-24 _____

_____

_____

Look up Romans 3:20 _____

_____

Also Romans 7:7, and underline in your Bible.

(11) God Gave to Moses the Pattern for the Tabernacle (Exodus 25 through 40).

   (a) The pattern for the tabernacle is in chapters 25-31.

(b) Aaron and the people made a golden idol and Israel again slipped into idolatry and immorality. Moses interceded for them, but as he came down from Mt. Sinai, he saw the calf of gold and he was angry; so angry he broke the two stones containing the law. Moses interceded again for his people and then ascended back up Sinai. He descended, carrying a new copy of the law, and "his face did shine so that the people could not look upon him." He had been with God and it was visible (chapters 32-34).

(c) Moses finally instructed the people to build and assemble the tabernacle. The people gave more than enough to finish the tabernacle, the place where God could dwell with His people (chapters 35-40).

The tabernacle pointed to and was a symbol of Christ and His atoning work on the cross.

(12) Moses Never Went Into the Promised Land.

In Numbers 27:18-23, Joshua was selected to be his successor and it was Joshua who led Israel back into Canaan.

Only 70 Israelites had gone down into Egypt. After 400 years, it is estimated that more than two million (600,000 men, plus women and children) came out of Egypt.

Look up Deuteronomy 34:10 _____

_____

Look up Deuteronomy 31:2 _____

_____

Look up and underline Deuteronomy 29:29.

5. **WHAT THE NEW TESTAMENT SAYS ABOUT MOSES:**

(1) Stephen, again, tells us a great deal about Moses.
Look at Acts 7:22-46. Underline verses 23 and 30.

(2) Jesus ascribes the Pentateuch (first five books of the Bible) to Moses in Luke 24:44

_____

_____

(3) Look up John 3:14, and compare with Numbers 21:8-9.

(4) Jesus compares the bread given in the wilderness with the Bread of Life.

Look at John 6:31-35, and write in verse 35 _____

_____

(5) In Hebrews 3:1-19, we see that Christ is our High Priest.
He, God's Son, is better than the servant, Moses. Notice verse 5

_____

_____

Then verse 6 _____

_____

Underline verse 1 in your Bible.

(6) In Hebrews 11:23-29, five times we read "by faith."

Write in verse 25 _____

_____

Notice in verse 27 the words, "as seeing him who is invisible." Who was the "invisible" one? He was Jesus Christ, as you see in

48

verse 26. Moses had faith in the "seed of woman." Moses had a sixth sense, *Faith.*

6. **THE LESSONS WE SHOULD LEARN FROM THIS LESSON:**

(1) God selects and elects those who are to be His leaders in every generation.

(2) The Lord will sometime place us on the "backside of the desert" to teach us His will and patience.

(3) The Lord calls all of us, who have accepted Him, to a place of service, regardless of how small or great.

(4) All of us, in our carnal nature, will offer excuses to the Lord just as Moses did when he was called.

(5) In God's own time, He always has a way out for His people. Remember the ten plagues?

(6) The Lord provides only what we need; all we need to do is His work.

CAN YOU REMEMBER?

1. Moses' life was divided into three periods. What were they?

2. The excuses given by Moses sound like excuses today in the Christian world. Can you name them?

3. What was the purpose of the plagues?

4. God provided a way of escape for His people. What was it called? (Exodus 12).

5. What are the three divisions of the law?

6. Which books of the Bible did Moses write?

7. What did the tabernacle portray? What did it picture?

YOUR NEXT ASSIGNMENT:

1. Read Exodus 4 through 17; 24 and 30; Numbers 17 and 20; Leviticus 8, 9, 10, 16, and 17; Psalm 106; Hebrews 4:14 and 5:4; Hebrews 7:4-19; Hebrews 9:1-15.

2. The character for our next study is Aaron. Read all the assigned Scripture and other readings you may find on Aaron.

3. Review your study of Moses.

4. Mark your Bible where new truths are learned.

Lesson 12
"Aaron"

(Where lines are provided, look up the Scripture and write it or its meaning in the space provided.)

1. **THE MEANING OF THE NAME:**
   Aaron means "enlightened, bright, or mountain of strength."

2. **BASIC SCRIPTURES:**
   Exodus 4 through 17; 24 and 30; Numbers 17 and 20; Leviticus 8, 9, 10, 16, and 17; Psalm 106:8-16; Hebrews 4:14 to 5:4; Hebrews 7:4-19; Hebrews 9:1-15.

3. **FAMILY BACKGROUND:**
   Aaron was the brother of Moses. In our study, one cannot separate these two great leaders for God. Aaron was three years older than Moses (Exodus 7:7). He was a descendant of Levi through Kohath and Amram (Exodus 6:16-20). Aaron was the fourth generation from Levi.

   It is assumed that he was born before the terrible edicts of the Pharaoh dooming the Hebrew male children to death.

   Aaron married Elisheba (of the tribe of Judah), and she bore him four sons; Nadab, Abihu, Eleazar, Ithamar (Exodus 6:23). You should remember the first three of these sons of Aaron.

4. **WHAT THE OLD TESTAMENT SAYS ABOUT AARON:**

   (1) When Moses was called as the deliverer of the Israelites out of Egypt, he gave the Lord God excuses as to why he should not be the one chosen.

   Moses said, "I am not eloquent, I am slow of speech, and of a slow tongue" (Exodus 4:10). The Lord then selected his brother, Aaron, to be the spokesman. God would use Moses' head and heart and the mouth of Aaron. Note Exodus 4:14-16 and underline in your Bible. Aaron became the "prophet" for Moses. Look up Exodus 7:1 and write in the verse: _____

   _____

   The word "prophet" here means "one who speaks in place of another." The word "pro" in "prophet" does not mean "beforehand," as in the word "provide," but it does mean "in place of." The remainder of the word "prophet" is from the Greek, "phemi," which means "to speak." When the Lord God said that Aaron "shall be thy prophet," He meant just that.

   (2) Aaron and Moses met and embraced (Exodus 4:27).

   Returning to Egypt from Midian, they gathered the elders of Israel and told them of the approaching deliverance from bondage (Exodus 4:29-31).

   (3) Aaron acted as the agent and spokesman for Moses and carried the "rod of God" which had been given to Moses.

   Aaron used the "rod" (given by God as a "sign" of Divine authority, Exodus 4:17), in the first talks with the elders and Pharaoh. Look up Exodus 7:9, 19; 8:5, 16.

   Moses finally took the rod in his own hand and did as the Lord commanded, Exodus 9:23; 10:13,23.

   Look up Exodus 14:16 and write in _____

Turn to Exodus 17:5-6 and underline in your Bible. (The rod will appear again later in this lesson.)

(4) Aaron was to be the high priest and his sons were to be priests.

This was according to the instructions of God to Moses. After the tabernacle had been completed, Aaron and his four sons were consecrated to the priesthood by the anointing of oil and clothed in beautiful garments (Exodus 28:1-3). Notice that God appointed Aaron and his sons, and the people were to make the garments to "consecrate" Aaron to minister to the Lord God. That word "consecrate" means "to set apart for God" or "sanctify."

(5) The Consecration of the Priests (Leviticus 8).

The high priest (Aaron)	**The other priests (his sons)**
• Cleansed (verse 6)	• Cleansed (verse 6)
• Clothed (verses 7 and 8)	• Clothed (verse 13)
• Crowned (verse 9)	• Charged (verse 35)
• Anointed (verse 12)	• Anointed (verse 30)

Aaron was anointed *before* the blood sacrifice in Leviticus 8:11 (the sacrifice is in verses 14 through 24), prefiguring Jesus Christ.

His sons were anointed *after* the blood sacrifice (verse 30), prefiguring believer priests-Christians.

(6) The Ministry of the Priests (Leviticus 9).

God always has His leaders and He blesses through leaders. (Read Leviticus 9:22-24 and underline.)

(7) The Sin of Presumption by Two Priests (Leviticus 10).

Two sons of Aaron, Nadab and Abihu, went ahead of the Lord and offered "strange fire" from the altar of burnt offering "*before* the Lord which He commanded them *not*" (verse 1).

God punished them in verse 2. They were not to misuse or abuse the office God had given to them.

(8) God's Atonement Through Blood (Leviticus 16).

This is the great chapter on "atonement." That word means "to cover." In the Old Testament, "atonement" covered sin until the one *real atonement* was offered by our Great High Priest, Jesus Christ.

God gave Aaron strict instructions as to the time and circumstances when Aaron could enter the "Holy of Holies." Read chapter 16 and underline verse 2. Write in verse 34 _____

_____

_____

The word "atonement" is used *sixteen* times in this chapter. Find them and underline the word.

In Leviticus 17, we see the place of sacrifice. The place was always "the altar." The one verse you should memorize is verse 11 _____

_____

Note also verse 2. The Lord gave the orders to Moses, who gave them to Aaron. Notice, "This is the thing which the Lord hath commanded." One thing God required, as always: *Blood applied upon the altar, "for it is the blood that makes atonement."*

(9) Aaron's Rod That Budded (Numbers 17).

After the attack on the priesthood of Aaron in chapter 16, God did a magnificent thing. He took a "stick" called "the rod of Aaron" and caused that rod to bud and blossom and yield almonds. Look at verse 8 and underline; also verse 10. In verse 10 the Lord said "Bring Aaron's rod again before the testimony (Ark), to be kept for a sign."

This rod becomes significant. Consider that each of the heads of the tribes brought a dead rod. Only "the rod of Aaron for the house of Levi was budded." God put life into only one rod, Aaron's.

This is a beautiful picture of Christ in resurrection. (Look up Hebrews 9:1-4 and you find what was in the Ark.)

(10) The Sin Of Aaron and Moses (Numbers 20).

As usual, the people complained because there was no water. God told Moses exactly what to do.

Write in verse 8 _____

_____

God said "speak" and He did not say "smite." This was a sin (fully explained in the New Testament), and God told Aaron and Moses that they would not go into the Promised Land. Look at verse 12, and underline in your Bible.

(11) Aaron's Death (Numbers 20).

Beginning at verse 23, we read of the death of Aaron, and God repeated the reason Aaron did not go into the land in verse 24.

Eleazar, Aaron's son, became the high priest (verse 28).

Aaron was the first high priest and filled that office nearly forty years.

5. **WHAT THE NEW TESTAMENT SAYS ABOUT AARON:**

(1) Paul tells us that the things that happened to Israel in the wilderness are examples, pictures, types for us during the church age.

Look up I Corinthians 10:6 and write in the verse _____

_____

Also verse 11 _____

_____

While you are in I Corinthians 10, you will discover something about the "rock in the wilderness." Write in verse 4 _____

_____

(2) Aaron, the first high priest, *was a picture of Jesus Christ,* **our High Priest.**

Underline Hebrews 4:14.

Jesus was "after the order of Melchizedek," or everlasting. This "order" is described in Hebrews 7:11-28. Write in Hebrews 7:27

_____

Underline Hebrews 8:1-2. Also verse 5.

Jesus executes His office of High Priest after the pattern of Aaron. This is detailed for us in Hebrews 9:1-15. Notice especially the first ten verses of this chapter and write in verses 7, 8, and 9 ____

_____

_____

(3) Aaron, according to the above verses, was sinful (verse 7).

He functioned in the earthly tabernacle, "which was a figure (picture) for the time then present." The tabernacle and priestly ministry of Aaron was, according to verse 8, "the Holy Spirit sign-i-fying that the holiest of all was not yet made manifest (visible), while the first tabernacle was yet standing."

(4) "But Christ," The Better Way (Hebrews (9:11-15).

Jesus Christ is our High Priest and no longer is it necessary to offer the blood of animals for sin. In verse 12, "by His own blood, He entered once into the holy place, having obtained eternal redemption for us." (Redemption means "we have been bought with a price paid by someone else.")

Underline Hebrews 9:14.

6. THE LESSONS YOU SHOULD LEARN FROM THIS STUDY:

(1) When God calls a person, He provides them with the ability to perform that service.

(2) A "prophet" is "one who speaks in place of another." In that sense, we can all be "prophets" and speak for the Lord Jesus.

(3) Aaron was the high priest and his sons were priests. This was a figure of Christ, as our High Priest, making all who believe in Him priests. Jesus is the only mediator between God and man (I Timothy 2:5).

(4) The "rod" was God's symbol of authority. We have the "rod" of God, His Word.

(5) Aaron was called of God, yet human. He was sinful and he never went into the Promised Land. Yet, he belonged to the Lord God. Look at Psalms 106:16.

(6) We have the authority, if we believe in Jesus, to come boldly to Him to find grace, obtain mercy and find help in time of need (Hebrews 4:14-16).

CAN YOU REMEMBER?

1. Aaron came from the tribe of _____.

2. Why did God place Aaron with Moses?

3. How did Aaron become the high priest?

4. The tabernacle and the priestly function was placed in the Word of God for a purpose. What was that purpose?

5. What (or who) was that ROCK in the wilderness?

6. Aaron was called, yet he was not sinless. Can you name two things he did wrong?

YOUR NEXT ASSIGNMENT:

1. Read Exodus 17:8-16; 24:12-18; 33:11; Numbers 13, 14, and 27; Joshua 1 through 7; Joshua 10, 13, 23, and 24; Acts 7:44-46; Hebrews 4:6-8; Hebrews 11:30.

2. The character for the next lesson will be Joshua. Read all you can find about him.

3. Review your study of Aaron.

4. Mark your Bible where new truths are learned.

Lesson 13
"Joshua"

(Where lines are provided, look up the Scripture and write it or its meaning in the space provided.)

1. **THE MEANING OF THE NAME:**

   Joshua means "Jehovah is salvation."

2. **BASIC SCRIPTURES:**

   Exodus 17:8-16; 24:12-18; 33-11; Numbers 13,14,27; Joshua 1 through 7, 10, 13, 23, 24; Acts 7:44-46; Hebrews 4:6-8: Hebrews 11:30.

3. **FAMILY BACKGROUND:**

   All that we know about Joshua is that he was born as a slave in Egyptian bondage. He was born the son of Nun, an Ephraimite (Numbers 13:8). Nothing is mentioned in Scripture of his mother but, without doubt, Joshua's parents feared the Lord God of Israel.

   There are several names used in Scripture for Joshua. You have noticed one in Numbers 13:8; the name "Oshea." In Deuteronomy 32:44, he is "Hoshea." Other names used for him are "Jehoshua" in I Chronicles 7:27. In Hebrews 4:8, his name is translated Jesus. In Nehemiah 8:17 you find "Jeshua." *That term, "Jeshua," was Grecianized and appears as "Jesus."* When you look again at the "meaning of the name," you can understand why Joshua and Jesus are so closely identified in name.

4. **WHAT THE OLD TESTAMENT SAYS ABOUT JOSHUA:**

   (1) He was Moses' Minister (Exodus 24:13).

   Joshua had the unique privilege to go with Moses to Mt. Sinai. Joshua was actually an assistant to Moses. Moses would have selected a close associate prayerfully. Joshua felt it his reponsibility to care for Moses' reputation, character, and physical needs. In Exodus 33:11 Joshua, the servant of Moses, stayed in the tabernacle as though there might be further instructions from the Lord.

   It is hard to be a "second fiddle," but it was in this capacity that Joshua had great ability. He was second to Moses and a servant to Moses, but Joshua was first and foremost "the servant of the Lord," as is recorded in Joshua 24:29. A "second fiddle," or a second man, called of God, can perform a service of great distinction if that person can kill self-pride. Joshua must have conquered pride.

   (2) Joshua was Successor to Moses (Numbers 27:15-19).

   By divine appointment, Joshua was to lead Israel after Moses. Look up Numbers 27:18 and write in _____

   _____

   _____

   God gave to Joshua the power to lead with authority. God gave him the ability and Joshua had great faith.

   (3) The Call and Commission of Joshua (Joshua 1:1-9).

   Joshua was God's choice after the death of Moses. He was to lead the children of Israel out of Egypt and *into* the land God had given to Abraham. The Pentateuch of Moses only led Israel *up to* Canaan. Joshua was to lead them *into* Canaan.

Note his call (Joshua 1:1-2) and write in verse 2 _____

_____

In the call and commission of Joshua, the Lord gave him a promise of possession of the land (verses 3 and 4). In the call God gave Joshua full assurance, "As I was with Moses, so I will be with thee: I will not fail thee, nor forsake thee" (verse 5).

Joshua's commissioning service was conducted by the Lord God Himself (verses 5 through 9). Four times in chapter 1, Joshua was told to be strong and courageous (Joshua 1:6, 7, 9, 18). Notice the words in the commission:

(a) "Be strong and of good courage" to divide the land (verse 6).

(b) "Be strong and very courageous" to do all the law (verse 7).

(c) Write in the secret of success (verse 8). _____

_____

(d) God repeats His assurance to Joshua (verse 9).

The important thing for us to remember is the *emphasis God placed on the Word of God in verse 8,* which is God's secret of success for anyone.

(4) A Leader in War (Joshua 2 through 11).

Joshua sent two spies to look over the key to victory, which was Jericho (chapter 2). Joshua used **means** as well as **faith.** (The writer of Hebrews confirms this as we shall see in the New Testament section of this lesson.)

A critical moment for Israel was at the crossing of the Jordan (chapter 3). Joshua was ready and the Lord assured him. Underline verse 7; also notice verses 3, 5, 13, and 17. They were to watch the Ark, follow the priests and Levites, and cross over on dry ground.

In chapter 4 the Lord told Joshua to raise memorials in the river Jordan (verse 9) and a memorial at Gilgal (verses 19-20). These memorials were to remind them of the power of God in holding back the waters, and the faithfulness of God in bringing them into the land.

The first thing Joshua faced after going into the land was Jericho. At that precise moment God revealed Himself to Joshua (Joshua 5:13-15). **This is an appearance of Jesus Christ, preincarnate.** This is called a "theophany," an appearance, a manifestation, an epiphany of Jesus Christ. The "man" Joshua saw identified himself as "the captain of the host of the Lord." Note and underline the last part of verse 15. The *same words* were used when God called Moses and God appeared and talked out of the burning bush (Exodus 3:3-5).

With this encouragement, Joshua was assured of Jericho if Israel would do as the Lord commanded. The whole thing was a venture of faith (chapter 6). You know the song about "the walls came tumbling down." This is the real account of what God did for Israel. This victory inspired Israel with confidence and enthusiasm and at the same time struck terror into the hearts of the Canaanites and actually conditioned them for defeat.

In chapter 7 Joshua had to deal with individuals, as well as armies and crowds. In this chapter the sin of Achan is described. Notice that the sin of one affected all of Israel (verses 10-11). The Lord said to Joshua, "Get thee up, Israel hath sinned." Achan wanted all he could get for himself. Notice verse 21: "I saw, I coveted, I took, I hid."

The next four chapters give the account of victories for Joshua and Israel. Turn to Joshua 11:23 and write in: _____

_____

(5) Joshua Was a Diplomatic Spiritual Leader (Joshua 13-24).

Joshua used diplomacy in his ability to divide the land among the tribes (chapter 13).

The division of the land was "by casting lots before the Lord" (Joshua 18:6-7). They were slow to actually possess the land (Joshua 18:3).

This should teach us to possess all that He has for us in Christ Jesus.

The great passage in this section is Joshua 21:43-45. Underline these verses and realize that God did all that He had promised.

In Joshua's farewell message, he exhorted the people to abide by the Word of God (Josha 23:6); to keep themselves separated from other nations (verse 7); to "cleave unto the Lord" who had given the victory (verses 8-11); to "guard against apostasy" (verse 13).

His testimony of his trust in God is given in Joshua 23:14. Underline in your Bible.

In Joshua's last words to his people he challenged them to serve the Lord.

Write in Joshua 24:14 _____

_____

In verse 15 Joshua's famous words are recorded: *"Choose now this day whom you will serve, but as for me and my house, we will serve the Lord."*

Joshua died at the age of 110 years (Joshua 24:29).

5. **WHAT THE NEW TESTAMENT SAYS ABOUT JOSHUA:**

(1) Again, Stephen's sermon before the council refers back to all that happened to Israel and their God-appointed leaders.

In Acts 7:44-45 Stephen speaks of the tabernacle and says in verse 45, "Which also our fathers that came after brought in with Jesus (Joshua) into the possession of the Gentiles, whom God drove out before the face of our fathers." In naming Joshua here, which in Greek is Jesus, there is the intimation that as the Old Testament Joshua brought in that typical tabernacle, so the New Testament Jesus should bring in the true tabernacle, a "house not made with hands, eternal in the heavens" (II Corinthians 5:1). Look at Hebrews 8:2 and underline.

(2) In Hebrews 4:8 we see the same wording.

The verse should read, "For if Joshua had given them rest." This teaches us that our rest is in Christ Jesus. *Joshua could only bring the people to a rest in Canaan, while Christ brings all believers to the true rest of God.* Look at Hebrews 4:3 and 9.

(3) Joshua is a good lesson on FAITH.

In Hebrews 11:30 we read: *"By faith* the walls of Jericho fell down."* When you look at Joshua 1:5 and 9 you can understand the faith of Joshua.

Write in I John 5:4 _____

_____

(For more study on the parallel between Joshua and Ephesians see "Through The Bible In One Year," Basic Study, Vol. 1, page 29.)

6. **THE LESSONS YOU SHOULD LEARN FROM THIS STUDY:**

(1) Joshua is a good example of being the ideal "second man." This takes more grace than being the leader.

(2) Joshua was a servant of Moses, but first and foremost a servant of God.

(3) There is no sign of self-pride in the life of Joshua.

(4) After the death of Moses, Joshua became the leader and it did not

change him. In fact, he became closer to the Lord and His guidance.

(5) Joshua placed great emphasis upon the Word of God. A good example for our leaders and for us, who might be followers.

(6) Joshua was a diplomat, yet spiritual. He teaches us that we should possess all of our possessions in Christ, just as he told Israel to possess the land.

CAN YOU REMEMBER?

1. What does "Joshua" mean?
2. What was Joshua's main duty as described by the Lord?
3. How did the children of Israel cross the Jordan River?
4. What did they do after they crossed the Jordan?
5. How did Joshua and his people conquer Jericho?
6. How did Joshua divide the land?

YOUR NEXT ASSIGNMENT:

1. Read Joshua 2 and 6; Matthew 1:5; Hebrews 11:31; James 2:25.
2. The next character is Rahab, a harlot. What? A harlot in the Bible that teaches spiritual truths? Yes!
3. Review your study of Joshua.
4. Mark your Bible were new truths are learned.

Lesson 14
"Rahab"

(Where lines are provided, look up the Scripture and write it or its meaning in the space provided.)

1. **THE MEANING OF THE NAME:**

   Rahab means "insolence," "fierceness," "spaciousness."

2. **BASIC SCRIPTURES:**

   Joshua 2 and 6; Matthew 1:5; Hebrews 11:31; James 2:25.

3. **FAMILY BACKGROUND:**

   Rahab was an Amorite, who were an idolatrous people. Her parents, brothers and sisters were alive at the time of the conquest of Jericho. We are not given any of her family by name, but she mentions their relation to her in Joshua 2:13. (The Rahab mentioned in Psalms 87:4; 89:10; Isaiah 30:7; Isaiah 51:9 is not the Rahab of this study. The name in these references was a poetical name in Egypt and is parallel to the word "dragon." *Do not confuse these Scriptures with the Rahab of this lesson.*)

   Rahab was known as a "harlot." Her house was on the city wall of Jericho. It was built of sun-dried brick and her window looked to the outside of the wall. Some interpreters have suggested that the word "harlot" could be translated "innkeeper." The Bible never makes an attempt to call her by any other title except "harlot."

   Her family changed after the events of Jericho, and the family changes are discussed in this lesson.

4. **WHAT THE OLD TESTAMENT SAYS ABOUT RAHAB:**

   (1) Her Character — Joshua 2

   Three times in the Book of Joshua Rahab is referred to as a "harlot" (Joshua 2:1; 6:17, 25). She lived alone, as is indicated in (Joshua 2:18). Her family was to be in her house if they were to be saved. She had a house located so that the people of Jericho could see men entering and leaving. The word for "harlot" in both Hebrew and Greek means just one thing: "harlot." Her character was not good.

   Joshua sent two men to "spy secretly" on the city of Jericho (Joshua 2:1). The location of Rahab's house attracted their attention and they went there. We are not told why they went to Rahab's house but when you have read all the Scripture in the lesson assignment, a reason jumps out. That reason can be found in one verse, Romans 8:28 _____

   _____

   _____

   The Lord knows where to lead us and He prepares the way in advance.

   (2) Her Works — Joshua 2

   First, Rahab took a stand against the king of Jericho (verses 3-6). Rahab hid two men who were a part of the "enemy" of Jericho. She even lied to the king's representatives in order to protect the two spies. She had heard of the exodus of Israel out of Egypt, the miracle of the Red Sea and the overthrow of the two kings of the

Amorites, Sihon and Og (verse 10). (See Numbers 21:21-35.)

Second, Rahab planned the protection and the escape of the two spies (verses 4 and 6). She covered them with stalks of flax (used to make cloth material). She told them where to go and how long they should hide (verse 16). The escape of the two spies was through a window using a heavy scarlet thread or rope. The window was on the outside wall (verse 15).

(3)   Her Faith — Joshua 2:9-11

Rahab had been a sinful woman, *yet she had a remarkable understanding of the work and sovereign will of God.* Her own words indicate this fact. Notice and write in her words in verse 9 _____

_____

_____

Look at verse 11 and write the last part of the verse:

"for the Lord your God _____

_____ ."

Her faith was a simple faith. So strong was this faith that she was willing to risk her own life in order to save two Israelites, trusting that she would be saved by them. Her faith is also expressed in the two words of verse 9, "I know . . ."

(4)   Her Requests — Joshua 2:12-13

Rahab only requested that when Israel came into Jericho that she and her father, her mother, her brothers and sisters and "all that they have," meaning their children, be saved from death (verse 13). She made the request on the basis of what she had done for the spies (verse 12).

Notice the men's reply to her request (verse 14) _____

_____

_____

(5)   Her "True Token" — Joshua 2:12, 15, 18, 21

The *"true token"* or sign Rahab requested was one made by her own hands. It was the scarlet thread or rope which the men used to go down the wall. *That scarlet rope has great and significant meaning. It meant that Rahab had faith in the "men of god" and it was a sign of her faith in the Lord God of Israel.*

The scarlet rope was to be placed outside the window for Joshua and his men to see. It was Rahab's mark of identification as one to be saved in the day of calamity. *Therefore, it speaks of our safety in Jesus because of His sacrifice.* Look up and underline Hebrews 9:19-22.

We studied in Exodus 12 the Passover. Here in Joshua it is a like promise. Rahab and her family might not have felt perfectly safe within her house but the same promise held true, "When I see the blood, I will pass over you."

The scarlet rope was the token requested in verse 12. It was the same cord which had already saved the two spies and it was to be visible in the window. It was *scarlet, red.* It saved Rahab and her family.

As Dr. W. A. Criswell says, *"It is a part of the Scarlet Thread of Redemption."*

(6)   Rahab Was Saved Alive — Joshua 6:17, 22, 23, 25

Rahab loved her family and included them in her request for safety. When Joshua entered the city of Jericho, he respected the promise made to Rahab by the spies. With the scarlet line of redemption in the window, the two men were told by Joshua to go to the harlot's house and save her and all her kindred (verse 22).

The statement, "saved Rahab alive," (verse 25) might raise some questions. Some ask how her house, which is said to have been

60

"upon the wall" in chapter 2:15, escaped falling with the wall. We are sure that it did escape, for Rahab and her family were safe inside. The wall of Jericho fell down flat, according to Joshua 6:20. Matthew Henry states, "rather that part of the wall on which her house stood fell not."

So, Rahab and her family were saved miraculously by the power and sovereign will of God. Rahab was not only "saved alive," *but saved to live.* She knew that the spies from Israel were servants of the Lord, therefore she protected them and, in turn, was saved because of her faith in "the God of heaven above and in earth beneath" (Joshua 2:11).

5. **WHAT THE NEW TESTAMENT SAYS ABOUT RAHAB:**

   (1) **Rahab Became An Ancestress of Jesus — Matthew 1:5**

   Rahab's faith was a saving faith and she became the wife of Salmon, from the tribe of Judah. Some think that Salmon was one of the two spies who went to Rahab's house, and it could be, but nowhere is this stated in Scripture.

   Write in Matthew 1:5 _____

   _____

   The King James version says "Boaz of Rachab" and should read, "Boaz by Rahab." Notice in this verse that Boaz, Rahab's son, married Ruth and Obed was their son. Obed, Rahab's grandson, became the father of Jesse. Jesse, Rahab's great grandson, was the father of David, the king.

   Turn to Isaiah 11:1 _____

   _____

   Jesus is the "rod out of the stem of Jesse." Jesus is the "Branch out of his roots."

   Look at Jeremiah 23:5 and underline. In this verse the Branch, who is Jesus Christ, was raised from David. *These prophecies are all fulfilled in Matthew 1:5-6.* Paul says in Romans 1:3, "Jesus Christ our Lord, which was made of the seed of David according to the flesh."

   For further study you may look up Zechariah 3:8 and 6:12-13.

   (2) **Rahab's Faith Confirmed — Hebrews 11:31**

   Rahab's faith gave her a place in the great "Hall of Faith" of Hebrews 11. Now, write in Hebrews 11:31 _____

   _____

   Notice "Rahab perished not *with them that believed not.*" The secret of her safety and security can be found in the first two words, "By faith." Also notice the last two words of the verse, "with peace." She had a faith in the Lord God of Israel and an assured peace that she and her family would be saved.

   Rahab is the only woman besides Sarah listed in this faith chapter (Hebrews 11).

   While her faith is magnified in Hebrews 11, did you notice that the author of Hebrews is careful to put in the word "harlot?"

   (3) **Rahab's Faith Produced Works — James 2:25**

   Turn to James 2:25 and write the verse _____

   _____

   _____

   James says that Rahab was justified **by works,** while Paul says in Hebrews 11, she was justified **by faith.** *These do not contradict because faith justified Rahab and works justified the faith.*

   What Rahab did for the spies was **faith in practice.** She believed with the heart, confessed with the mouth (Romans 10:9-10), and acted at the risk of her life. (For the definition of faith, turn to Hebrews 11:1.) *Rahab could not see, but the substance was in her heart.* James does not let us forget that she was a harlot.

6. **THE LESSONS YOU SHOULD LEARN FROM THIS STUDY:**

    (1) Rahab, a harlot, was in the line of Christ. Jesus came in behalf of sinners and he identified Himself with sinful man. Just glance at the line of Christ in Matthew and Luke.

    (2) Christ magnified His grace when He came from such as Judah, Pharez, Tamar, Rahab and others.

    (3) Rahab teaches us that it is not the **amount** of truth one has that saves, but it is **obeying the truth** one has that saves.

    (4) Saving faith is that faith that produces works.

    (5) *God saves because of faith, not righteousness.*

    (6) What Rahab was is not as important as what she became. All of us are sinners, with sins as scarlet; but if we have believed, we have been saved by the "Scarlet Thread of Redemption," a token of grace from our Lord Jesus Christ.

CAN YOU REMEMBER?

1. Why do you think so much empahsis is placed on Rahab, the harlot?
2. What were some of her works?
3. Why did she perform these works?
4. What was the sign or token in the window and what did it indicate?
5. How many women are in the "Hall of Faith" in Hebrews 11? Name them.

YOUR NEXT ASSIGNMENT:

1. Read the four chapters of the Book of Ruth; Matthew 1:5
2. Review your study of the lesson on Rahab.
3. Mark your Bible where new truths are learned.
4. Read all you can find on Ruth, our character for the next lesson.

Lesson 15
"Ruth"

(Where lines are provided, look up the Scripture and write it or its meaning in the space provided.)

1. **THE MEANING OF THE NAME:**
   Ruth, "a sight worth seeing," "beauty," "friendship."

2. **BASIC SCRIPTURES:**
   Ruth 1-4; Matthew 1:5.

3. **FAMILY BACKGROUND:**
   All that we find recorded about Ruth is the fact that she was a young lady in Moab. Five times, in this short book, she is called "Ruth the Moabitess." She is also called "the woman of Moab" and "the Moabitish damsel."

   There is no record of her family, nor her past.

   The book of Ruth belongs to the period of the Judges, 1:1. The record is a true story of a young Gentile girl with qualities admired by Jew and Gentile down through history.

   Only two books in the Bible bear the names of women. They are Ruth and Esther. Ruth was a Gentile who married a Hebrew. Esther was a Hebrew who married a Gentile.

   When God writes the history of a life, He does it with a purpose, to teach us some lesson or illustrate some truth we should know. The life of Ruth does both, as we shall see in our study.

4. **WHAT THE OLD TESTAMENT SAYS ABOUT RUTH:**
   All four chapters of the Book of Ruth deal with her and reveal four stages in her life. *These correspond to the four stages in the spiritual life of a Christian.* The first two chapters show our part, and Ruth's; the last two chapters show God's part.

   (1) Ruth's Decision - Chapter 1
   Ruth had married a Hebrew named Mahlon (Ruth 4:10). After only ten years (Ruth 1:4) Mahlon and his brother, Chilion, died. This left Ruth and Orpah, Chilion's wife, widows. Their mother-in-law, Naomi, had lost her husband and then her two sons. Naomi and her family were Hebrews who had left their own land. While in Moab the two Hebrew sons married Moabite girls, ignorant of God and God's ways.

   Naomi had heard that the Lord had visited His people in Canaan and that the famine was over (Ruth 1:6). She and her two daughters-in-law start toward Canaan and the city of Bethlehem. Orpah, Ruth's sister-in-law decides she can not turn her back on her past, her country, her friends and her idols (Ruth 1:15). At the border, Orpah turns back. It would cost her too much.

   Ruth made her decision to go with Naomi. Ruth loved her mother-in-law and she was loyal to her. Two of the most beautiful verses in Scripture are Ruth 1:16-17. The verses are long but should be remembered and memorized if possible. Write them _____

   _____

   _____

   _____

The chief point of Ruth's decision was that she took the God of the Hebrews to be her God. Notice in Ruth 2:12 the past tense. She had already "come to trust" in the Lord God of Israel.

By her decision, Ruth became one of God's people and she and Naomi arrived in Bethlehem (Ruth 1:19).

So, in chapter one Ruth's decision was for God. "Thy people shall be my people, and thy God my God."

(2) Ruth's Service - Chapter 2

Ruth was young and excited over her new opportunity to work and care for Naomi. Naomi had a "kinsman" named Boaz and, by marriage, Boaz was also the kinsman of Ruth. He was a man of wealth and had fields of corn. God wisely orders small things and Ruth just "happened" to "light on a field belonging to Boaz" (verse 3).

Boaz noticed Ruth and invited her to stay in his field to glean (pick up the leftovers after the reapers). He also told her to stay near his women working in the field so that the young men would not touch her. Notice verses 11 and 12 and underline. Boaz saw her goodness and beauty and told his men to let Ruth work in the best part of the field and to give her "handfuls on purpose."

NOTE: *(In the Old Testament a kinsman had the right and obligation to redeem a relative. This is known as a "kinsman-redeemer" and the law is in Leviticus 25. The person and the inheritance could be redeemed by the near kinsman. The Hebrew word for "kinsman" is GOEL," one who could redeem, "to free by paying," becoming the redeemer, "the one who pays." In the case of Ruth, Boaz was the "GOEL" or the kinsman-redeemer.)*

Under the law, there were three requirements of the kinsman:

First, he must be willing to redeem (Leviticus 25:25; Galatians 4:4-5). _____

_____

_____

_____

Second, he must be a kinsman to have the right to redeem (Leviticus 25:48-49; Ruth 3:12-13; Hebrews 2:11). _____

_____

_____

Third, he must have the power, the means to redeem (Ruth 4:4-6; John 10:11-18). _____

_____

All of the above parenthetical statement is necessary for you to understand the actions of Boaz. It will be necessary for you to remember that statement when we reach the New Testament section of this lesson.

(3) Ruth's Rest - Chapter 3

This chapter seems strange to us and there is not the slightest indication of impurity in the story. The actions were in full agreement with Hebrew custom (Deuteronomy 25:5-6).

When Naomi sent Ruth to Boaz to lie at his feet, she was only appealing to Boaz to honor the Israelite law and give love and shelter, as a husband, to Ruth. This was to honor the name of Mahlon, Ruth's deceased husband.

Boaz understood Ruth's intentions, as his words show in Ruth 3:10-13.

Ruth rested in the fact that Boaz would keep his word as the near kinsman. Notice the word "rest" in verse 1 and verse 18.

Write in the last part of verse 13, "I do the part _____

_____ "

Do not read into this chapter what is not there. Ruth was a virtuous woman and Boaz said so (verse 11).

(4) Ruth's Reward - Chapter 4

Ruth became the bride of Boaz because he bought all that had belonged to the husbands of Naomi, Ruth and Orpah. Notice verse 9 and 10 and underline. There was a kinsman (not named) before Boaz who refused to take a Moabitess to be his wife. He handed over the right to Boaz, in public (verses 5-8).

Ruth and Boaz had a son whose "name may be famous in Israel" (verse 14).

The son was named Obed (verse 17).

Notice the interesting, exciting genealogy listed in verses 17-22:

Ruth, a *Gentile,* the mother of Obed . . .

Obed became the father of Jesse . . .

Jesse became the father of David, the king . . .

Ruth was the grandmother of David . . .

(Don't forget that Boaz was the son of Rahab and Salmon.)

5. WHAT THE NEW TESTAMENT SAYS ABOUT RUTH:

(1) In only one place is her name mentioned.

That is found in the genealogy in Matthew 1:5. Therefore, Ruth, the virtuous Gentile, was in the line of Christ. Of the four women in the line of our Lord, only Ruth was virtuous, while the other three were far from being like Ruth. They were Tamar, Rahab and Bathsheba.

(2) The lessons in Ruth abound with New Testament teaching in picture and type.

- Ruth's decision (chapter 1) and service (chapter 2) were her part. Also these are our parts.
- Her rest (chapter 3) and reward (chapter 4) were God's part.
- Boaz is a picture of our Kinsman Redeemer, Jesus Christ. He met the requirements of a "goel," which were:

First, he must be willing to redeem (Leviticus 25:25 and Galatians 4:4-5). Write in Galatians 4:4-5 _____

_____

Second, he must be a kinsman to have the right to redeem (Leviticus 25:48-49). Look up Philippians 2:5-8 and write in verse 7 _____

_____

Third, he must have the power, the means to redeem (Ruth 4:4-6; John 10:11 and 18). Write in verse 11 _____

_____

Verse 18 _____

_____

_____

- **Ruth is a picture of the church, the bride of the Redeemer.**
  When Ruth had no hope in anyone other than Boaz, when she knelt at his feet, he graciously received her.

So, today Jesus Christ is our near Kinsman and He is our Redeemer. The Church is His bride.

(3) The names in the Book of Ruth reveal much to us, and you should learn and record their meanings.

- "Bethlehem" means "house of bread"
- "Elimelech" means "my God is King"
- "Naomi" means "pleasantness"
- "Ruth" means "beauty, friendship"
- "Boaz" means "strength"

Jesus is our strength. The saved ones, the Church, is His bride and He loves us. In His sight we are beautiful and closer than mere friends. Our Kinsman Redeemer willingly paid the price to redeem us and to give us everlasting life.

Just think, the Bread of Life, Jesus, came to The House of Bread, Bethlehem.

6. **THE LESSONS YOU SHOULD LEARN FROM THIS STUDY:**

(1) A Hebrew family left Canaan and as a result the sons married "heathen" wives. They had left the place God had given them. We do the same thing and wonder why things happen to us.

(2) God always receives and restores those who come back to Him (as did Naomi).

(3) Love should abound for our loved ones; yes, even our mothers-in-law.

(4) When we place ourselves at His disposal and serve Him, He rewards us with spiritual blessings.

(5) We should not be like Orpah, who turned back because it would cost her too much.

(6) The Lord provides for all our needs if we ask, believe and work for Him.

CAN YOU REMEMBER?

1. What is significant about Ruth?

2. What was Ruth's most important decision?

3. Where did Ruth and Naomi go, and why?

4. What is a kinsman-redeemer?

5. Who is our Kinsman-Redeemer?

6. What were Ruth's qualities?
   She was the grandmother of _____.

YOUR NEXT ASSIGNMENT:

1. Read I Samuel 1 and 2.

2. Read all you can find about Hannah.

3. Review your notes on your study of Ruth.

4. Mark your Bible where new truths are learned.

Lesson 16
"Hannah"

(Where lines are provided, look up the Scripture and write it or its meaning, in the space provided.)

This lesson is an integral part of the next lesson on the character Samuel. The two lessons really go together; therefore, it is imperative that you be in attendance for both.

1. **THE MEANING OF THE NAME:**
   Hannah means "gracious," and by a slight change becomes Anna or Ann.

2. **BASIC SCRIPTURES:**
   I Samuel 1 and 2.

3. **FAMILY BACKGROUND:**
   All we are told about Hannah is found in the two chapters of I Samuel. Her background is not recorded. The family life of Hannah, after marriage, is recorded and we shall consider that part of her life. Hannah's husband, Elkanah, was a Levite and belonged to one of the most honorable families of the priestly tribe, the Kohathites. Elkanah was an undistinguished priest who followed the common custom of polygamy in those days. His other wife was Peninnah and she could have children. Hannah was barren. Peninnah made light of Hannah and made cruel remarks about her. There was probably a bit of jealously in her remarks, as seen in I Samuel 1:6, because Elkanah loved Hannah (I Samuel 1:5).

   Hannah never showed a sign of revenge and her beautiful spirit, in spite of the bad treatment, caused no conflicts in the family. From such a home life, Hannah was to become an outstanding personality in the Old Testament, making an impact upon the world.

4. **WHAT THE OLD TESTAMENT SAYS ABOUT HANNAH:**

   (1) Her Grief - I Samuel 1:3-10

   Each year the family would go to Shiloh to the temple and offer sacrifice, and worship the Lord of hosts. As they made their way to Shiloh, Hannah had to take the ridicule of the second wife. This fact, along with the fact that Hannah was childless, caused her deep sorrow and grief.

   Write in verse 8 _____

   _____

   Her husband was good to her and loved her. The agony of a Jewess with no children is hard for our culture to understand.

   Hannah was bitter in her soul as she made her way to the temple and found Eli, the priest, sitting by a post of the temple.

   Her grief was caused by her barren condition, as is indicated in verse 15, "I am a woman of a sorrowful spirit."

   Hannah was the fourth great woman in the Bible who grieved because she had not conceived and, of the four, she was the most prayerful. Note the others:

   - Sarah laughed when told a child would be hers in old age.
   - Rebekah was barren and Isaac prayed for her to have children. Twenty years after marriage she had Esau and Jacob.
   - Rachel was barren and said, "Give me children or else I die."

- Hannah, grieved, took her problem to God and depended upon Him for a child.

Her first step toward overcoming her grief was taken when she made her way to the temple. *What a lesson for all of us, "take our burdens to the Lord and leave them there."*

(2) Hannah's Prayer and Promise - I Samuel 1:11-19

Hannah, in the temple, prayed. In the prayer she made a vow with the Lord.

Write in part of verse 11: "give unto thine handmaid _____

_____

_____

Notice her promise in verse 11: "If thou wilt, I will give him to the Lord all the days of his life." She took her sorrow to God in prayer. She gave herself to prayer until she knew He had heard her request.

In Hannah's request, she promised to give the man child back to the Lord and "no razor would touch his head." See verse 11. This was a pledge to the Lord that the boy would be as a Nazarite. Turn to Numbers 6:2-5. Write in verse 2 _____

_____

Also verse 5 _____

_____

_____

Hannah, before the child was conceived, made this promise. What is a Nazarite? A Nazarite was a person totally separated to the Lord. The long hair was a visible sign of the Nazarite's separation and his willingness to bear reproach for the Lord's sake.

It may be that Hannah looked beyond her own longing for a child and saw how desperately the nation of Israel, in a time of religious decline, needed a man totally separated to God.

God can always trust His own with gifts when they are willing to give them back to Him.

The prayer Hannah prayed in God's house at Shiloh was a prayer of supplication without external speech. Her lips moved but there was no audible sound. Her prayer was internal, from her heart and soul. Eli, the priest, watched her mouth and thought she was drunk. Underline verses 12 and 13. The words of Eli only added to her troubles. Her answer was a masterpiece in verse 15, "I am a woman of a sorrowful spirit: I have drunk neither wine nor strong drink, but have poured out my soul before the Lord." Eli answered in verse 17, "Go in peace." _____

_____

_____

Notice verse 18. Hannah left the house of God happy. Her countenance was no more sad. She even started eating again. She was assured in her heart that God would give her a son.

Then a miracle of God happened (verse 19). When they returned home, Elkanah **knew** his wife and she conceived. (Parents, that is a good word to use when answering your children about sex. "He **knew** his wife.")

(3) Hannah's Promise Kept - I Samuel 1:20-28

Hannah had a son and she named him Samuel, meaning "asked of the Lord." In her prayer she had promised Samuel to the Lord. She nurtured him, loved him until he was weaned (verse 23).

Samuel was very young when Hannah took him to "the house of

the Lord in Shiloh. *Again she prayed and told the Lord she had not forgotten her promise, nor God's gift to her.* Her words are precious in verse 28. _____

_____

_____

Hannah had no fear for her son. She had placed him in God's hands and there he was safe. Oh, for more Hannah's in our day.

(4) Hannah's Praise To God - I Samuel 2:1-10

Before she left Samuel with Eli, Hannah prayed a triumphant prayer which has been called the forerunner of the Magnificat of Mary, the mother of Jesus.

Compare I Samuel 2:1-10 with Luke 1:46-53.

These two prayers have stirred the hearts of Christians through the years.

(5) God Gave Fruit of the First Fruits - I Samuel 2:18-21

Because Hannah had been faithful to the Lord and had "lent" or given Samuel, the first fruit of her womb, to Him; *the Lord gave her even more fruit.* Write in verse 20 _____

_____

Hannah was visited by the Lord, and she had three sons and two daughters (verse 21). *The Lord always does "exceeding abundantly above all that we ask or think, according to the power that worketh in us" (Ephesians 3:20).*

(6) The Child Samuel - I Samuel 2:11, 18, 19, 26

The child grew and ministered before the Lord. During those early years, Hannah went to see Samuel and took him a little coat each year. Hannah's biography ends in this chapter and she slipped into the background to become immortal through her son.

5. WHAT THE NEW TESTAMENT SAYS ABOUT HANNAH:

(1) Hannah is not mentioned one time in the New Testament.

Her life and influence flows through the pages of the New Testament because of her son, Samuel.

(2) The Bible sometimes speaks the loudest when it is silent on a subject.

We shall see this truth in the next lesson.

For instance, Hannah, not mentioned, influenced the life of the mother of our Lord.

She is anonymous through the pages of the New Testament. Because Samuel started the first school of the prophets, he had a great influence on all the writers of the Scripture.

6. THE LESSONS YOU SHOULD LEARN FROM THIS STUDY:

(1) God sometimes withholds good things until we are submissive to His will.

(2) When cruel remarks are made without cause, we should take them as a Christian and not ruin our testimony.

(3) When we pray, as Hannah prayed, we must know that God answers in His own way and at His set time.

(4) Every sorrow we have, the Lord can handle. He did in the life of Hannah.

(5) What we promise and then give to the Lord, He magnifies and sends abundant blessings upon us.

(6) In every thing we should rejoice. Hannah praised the Lord for her child, Samuel, knowing she would give him back to the Lord.

CAN YOU REMEMBER?

1. Why was Hannah so dependent on the Lord?
2. Where did Hannah find peace of soul?
3. Who criticized her at home and at the temple?
4. What is a Nazarite?
5. Why is Hannah so well known to this day?
6. What was her supreme characteristic?

YOUR NEXT ASSIGNMENT

1. Read I Samuel 1 - 10; chapters 16 and 19; I Chronicles 9:22; 26:28; 29:29; Acts 3:24; 13:20; Hebrews 11:32-34.
2. Review your study of Hannah.
3. Mark your Bible where new truths are learned.
4. Read all you can find on Samuel, our next lesson.

Lesson 17
"Samuel"

(Where lines are provided, look up the Scripture and write it or its meaning in the space provided.

1. **THE MEANING OF THE NAME:**

   Samuel means "asked of God" or "appointed by God."

2. **BASIC SCRIPTURES:**

   I Samuel 1 - 10; chapters 16 and 19; 25:1; I Chronicles 9:22; 26:28; 29:29; Acts 3:24; 13:20; Hebrews 11:32-34.

3. **FAMILY BACKGROUND:**

   As we saw in the last lesson, Samuel was the firstborn of Hannah and Elkanah. He was an answer to his mother's prayer. God heard her request and gave her Samuel, "asked of God." His father was a Levite from the family of Kohath. He was a man of the hill country of Ephraim, because the family had been assigned residence in that tribe. Look up Joshua 21:5 and 20. Samuel was born into a family where there were two wives and other children by Elkanah's other wife. He did not stay in that household long because Hannah had promised to give Samuel back to the Lord. **All that Hannah gave to God, were first His gifts to her.** The same is true in our lives.

   Notice in I Samuel 1:28, Hannah did not give him to the Lord for a little while but "as long as he liveth." Samuel was presented to the Lord at a very young age. In Samuel 1:24 the Scripture says, "when he was weaned, the child was young." Most of the Jews who ponder this verse say that he was three years of age. This should teach us a lesson; we cannot begin too soon in the spiritual training of our children.

4. **WHAT THE OLD TESTAMENT SAYS ABOUT SAMUEL:**

   (1) Samuel, A Levite and Nazarite — I Samuel 1:1 and 1:11

   By birth, Samuel was a Levite (I Samuel 1:1). He was born in Ramathaim-zophim. Zophim means "watchmen." Prophets are called watchmen, a point to remember. "Rama," when translated to Greek, is Arimathea. (These two thoughts should stir your mind to search more Scripture and a Bible dictionary.)

   By vow, Samuel was a Nazarite (I Samuel 1:11).

   The vow of Hannah, Samuel's mother, before he was conceived was the vow of the Nazarite. That vow can be found in Numbers 6:1-5. The vow meant:

   (a) one totally separated to the Lord (Numbers 6:2)

   (b) one who takes not of strong drink and wine (Numbers 6:3)

   (c) one who uses not a razor (Numbers 6:5), the long hair naturally being a reproach to man (I Corinthians 11:14). The Nazarite wore long hair as a visible sign of his separation to the Lord and his willingness to bear reproach for the Lord's sake.

   (d) one who avoided contact with a dead body (Numbers 6:5-6). This was a sign of absolute purity of life.

   (2) Samuel's Call From God — I Samuel 3:1-18

   Samuel was called by the Lord when he was very young. Notice verse 1: "And the Word of the Lord was precious (unusual) in those days." So the Lord God called this young man to be a spokesman for Him. Look at 3:4 and write in _____

Now write in verse 10 _____

_____

(3) Samuel, A Prophet — I Samuel 3:19-21

Samuel was called to be a prophet, "a spokesman for God, a seer, a watchman." Look at that precious verse 20 _____

_____

Samuel had been faithful in revealing to Eli the first words God had told him in a vision (I Samuel 3:11-18). This was a hard thing for a young boy to do but he did as the Lord said.

Samuel marks the beginning of the prophetic office. There were those in the past on whom the mantle of prophecy had fallen, such as Moses in Deuteronomy 18:18. *Scripture indicates that the prophetic order was founded by Samuel.* Look at I Samuel 9:9, 18, 19. Underline verse 9. We learn that a "seer" and a "prophet" were the same. Samuel was both.

Look up I Samuel 10:5, "that thou shalt meet _____

_____

Now, I Samuel 19:20 _____

_____

From these verses, we learn that Samuel started the first school of prophets and he was over them. Alexander Whyte, in his book "Bible Characters" (p. 226), says, "Samuel devised and founded and presided over a great prophetical school in his old age. How much of the Old Testament itself we owe to the prophets, and the preachers, and the psalmists, and the sacred writers, and other trained students of Samuel's great school, we have not yet fully found out."

(4) Samuel, the Intercessor

Turn to I Samuel 7;5-8. Notice Samuel says, "I will pray for you unto the Lord" (verse 5). Write in verse 8 _____

_____

Look up I Samuel 12:18-23. Underline verses 18 and 19. Write in verse 23, one of the great verses on prayer _____

_____

(5) Samuel, a Priest

By birth, Samuel was a Levite and the Lord gave him the duties of the priest. He was ranked with Moses and Aaron in the office. Turn to Psalm 99:6 _____

_____

His priestly functions were:
* the offering of sacrifice (I Samuel 7:9-10)
* praying for his people (I Samuel 7:9)
* the anointing of kings (I Samuel 10:1; 16:13)

(6) Samuel, A Judge

Samuel was a prophet and performed the functions of a priest, but he was also a judge. Samuel was the last of the judges and he anointed the first king, Saul. The Lord had His man serve in all of these capacities because "a Word from the Lord was unusual in those days and there was no open vision" (I Samuel 3:1).

Samuel judged Israel. Look up I Samuel 7:15-17. Write in verse 15 _____

In verse 16 and 17 the word "judged" is used. Underline the word in your Bible.

Chapter 7 positively identifies Samuel as a prophet, priest and judge:

- in verse 3, he proclaims as a prophet.
- in verse 5, he prays as a priest.
- in verse 6, he judges.
- in verse 9 and 10, he sacrifices, a priest.
- in verse 12, a prophet.
- in verse 15 and 16, a judge.
- in verse 17, a judge and priest.

(7) The Death of Samuel — I Samuel 25:1

Samuel died, having seen Israel turn from a theocracy to a monarchy. Samuel was sad over this but followed the will of God. Israel had not rejected Samuel, but God. One of the important verses in I Samuel is 8:7 _____

_____

The people loved Samuel and mourned his death.

The life and story did not end at chapter 25. In chapter 28 Saul fell into witchcraft and sent for the witch of Endor. In I Samuel 28:11-20 a dead man speaks. The man who spoke was Samuel. He re-emphasized the message of the Lord he had spoken in I Samuel 15:22-28.

So the great prophet Samuel leaves his impression on all of us. We hold in our hands the Book, greatly influenced by this man.

5. WHAT THE NEW TESTAMENT SAYS ABOUT SAMUEL:

(1) Peter, in his second sermon, established Samuel as the leader of the prophets.

Look at Acts 3:24 _____

_____

(2) Paul established Samuel as a prophet in Acts 13:20 _____

_____

_____

_____

(3) In Hebrews 11:32, Samuel is listed in the hall of faith.

Underline verse 32.

6. THE LESSONS YOU SHOULD LEARN FROM THIS STUDY:

(1) A child given to the Lord in prayer and faith will make an impact for the Lord.

(2) Early training in the things of Christ will have a lifelong influence upon our children.

(3) The influence of a godly person will affect future generations, just as Samuel did.

(4) We should never cease to pray for those who need Christ, for Christian leaders, for our nation, as Samuel never ceased in praying for Israel.

(5) The Lord honored Samuel's mother, Hannah, and granted her a son. Through her son, she has lived through the centuries as a model of motherhood. The Lord is the same yesterday, today and forever.

CAN YOU REMEMBER?

1. What was Samuel by birth? By a vow?
2. What was a Nazarite?
3. What did Samuel begin? What was his main title?
4. What institution did he establish?
5. Samuel ended the period of the _____

   and headed the order of the _____
6. Samuel anointed two kings. Who were they?

YOUR NEXT ASSIGNMENT:

1. Read I Samuel 8 through 31; I Chronicles 10; Acts 13:21.
2. Read all you can find on Saul, the first king of Israel. He is our next character study.
3. Review your notes on Samuel and Hannah.
4. Mark your Bible where new truths are learned.

Lesson 18
"Saul, the King"

(Where lines are provided, look up the Scripture and write it or its meaning in the space provided.)

1. **THE MEANING OF THE NAME:**
Saul means, "asked for" or "demanded."

2. **BASIC SCRIPTURES:**
I Samuel 8 through 31; I Chronicles 10; Acts 13:21.

3. **FAMILY BACKGROUND:**
Saul was the son of Kish, a Benjamite. In the New Testament the name is "Cis," an imitation of the Greek. Benjamin was the youngest of the twelve sons of Jacob. From this tribe sprang *two* Sauls. *Saul, the king; and Saul, the Apostle to the Gentiles, whom was know as Paul, the Apostle.*

Nothing else is given to us about the family of Saul. He was an obedient son (I Samuel 9:1-3).

4. **WHAT THE OLD TESTAMENT SAYS ABOUT SAUL, THE KING:**

(1) **The people demanded a king (I Samuel 8:5).** _____

_____

Samuel had been the prophet and judge and priest. Israel wanted to be like other nations and they rejected the theocracy (God as King, Supreme Power). In I Samuel 8:7 the Lord told Samuel _____

_____

They had not rejected Samuel, but God. God granted them their own selfish desire in I Samuel 8:22.

(2) **God selected Saul as the king and told Samuel what he should do (I Samuel 9:15-17).**

The Lord selected a young man with a striking physical appearance. Note his description in I Samuel 9:2. _____

_____

The Lord told Samuel that Saul would come to him, and Samuel was to anoint him as the **first king of Israel.** Read I Samuel 9:18-20.

Saul was, at that time, humble and modest. Note I Samuel 9:21:

"I am a Benjamite . . .
"of the smallest of the tribes of Israel . . .
"my family is the least of all the families of the tribe of Benjamin ﹨ . .
"Why do you speak to me?"

His humility is seen again in I Samuel 10:22. This was the day of his presentation to the people, but Saul "hid himself among the stuff."

He had a degree of self control as noted in I Samuel 10:27. When "the sons of Belial" despised Saul and criticized him, the Scripture says, "But he (Saul) held his peace."

(3) **The Lord gave Saul a new heart.**

He became another man.

Look at I Samuel 10:6, the last phrase _____

_____

_____

Then I Samuel 10:9 _____

_____

When the Lord calls a person to a work, He gives to that person all that is required. This is a good example for us in the life of King Saul.

Saul was changed inwardly first and then presented to the people. When they saw Saul, standing head and shoulders above all others, the people responded by shouting, "God save the king."

Saul was provided with outward help and assistance. God gave him men. Note I Samuel 10:26 _____

_____

God not only provided Saul with inward and outward gifts, He also gave him a great and successful victory in defeating the Ammonites (I Samuel 11:1-11). This gave the people great hope and confidence in their king (I Samuel 11:12).

Thus far we have seen the good side of Israel's first king. Saul had the natural ability, then an inward spiritual ability which God gave him. He had the opportunity to do great things for his people and for the Lord. *But the Adamic nature took over and Saul started the downward path to ruin.*

(4) The downfall of a King caused by "selfism."

First, the sin of presumption and impatience. Look back at I Samuel 10:8 and underline. Samuel had told Saul to go to Gilgal and to wait seven days and that he (Samuel) would offer sacrifices to the Lord.

Now turn to I Samuel 13:8 _____

_____

Saul, impatient, violated the priestly function by offering a sacrifice to the Lord. Samuel arrived, just as he had promised, but it was too late for Saul. *He did what he wanted to do.* Notice the last part of I Samuel 13:12. Now write in verse 13 _____

_____

Because of Saul's self will and impatience, the Lord rejected him as king. Underline verse 14.

Second, Saul was disobedient and rebellious. In chapter 15, Saul partially carried out the Lord's instructions. He was to destroy the Amalekites. He did, but he also took the best sheep and oxen and all that was good. The king of the Amalekites, Agag, was spared and taken by Saul.

Third, Samuel was told by the Lord, "I am sorry, my mind is changed, that I have set up Saul to be king" (I Samuel 15:11). Samuel's rebuke begins in verse 17 and continues to verse 23 and then verse 28.

Underline I Samuel 15:17. Now write in verses 22 and 23 _____

_____

_____

_____

Underline verse 28 in your Bible.

Notice that Samuel called sin, **sin** and did not cover it as we have a tendency to do in our day.

In I Samuel 13:14 and 15:28 the kingship is to be taken from Saul.

Fourth, "The Spirit of the Lord departed from Saul, and an evil spirit from the Lord troubled him " (I Samuel 16:14).

Fifth, Saul became insanely jealous of David (I Samuel 18:8) —

He even tried to kill David three times: I Samuel 19:1,10; 23:8. Twice David spared Saul's life.

Sixth, Saul turned to witchcraft (I Samuel 28:7).

Saul, handsome, man with natural ability, a new heart, a new person, great opportunity; what happened? **He refused to obey God and he wanted his own way, selfism.** He went down, down to the lowest depths of sin and sought out the witch of Endor. *He went from the highest to the lowest.*

All of these steps form a familiar story of egotism, pride, abuse of power, jealousy; leading to moral decay.

Seventh, Saul was wounded in battle and then killed himself by falling on his own sword (I Samuel 31:4; I Chronicles 10). This giant of a man had gone from the position of king to the pits of unbelief in the secret session with the witch of Endor. Selfism, ego, whatever one might call it, finally conquered Saul, Israel's first king.

Saul's own words, in one of his pleas and confessions to David, tells the story for us. Look at I Samuel 26:21; "I have sinned . . . behold I have played the fool and erred exceedingly. "

5. WHAT THE NEW TESTAMENT SAYS ABOUT SAUL:

(1) The New Testament mentions this Saul one time.

The Apostle Paul, in his sermon at Antioch, mentions Saul in Acts 13:21. Write in this verse _____

This Scripture tells us how long Saul reigned as king. Nowhere in the Old Testament is this stated. Paul tells us that Saul reigned 40 years (Josephus also says 40 years in Antiquities book 6, chapter 14, paragraph 9.)

(2) We could not leave this study without reminding you that the Saul of the New Testament was also from the tribe of Benjamin (Romans 11:1 and Philippians 3:5).

The Saul of the New Testament became Paul, the Apostle.

(We shall study Paul in the characters of the New Testament).

6. THE LESSONS YOU SHOULD LEARN FROM THIS STUDY:

1. It takes more than a good family background, a handsome physical appearance to be a godly servant.
2. Ability to understand the Word of God is as important as great opportunities.
3. Obedience to the Lord is far more important in achieving success than any other factor.
4. Self and ego should be placed on a shelf in a locked room and left there to rot.
5. Being in the highest office in the land did not give Saul authority to do as he pleased and disregard God.
6. When we start down into sin and more sin, it is almost impossible to turn around by our own will. It takes the grace of our Lord Jesus Christ to turn us around.

CAN YOU REMEMBER?

1. Why was Saul made king over Israel?
2. What were his qualities as a leader?
3. What made Saul go from good intentions to bad deeds?
4. In one word, what was Saul's "greatest sin?"

5. Did Saul ever confess sin? What did he say?

YOUR NEXT ASSIGNMENT:

1. Read I Samuel 13, 14, 18, 19, 20, 23, 31; II Samuel 1 and 9.

2. Read all you can find about Jonathan, the son of Saul. (There are about 14 Jonathans in Scripture.)

3. Review your notes on Saul, the King.

4. Mark your Bible where new truths are learned.

Lesson 19
"Jonathan, the Son of Saul"

(Where lines are provided, look up the Scripture and write it or its meaning in the space provided.)

1. **THE MEANING OF THE NAME:**
   Jonathan means "whom Jehovah gives" or "the Lord gave."

2. **BASIC SCRIPTURE:**
   I Samuel 13, 14, 18, 19, 20, 23, 31; II Samuel 1 and 9.

3. **FAMILY BACKGROUND:**
   Jonathan was the oldest son of King Saul. The only background given in Scripture is found in I Samuel 14:49-51. His mother was Ahinoam. Jonathan had two brothers and two sisters. His father, Saul, also had a concubine named Rizpah, who had two sons by him (II Samuel 21:8 and 11). In Jonathan's own family he was the heir apparent to the throne of Israel. He was endowed with great mental ability, high and noble morality, a handsome physique and a heart of love. He was suited for such a position as king.

   But for his father's transgressions he would have been the second king of Israel, but Jonathan knew he would never be the king. Samuel revealed this fact to Saul in I Samuel 13:14 and again in I Samuel 15:23 and 28.

4. **WHAT THE OLD TESTAMENT SAYS ABOUT JONATHAN:**

   (1) Jonathan, a Man Without Fear - I Samuel 13:2-3; 14:1-45

   Jonathan was assigned 1,000 men to smite the Philistines. His background is not even mentioned. His first appearance in Scripture is as a warrior, a man of valor.

   Again in chapter 14, Jonathan and one armor bearer climbed the steep side of the rocky gorge of Michmash and killed 20 Philistines. When Saul came to attack the Philistines, he found them in panic and fighting each other because Jonathan had caused great confusion by his attack (I Samuel 14:1 through 23).

   Saul pronounced a curse upon any who would eat during the pursuit to kill all the Philistines. Jonathan was not aware of his fathers orders and ate a bit of wild honey. For this Saul told his own son, "thou shalt surely die" (verse 44). The people, knowing that Jonathan had actually saved Israel with the help of God, said to Saul, "not one hair of his head shall fall to the ground. So the people rescued Jonathan" (verse 45).

   The first impression of Jonathan is of a fighter and warrior. He was strong and had great mental ability, but his greatness was not only on the field of battle but also in his love and abiding faith in the Lord God.

   (2) Jonathan's Covenant With David - I Samuel 18:1-4

   David had just killed Goliath (chapter 17) when King Saul inquired as to who he was. David answered with great pride in I Samuel 17:58 _____

   _____

As David spoke to King Saul, Jonathan felt in his heart an abiding love that went out to David. Scripture I Samuel 18:1 says it best; "the soul _____

_____

_____

NOTE: The *soul* of Jonathan was **knit** to the *soul* of David. You knit things that are of the same substance, the same fiber, texture and strength. Bone will knit to another bone, tissue to the same kind of tissue.

Jonathan loved David as he loved his own soul, a pure, godly love.

Their pattern of friendship has been the perfect example of all true friendships since.

The covenant Jonathan and David made was one sealed by Jonathan, the son of the king, giving his robe and garments and sword to David, the soon-to-be king. David was God's choice (I Samuel 16:1) _____

_____

The seal of the covenant was as real as any seal of any covenant in Scripture. Jonathan was a God-loving, spiritual man, having been trained early by Samuel. He made the covenant with David and at the same time placed faith in the Greater David, Jesus Christ. He knew David's God.

Jonathan, the son and heir of Saul, stripped himself in order to seal David to the throne of Israel. Jonathan, as far as was in his power, did that day all that Jesus Christ did in the fullness of time (Philippians 2:6-8; Colossians 4:4-5). Jonathan was only the sinful son of a sinful father while Jesus came as the Son of God. Jesus stripped himself bare so that He might clothe us with His robe of righteousness, that we might share His Glory.

There is another lesson here for us today: when we love Jesus, the Greater David, as we love our own soul, we will give up all we have—strip ourselves—and place all we have on His shoulders as our Lord and King. That is exactly what loving, kind, generous, humble Jonathan did.

(3) Jonathan Defended David - I Samuel 19:1-7

All of Jonathan's life was wrapped up in two men—the king, Saul, and the future king, David. We cannot separate his life from these two men.

Saul, the father of Jonathan, wanted to kill David because of jealousy which started immediately after David's confrontation with Goliath. Look at I Samuel 18:7 _____

_____

Underline I Samuel 18:8-9. This was King Saul's reaction to David. The jealousy grew to the point of hatred. Murder was number one on Saul's agenda.

In chapter 19:1-7, Jonathan took steps to protect David:

First, Jonathan told David of Saul's plan to kill him (verse 2).

Second, he cared for David's security, "take heed until morning" (verse 2).

Third, Jonathan interceded for David (verses 4-5).

Fourth, his appeal changed the heart of the king (verse 6).

Fifth, Jonathan brought David to Saul. David was once again in the king's court (verse 7).

Jonathan was an intercessor, a peacemaker, an instrument in the hand of God.

(4) Jonathan Protects David - I Samuel 20:1-42; 23:15-18

All of chapter 20 is the record of Saul's wrath against David, and Jonathan protecting David. The friendship became stronger with every adversity. Note I Samuel 20:17 _____

_____

Underline I Samuel 20:42.

In chapter 23:15-18 we see one of the jewels of Scripture. David had been running from Saul. In the wilderness of Ziph, Jonathan appeared on the scene. Note the first thing he does (verse 16). __

_____

Jonathan proclaimed David's advancement to the throne, which was Jonathan's birthright. Note verse 17:

"Saul shall not find thee . . ."
"thou shalt be king over Israel . . ."
"I shall be next to thee . . ."
"Saul knows this . . ."

They made a covenant before the Lord (verse 18). This was true devotion, giving and receiving assurance of their love and friendship. We should do the same with those we love; but, far greater is our need to renew our covenant, our devotion and our love to the Lord Jesus.

Jonathan and David parted at verse 18 and never saw each other again.

(5) The Death of Jonathan - I Samuel 31:2

Jonathan died at the hands of the Philistines. He and his father, Saul, were killed in the same battle.

In II Samuel 1:17-27 David mourned the death of both Jonathan and Saul. David said only good about Saul. His devotion to Jonathan is found in verse 26 (underline it).

5   **WHAT THE NEW TESTAMENT SAYS ABOUT JONATHAN:**
There is no mention of this noble character in the New Testament; yet he played an important role in the life of David. Jonathan was the son of King Saul, whom the people demanded as king. Saul was not from the "house of Jesse." After rejecting Saul, the Lord God said that "He had provided a king" from one of Jesse's sons (I Samuel 16:1).

Dr. Herbert Lockyer, author of All the Men of the Bible, says "Jonathan personified all of the Christian virtues or graces that Peter wrote about in II Peter 1:5-7."

List the graces: _____, _____, _____,

_____, _____, _____, _____,

_____, _____,

6.   THE LESSONS YOU SHOULD LEARN FROM THIS STUDY:

(1)   Jonathan was a perfect example of a godly friend.
(2)   He could take second place without jealousy.
(3)   He never begrudged David's selection by the Lord to be king over Israel.
(4)   He "strengthened the hand of David in God."
(5)   Jonathan was not strange, as some might think in our day. His love for David was pure, holy, real. All of us should have such godly friends.
(6)   Self-sacrificing friendship is a virtue we should attain through Christ. Jonathan and David were the prime examples of friendship in Scripture.

CAN YOU REMEMBER?

1.   "Jonathan loved David _____."
2.   What can you "knit together?"
3.   What was the seal of the covenant Jonathan made with David?

81

4. Why was Jonathan constantly defending David?

5. What did Jonathan do when he met David in the wilderness of Ziph?

YOUR NEXT ASSIGNMENT

1. You should have read I Samuel 16 - 31 in the last lesson. Now read II Samuel, the entire book. Also, I Chronicles 15 and 25; I Kings 1 and 2; Matthew 1:1; 22:41-45; Mark 11:10; Luke 1:32.

2. The next study will be on David, the king. There is so much in Scripture about him. Read all you can find in your Bible.

3. Review your notes on Jonathan.

4. Mark your Bible where new truths are learned.

Lesson 20
"David, the King"

(Where lines are provided, look up the Scripture and write it or its meaning in the space provided.)

1. **THE MEANING OF THE NAME:**
   David means "well beloved."

2. **BASIC SCRIPTURES:**
   I Samuel 16 through 31; the book of II Samuel; I Chronicles 15 and 25; I Kings 1 and 2; Matthew 1:1; 22:41-45; Mark 11:10; Luke 1:32.

3. **FAMILY BACKGROUND:**
   David was the youngest of the eight sons of Jesse. He was from Bethlehem, meaning "the house of bread." Nothing is mentioned in Scripture about the mother of David.

   Here we see some of the many prophecies of past lessons come to pass. Do you remember the line through which the Messiah, Jesus, was to come? Do you remember in former studies the names of Abraham, Isaac, Jacob, Judah, Tamar, Salmon, Boaz and Ruth, Obed, Jesse, and now David? (God had made a covenant with Abraham and He worked His will to bring about the blessing through His Seed, Jesus Christ.)

   Samuel was used of God in the selection of David as the second king of Israel. Notice I Samuel 16:1 and underline. Now look at verse 7 of the same chapter and write in the last half of verse 7, "for the Lord seeth _

   _____

   Notice I Samuel 16:12 and 13. David was a handsome man. He was selected by the Lord and anointed to be king by Samuel. "The Spirit of the Lord came upon David."

   David was not enthroned to be king until *after* the death of Saul. Even though the Lord God had selected him, David took his place as a servant and as one despised by Saul. He was hated and hunted by Saul. From his experiences of fleeing and wandering, David wrote some beautiful Psalms. Among them are Psalms 54, 56, 57, and 59.

   David is the only character in Scripture called "the man after God's own heart." Turn to I Samuel 13:14 and underline the phrase. Now in Acts 13:22, find the phrase and underline it.

   We have glanced only at the background of David because our previous lessons have included a portion of his life. Now we shall take up the reign and rule of David as king of Israel.

4. **WHAT THE OLD TESTAMENT SAYS ABOUT DAVID:**

   (1) **David Mourned the Death of Saul and Jonathan - II Samuel 1:17-27**

   The song David wrote about Saul and Jonathan dwells on only the good in Saul. This passage shows deep reverence for the position Saul had occupied as the Lord's anointed king over Israel. There is no mention of Saul's faults or cruelty toward David. When David mentioned Jonathan, his heart overflowed (verse 26).

   (2) **David as King Over Judah - II Samuel 2 through 4**

   David reigned at Hebron seven years and six months over only Judah, II Samuel 2:11. See II Samuel 2:4: "and the men of Judah came and there they anointed David king over the house of Judah." The other tribes would not accept David as king and they decided to have their own king (II Samuel 2:8-10). This caused a civil war between the followers of Saul and the followers of David. Note II Samuel 3:1 _____

_____

(3) David, King of All Israel, At Jerusalem - II Samuel 5 through 11

After the death of Ish-bosheth, the king over Saul's followers, all the tribes came to David and anointed him king over all Israel (II Samuel 5:3).

David reigned as king 40 years. Look up II Samuel 5:4 and 5 ___

_____

He moved the capital to Jerusalem-Zion, the city of David (II Samuel 5:6-7). Underline verse 7.

The coronation of David as king over all Israel was huge. This is not described in II Samuel 5, but in I Chronicles 12:23-40. By adding all the numbers present at his coronation, there were about 340,000 armed men. They were all of one heart to make David king (I Chronicles 12:38).

(4) The Davidic Covenant - II Samuel 7:4-16

One of the great covenants of the Lord is this covenant with David. The Messiah was to come from the "seed of David according to the flesh" (Romans 1:3). This covenant confirmed to David the establishment of his throne forever.

There are several significant things we should remember about the Lord's covenant with David:

(a) *The Divine Confirmation of a place for Israel, (verse 10).*
(b) *The Divine Confirmation of the throne in Israel, (verse 13).*
(c) *The perpetuation of the Davidic rule, (verses 11-16). Here three things are secured:*

    1. "house" or posterity (verses 11 and 13). Write in verse 13:

    _____

    2. "throne" or royal authority (verse 13)
    3. "kingdom" or sphere of rule (verses 12 and 13)

    All three of these are secured forever by the Lord God in verse 16: _____

    _____

Psalm 89 gives an exposition of the Davidic Covenant. The covenant looks far beyond David and Solomon as we see in verse 27. Read and underline. "Higher than the kings of the earth" can only refer to the Lord Jesus, "the seed of David after the flesh." Notice in this Psalm verses 3 and 4. Underline these verses. Now verses 20-37 are so important. Read this passage and underline verses 20, 21, 28, 29, 34, 36, 37.

(d) *The covenant was unconditional because it was to be fulfilled in Jesus Christ. This was affirmed by the prophets in such passages as:*

    Isaiah 9:7 _____

    _____

    Isaiah 11:1 _____

    _____

    Jeremiah 23:5 _____

    _____

    Ezekiel 37:25 _____

_____

_____

(e) **The Davidic Covenant was a sure prophecy of Christ.** The **first** such prophecy was made to Adam in Genesis 3:15. ___

_____

The **second,** to Abraham in Genesis 22:18 (underline).
The **third,** to Jacob in Genesis 49:10 _____

_____

The **fourth,** to David in chapter 7 of II Samuel.
So first, God made the promise to a **race** in Adam.
Second, to a **nation** in the race, Israel.
Third, to a **tribe** in that nation, Judah.
Fourth, to a **family** in that tribe, the family of David.

(5) David's Great Sin - chapter 11

His first sin (verses 3 and 4) _____

_____

The first sin led to the second sin. In verses 15-17 David placed Uriah, Bathsheba's husband, in the forefront of the battle, where he was killed.

(6) David's Repentance - II Samuel 12:13-18 and 23

God used the wise preacher, Nathan, to awaken David. He did not mince any words. Note verses 7-12. David confessed and was forgiven (verse 13), but the consequences of sin had to be dealt with by David and Bathsheba. The baby died. Record David's words in verse 23 _____

_____

Then Solomon was born to David and Bathsheba (verse 24).

(7) David's Troubles - II Samuel 13 through 24

The remainder of the book of II Samuel is a record of David's troubles and heartbreak. His heartbreak was caused within his family, Absalom being the greatest heartbreak. In chapters 15 through 18 the rebellion of Absalom, culminating in his death (II Samuel 18:15) and David's sorrow (II Samuel 18:33) are set forth. This was the fruit of David's sin, according to II Samuel 12:11-12. Read and underline. Write in the sorrow of David in II Samuel 18:33_____

_____

The record of David in II Samuel closes with his purchase of the threshing floor of Ornan on Mt. Moriah, which became the sight of the temple. It was here, hundreds of years earlier, where Abraham offered Issac.

(8) David Secures The Throne for Solomon - I Kings 1 and 2

There is always a struggle for power. While David was on his death bed, he had to make critical decisions in order to secure the throne for Solomon. (Read I Kings 1.)

Solomon is anointed king (I Kings 1:39-40).

David charged his son, Solomon (I Kings 2:1-9). Notice verses 2-4 and underline.

(9) The Death of David - I Kings 2:10-11

Having served 40 years as king of God's people, seven years in Hebron and 33 years in Jerusalem, he was buried in the city of David.

5. WHAT THE NEW TESTAMENT SAYS ABOUT DAVID:

There are 57 references to David in the New Testament. We can only select a few to shed light on David and our Lord Jesus.

(1) **Jesus was the Son of David (Matthew 1:1)** _____

_____

(2) **There were 42 generations of sons from Abraham to Jesus (Matthew 1:17)** _____

_____

(3) **Jesus was constantly called "The Son of David."**
Look up Matthew 9:27; 12:23; 15:22; 20:30-31; 21:9. Look at Luke 1:32-33 and write in: _____

_____

_____

(4) **Paul shines positive light in his sermon in Acts 13:22-23.** Underline verse 22 and write in verse 23 _____

_____

Underline Romans 1:3 (Paul speaking).

(5) **John, the Apostle, speaks of the kingly character of Jesus in Revelation 5:5** _____

_____

(6) **Jesus identifies Himself in Revelation 22:16, in this final chapter of God's Word.**

Write in verse 16 _____

_____

God, the Father, will yet give to that thorn-crowned One "the throne of His father David," according to the above Scriptures and also by Peter's sermon in Acts 2:25-31. Underline verse 30.

6. **THE LESSONS YOU SHOULD LEARN FROM THIS STUDY:**
   1. Sometimes a person is "called" or "chosen" by the Lord, but has to wait for God's timing. David was a good example of this.
   2. He was "the man after God's own heart." In our day of grace in the Lord Jesus, we should pray and qualify for the same title.
   3. David was patient in taking the throne. He teaches us patience.
   4. The covenant God made with David is still unconditional. Jesus shall return and be on David's throne.
   5. The covenant was a sure prophecy of Christ. The prophecies of Scripture should inspire and encourage us. Do not run from prophetic utterances.
   6. David was Adamic in nature; he sinned, yet God used him. He was just like all of us.

CAN YOU REMEMBER?
1. How many times was David anointed?
2. How long did he reign? In Hebron? In Jerusalem?
3. When was David enthroned?
4. What does the Davidic Covenant mean to you?
5. What were David's great sins?
6. Who was the spiritual leader, minister, who advised David?

YOUR NEXT ASSIGNMENT:
1. Read I Kings 1 through 11; II Chronicles 1 through 9, Matthew 6:29; 12:42; John 10:23; Acts 5:12; 7:47.
2. The next study will be on Solomon, the wise man. Read all you can find about him.
3. Review your notes on David.
4. Mark your Bible where new truths are learned.

Lesson 21
"Solomon, The Man of Wisdom"

(Where lines are provided, look up the Scripture and write it or its meaning in the space provided).

1. **THE MEANING OF THE NAME:**

   Solomon means "peace or peaceable." In Hebrew the name would be "Shelomo."

   II Samuel 12:24-25 also gives another name, "Jedidiah," meaning "beloved of the Lord." This name was given to the babe by Nathan upon instruction from the Lord.

   Both names together have a profound meaning.

2. **BASIC SCRIPTURES:**

   I Kings 1 through 11; II Chronicles 1 through 9; Matthew 6:29; 12:42; John 10:23; Acts 5:12; 7:47.

3. **FAMILY BACKGROUND:**

   Scripture tells us of the children of David by Bathsheba. Those born to David in Hebron by different wives are given in II Samuel 3:2-5. Children by wives and concubines in Jerusalem are mentioned in II Samuel 5:13 through 15 (note verse 14).

   Solomon was given to David and Bathsheba by the Lord, after the death of the first child by Bathsheba.

   The Lord told David he would not build the temple but his son would build it (I Chronicles 22:8-12 and II Samuel 7:4-16). The Lord named Solomon and chose him to build the temple (I Chronicles 28:2, 3, and 6). So Solomon, the "beloved of the Lord" and "peaceable" one, was born to a fore-ordained work for God. We must not forget that his parents were sinful people; Bathsheba had a reputation of sensuality; David committed such acts as illicit sex and then had Bathsheba's husband killed. *Solomon was definitely born into the Adamic race. We should not expect him to be perfect.* We shall see his good and his bad in this study.

4. **WHAT THE OLD TESTAMENT SAYS ABOUT SOLOMON:**

   (1) Solomon Became King of Israel - I Kings 1:33-39.

   David, the father of Solomon, declared Solomon to be his successor. David knew that the Lord God had chosen Solomon to be on the throne. Look up I Chronicles 22:9 _____

   _____

   Underline I Chronicles 28:5.

   An older brother tried to seize the kingdom, as you will see in I Kings 1:5-9. Nathan and Bathsheba went to David, and orders were immediately carried out to anoint Solomon as king (underline I Kings 1:39).

   (2) The Charge To Solomon - I Kings 2:1-9.

   David charged (challenged) his son as he took the throne. Note I Kings 2:2 _____

   _____

Underline verses 3 and 4.

(3) Solomon's Prayer For Wisdom - I Kings 3:5-15.

In verse 5 the Lord said to Solomon, "ask what I shall give thee."

Solomon responded in verse 7, "I am but a little child." Actually he was about 20 years old, but he was like a child in this new responsibility. He knew he needed help.

His request of the Lord is in verse 9 _____

_____

Also turn to II Chronicles 1:10 and underline.

God responded by giving him all he requested (I Kings 3:12) and more (verse 13), "I have given thee that which thou hast not asked, both riches, and honor: so that there shall not be any among the kings like unto thee all thy days." But there is a condition the Lord places on long life. In verse 14, "If thou wilt walk in my ways, to keep my statues, etc."

(4) The Wisdom of Solomon - I Kings 4:29-30.

Underline verses 29 and 20.

Note verse 32 _____

_____

You will find 917 of Solomon's proverbs in the Book of Proberbs.

(5) Solomon Begins the *First* Temple - I Kings 5 and 6.

Solomon knew he would have to build the temple of the Lord. This was to be the first "house of the Lord." Heretofore the tabernacle was the place where the people met the Lord. Now a permanent temple was to be built on the very place where David had bought the threshing floor of Ornan. See II Chronicles 3:1 and I Chronicles 21:18-30.

This was the first of three temples in the history of Israel:

First - Solomon's Temple

Second - Zerubbabel's Temple

Third - Herod's Temple

In I Kings 5:5 Solomon stated his purpose _____

_____

In I Kings 6:1 the date of the beginning of the temple was 480 years after Israel came out of Egyptian bondage, or about 962 B.C. In I Kings 6:38 it took seven years to finish the building. Don't let verse 37 fool you. It refers back to I Kings 6:1, to the fourth year of Solomon's reign.

The pattern for the temple had been given to David by the Lord (I Chronicles 28:19); and David gave the pattern to Solomon (I Chronicles 28:11-12). Solomon made a new brazen alter, candlesticks, tables, lavers, pots and other articles, but he did **not** make a new Ark of the Covenant. The Ark of the Covenant which was brought into the new temple was the same one which had been made at Mt. Sinai.

Read I Kings 8:6 and underline.

Who filled the new temple? Look at I Kings 8:11 _____

_____

(The porch mentioned in I Kings 7:7 was used as a judgment hall. This porch is referred to in the New Testament. Also notice in I Kings 7:1 that Solomon took 13 years to build his *own* house.)

Read Solomon's prayer of dedication after his message at the ceremony (I Kings 8).

(6) The Second Appearance of the Lord to Solomon - I Kings 9:1-9 and II Chronicles 7:12-22.

The Lord God had appeared to Solomon at Gibeon (I Kings 3:5), when He said, "Ask what I shall give thee."

At the second appearance the Lord told Solomon that He had heard and answered his prayer concerning the temple (I Kings 9:3). The part of Solomon's petition concerning the continuation of the kingdom of Solomon was conditional (I Kings 9:4-7). Read and underline. This same event is also recorded in II Chronicles 7:12-22. One of the most familiar verses in all Scripture is given by God to Solomon and to us. Write in II Chronicles 7:14 _____

_____

The warning of the Lord was an exact prophecy which took place later in the history of Israel.

(7) Solomon's Sin Against God - I Kings 10 and 11.

In chapter 10 Solomon is described as he appeared to men; in chapter 11 as he appeared to God.

Solomon attracted people from all parts of the world. Among them was the Queen of Sheba (I Kings 10:1-13). This visit is also recorded in II Chronicles 9. Notice in II Chronicles 9:8 that the Queen of Sheba gave Solomon some advice he needed:

"God delighted to set thee on *His* throne . . ."

"to be king for the Lord thy God . . ."

"because thy God loved Israel . . ."

"made thee king to do judgment and justice . . ."

The remainder of I Kings 10 gives some idea of Solomon's enormous wealth. With all the peace, prosperity and power of Solomon, the wisdom of Solomon became earthly rather than heavenly.

The power and fortune led to Solomon's transgression against God. Notice the very first verse of I Kings 11. _____

_____

Now verse 3 _____

_____

The wives Solomon took were not all Israelites. Many were from other nations and "they turned away his heart after other gods and his heart was not sincere with the Lord his God."

Four and one-half centuries before, God had given the qualifications for the future kings of Israel. Turn to Deuteronomy 17:14-17. *Solomon disobeyed each of the four things forbidden a king:*

First - "He shall not multiply horses to himself" (Look at I Kings 10:26).

Second - "Nor cause the people to return to Egypt, that he should multiply horses" (Look at I Kings 10:28-29).

Third - "Neither shall he multiply wives to himself, that his heart turn not away" (Look at I Kings 11:3).

Fourth - "Neither shall he greatly multiply to himself silver and gold" (See I Kings 10:14, 23, and 27).

Solomon had disobeyed God in all of these areas. Also in Deuteronomy 17:18-20, the Lord required that the king read the Word and keep the words of the law. *Solomon simply neglected the plain Word of God.* His heart was turned away from God by "things."

(8) The Result of Solomon's Sin - I Kings 11:9-13 and 31.

God **does** get angry about sin (verse 9).

In verse 11 God told Solomon that the kingdom would be divided after his death. Jeroboam was to have ten tribes (I Kings 11:31).

Rehoboam, the son of Solomon, was to have the other two (I Kings 12:21).

The Lord God never fails to keep His Word, whether it be mercy or judgment.

There is no evidence in Scripture that Solomon was sorry for all he had done. There are no words of repentance, no tears of sorrow. In his own writing, the Book of Ecclesiastes, Solomon wrote of the vanities of life and closed the book with the "whole duty of man" (Ecclesiastes 12:9-14). *Nowhere do we read, "I am sorry for my sin."*

(9) Solomon's Death - I Kings 11:41-43.

Solomon died after a 40 year reign, not quite 60 years old.

5. **WHAT THE NEW TESTAMENT SAYS ABOUT SOLOMON:**

(1) "Behold a Greater than Solomon is here" - Matthew 12:42.

Solomon was indeed a wise man; but Jesus **is** wisdom itself, in "whom are hid all the treasures of wisdom" (Colossians 2:3). __

The Queen of Sheba came from afar to witness the wisdom of Solomon, while we have Christ among us and His Word in our hand. Jesus Christ is greater than Solomon. Jesus said so, and that is a fact.

(2) "Jesus walked in the temple in Solomon's Porch" - John 10:23.

There Jesus walked where the Sanhedrin held their proceedings. The porch was a place of judgment in Solomon's day. Jesus was in the temple, walking, meditating, available. *That is the lesson in this scripture.*

(3) The early church met on Solomon's Porch - Acts 5:12.

Peter preached there. Ananias and Sapphira died there.

"They were all of one accord in Solomon's porch." They met in the open place of the temple. This teaches us that the early church met in public worship. We should never cease to assemble in worship.

(4) "Solomon in all his glory was not arrayed as one of these" - Matthew 6:29.

Jesus spoke of our father's care for us and used lilies of the field as a comparison. Solomon did not have the beauty of one of the lilies.

"Behold, A Greater Than Solomon is Here!!"

6. **THE LESSONS YOU SHOULD LEARN FROM THIS STUDY:**

(1) The Lord God gives and takes away as He wills. He gave to Solomon the charge to build the temple.

(2) All great Bible characters were born into the Adamic race: there-fore, *we should not expect perfection.*

(3) God grants wisdom if we ask (James 1:5).

(4) God gives us more than we expect or deserve.

(5) Solomon is a good example that riches and things do not make a person happy.

(6) The Lord judges *all,* the great as well as the small. Jesus is our Advocate, our Savior, who saves us from the judgment (not the consequences), of sin.

CAN YOU REMEMBER?

1. What did Solomon pray for as he became king?
2. How many proverbs and songs did he write?
3. How long did it take Solomon to build the temple? His own residence?
4. What was placed in the temple that was old?
5. What happened to Israel when Solomon died?

90

YOUR NEXT ASSIGNMENT:

1. Read II Kings 11 and 12; II Chronicles 22-24; Matthew 23:35.
2. The next character will be Joash, son of Ahaziah. The line of Christ was destroyed, save one, Joash.
3. Review your notes on Solomon.
4. Mark your Bible where new truths are learned.

Lesson 22
"Joash, the Royal Seed Preserved"

NOTES

(Where lines are provided, look up the Scripture and write it or its meaning in the space provided.)

1. **THE MEANING OF THE NAME:**

   Joash means "Jehovah supports, hastens to help" or "Jehovah has given."

2. **BASIC SCRIPTURES:**

   II Kings 11 and 12; II Chronicles 23 and 24; Matthew 23:35.

3. **FAMILY BACKGROUND:**

   The reason Joash was selected for this series is simply that few Christians know anything at all about this significant person in the line of Christ. Joash was born the son of Ahaziah. Ahaziah was the son of Jehoram and his wife Athaliah. When King Ahaziah of Judah was killed by Jehu, the king of Israel (Northern Kingdom), Ahaziah's mother, Athaliah arose and destroyed all of the royal seed (from the seed of David), save one—Joash.

   The family background becomes more degenerate the farther back we trace it in Scripture.

   Athaliah was the daughter of Ahab and Jezebel: therefore, she was half Israelite and half Phoenician. Her parents gave her a reputation and character she lived up to quite well.

   Joash became a fulfillment of the words of the Lord in II Kings 8:19 ___

   _____

   A like passage is found in II Chronicles 21:7.

   God had promised David the continuation of his family. In Psalms 132:17 the Lord says:_____

   _____

   _____

4. **WHAT THE OLD TESTAMENT SAYS ABOUT JOASH:**

   (1) The line of David Almost Extinguished - II Kings 11:1

   You have just read Psalm 132:17. The lamp of David was almost extinguished and yet wonderfully preserved.

   In II Kings 11:1 the hatred and malice of Athaliah, the queen-mother, the grandmother of Joash, was exhibited when her son, Ahaziah, was killed by Jehu. See II Kings 9:27-28.

   This wicked grandmother was married to Jehoram, who killed all his brothers (II Chronicles 21:4). The Arabians killed all Jehoram's sons except Ahaziah (II Chronicles 22:1).

   Jehoram, the husband of Athaliah, died of stomach disease, predicted by the prophet Elijah (II Chronicles 21:12-20). He did not follow in the way of his father, but sinned against God and Judah. This left the throne open, upon the death of Ahaziah.

   Royal blood was profusely shed.

As if all the deaths were not enough, the queen-mother made sure that all the children in line for the throne of Judah were killed. She did such a wicked thing because she wanted to rule with complete authority with no threat of an heir to reign with her. She also murdered the royal seed from a spirit of revenge and rage against God. *She decided to destroy the line of David, a foolish attempt, because God promised to perpetuate the line of David.*

Can you imagine a grandmother killing her own grandchildren? Athaliah did. Look at her title in II Chronicles 24:7 _____

_____

Don't become confused with all of these names.

The main thing is to remember something like this:

- **Jehoshaphat**

- **Jehorum** (married Athaliah)

- **Ahaziah** Athaliah reigns as Queen of Judah after killing all legal heirs to the throne of David, *all but one*. Joash.

- **Joash**

These names are in the line of David.

(2) **The line of David preserved by Jehosheba, the aunt of the baby, Joash - II Kings 11:2-3**

Notice in verse 2, "Joash was taken from among the king's sons which were slain and hid him."

Joash was the only seed of David remaining. Only one child, and David's line would have failed had he been killed. But God's promises never fail. He had not forgotten His promise to David. His eye was on that infant, Joash.

Jehosheba, the wife of Jehoiada, the priest, was also the aunt of Joash. Notice in verse 2, she was the sister of Ahaziah.

Note where Joash was hidden in verse 3 _____

_____

By hiding Joash in the house of the Lord, he was under God's special care and protection.

David's words were made good to one of his seed. Look up Psalms 27:5 _____

_____

The seed of David was bound up in one life, hidden and unseen for six years. God placed that one life in the hands of a priest, Jehoiada, and his wife, who kept Joash in the temple.

Is this really important to us? Oh, yes, a thousand times yes. A.C. Gaebelein says, "It was one of the many attempts Satan made to exterminate the male offspring to make the coming ONE, the promised Saviour, the Seed of the woman impossible. Had he succeeded through Athaliah in the destruction of the royal seed of David, the promise made to David would have become impossible."

Athaliah reigned for the six years.

(3) **The Preparation for the Presentation of Joash - II Kings 11:4-11**

The priest, Jehoiada, was the leader and organizer of this secret affair.

Notice verse 4, "In the seventh year he gathered rulers of hundreds and the captains." These were men in office - religious, civil and military office. He gathered them, made a covenant with them and took an oath of secrecy from them. Then he showed them Joash.

Can't you see, as it were, the surprise on the faces of the select few? They saw and realized that there was hope in the promise of A Seed of David.

Jehoiada planned well the presentation of Joash. He skillfully divided and stationed the royal guard so that no possible harm could come to the infant king (verses 5-11). Jehoiada was beginning a revolution and the people followed.

(4)   The Presentation of Joash, King of Judah - II Kings 11:12

Jehoiada brought forth Joash, the king's son. The priest immediately began the coronation of the young king. Note the tokens of power, obligation, spiritual leadership given in the coronation in verse 12.

—"he put a crown upon him" (kingly power given)

—"he gave him the testimony" (a Bible to guide him)

—"he anointed him" (a token of spiritual blessing)

—"they made him king and clapped their hands" (hands of joy, relief from Athaliah)

—"they said, God save the king" (they made him their king)

(5)   The Opposition of Athaliah - II Kings 11:13-16

Like her mother, Jezebel, Athaliah heard the noise and went out to them. When she saw the king's place by the pillar occupied, the guards and trumpeters by him, and all the people rejoicing, she acted just like all guilty sinners. Notice verse 13, "She rent her clothes and cried, 'treason, treason.'"

Jehoiada ordered the officers to take her outside the temple area and kill her, and kill any who followed her (verses 15 and 16).

(NOTE: Joash is also spelled Jehoash - verse 21).

(6)   The Reign of Joash - II Kings 12 and II Chronicles 24

The reign of Joash began well and continued as long as Jehoiada, the priest, lived and instructed the young king.

Joash was only seven years old when he began to rule. Look at II Kings 12:1 _____

_____

Underline II Kings 12:2.

The most important work accomplished during the reign of Joash was the repairing of the temple, which had been broken down by Athaliah (II Chronicles 24:7-14).

Jehoiada, the priest, died at the age of 130 (II Chronicles 24:15-16). The nation lost a man of great influence.

King Joash, then a man over 30, should have been able to lead his people in the ways of God. He became a weak leader and listened to the princess' who were idolaters. Soon the house of the Lord was abandoned for worship in high places, with idols before them. The wrath of God came upon Judah and Jerusalem. God, in His mercy, sent them prophets but the people would not listen to them (II Chronicles 24:17-19).

Jerusalem was threatened by the king of Syria. Joash stripped the temple of its treasure and bought off the Syrain king for a time (II Kings 12:17-18).

Joash lost all sense of reverence and gratitude and killed the son of Jehoiada, the priest who had raised him. He had the son stoned in the temple on the Day of Atonement (II Chronicles 24:20-22). Write in verse 22 _____

_____

(7)   The Death of Joash - II Chronicles 24:25-27; II Kings 12:20

After the Syrian king returned and defeated Judah, Joash was

95

murdered by his own servants and denied burial with the other kings (II Chronicles 24:25).

His son, Amaziah, took the throne of Judah (II Chronicles 24:27).

Thus fell Joash, who began in the Spirit and ended in the flesh.

Please note: There are several men in Scripture named Joash or Jehoash. Do not let this confuse you. We are speaking here of Joash, the son of Ahaziah.

5. **WHAT THE NEW TESTAMENT SAYS ABOUT JOASH:**

   (1) Jesus spoke of the act of Joash in Matthew 23:35 (see II Chronicles 24:20-22).

   Jesus extends His warning from "the blood of righteous Abel unto the blood of Zecharias." This was not Zechariah the prophet, but Zecharias who was killed "in the court of the Lord's house." His father is called Barachias, which signifies the same as Jehoiada. This is the example Jesus used when He said He would "send unto you prophets, and wise men and scribes; and some of them you will crucify." Then He recalls the "blood of righteous Abel" to the "blood of Zecharias." Then Jesus goes on in verse 37 to give foundation to His warning, "Oh, Jerusalem, Jerusalem, thou that killest the prophets . . ."

   This is the only time any reference is made concerning the acts of Joash.

6. **THE LESSONS YOU SHOULD LEARN FROM THIS STUDY:**

   (1) The wickedness of the human heart is seen in Athaliah, the queen-mother who wanted power.

   (2) God promised David the continuation of his seed, "to give him always a light, and to his children" (II Kings 18:19). The Lord God always keeps His promise.

   (3) The Lord uses evil and turns it to His glory.

   (4) Regardless of how dark it may become (the seed of David down to one baby), God works within His timetable and His will.

   (5) Sometimes the jewels of God's goodness are hidden and unseen for a time (as was Joash).

   (6) The heart is Adamic in nature. Though trained by a priest, Joash went from revival to the fleshly path of sin. Have you gone from a spiritual mountain top down into the valley of sin?

CAN YOU REMEMBER?

1. Who was the wicked woman in this lesson?
2. What was her background?
3. Who was God's hero during this period?
4. Why is Joash so important in Scripture?
5. Why did Joash become worldy in his last years?
6. What promise did God make to David?

YOUR NEXT ASSIGNMENT:

1. Read I Kings 17 through 21; II Kings 1 through 8; Malachi 4:5-6; Matthew 17:1-13; Luke 4:25; 9:18-21; James 5:17-18; Revelations 11:3-12.

2. The next lesson will be on two of God's great prophets, Elijah and Elisha. Read all you can about these two men.

3. Review your notes on Joash.

4. Mark your Bible where new truths are learned.

Lesson 23
"Elijah and Elisha"

(Where lines are provided, look up the Scripture and write it or its meaning in the space provided.)

1. **THE MEANING OF THE NAME:**

   Elijah means "my god is Jehovah."

   Elisha means "God is salvation."

   (Elias is the Greek form of Elijah found in the New Testament.)

2. **BASIC SCRIPTURES:**

   I Kings 17 through 21; II Kings 1 through 8; Malachi 4:5-6; Matthew 17:1-13; Luke 4:25; 9:8-21; James 5:17-18; Revelations 11:3-12.

3. **FAMILY BACKGROUND:**

   All we know of Elijah, before his dramatic appearance as the prophet of God, is summed up in the words of I Kings 17:1; "Elijah the Tishbite, who was of the inhabitants of Gilead . . ."

   Elisha, the successor of Elijah, was the son of *Shaphat* and they lived in the Jordon valley (I Kings 19:16).

   The impact of these two men upon Biblical history was like a bright sun breaking through the black stormy clouds of Israel's dark hour of sin.

   The importance of Elijah's ministry may be gauged by the fact that *he appears on the pages of the New Testament more frequently than any other prophet of God, about 27 times.*

4. **WHAT THE OLD TESTAMENT SAYS ABOUT ELIJAH:**

   (1) Elijah Announced a Drought Upon Israel - I Kings 17:1

   In I Kings 16:28-34 Ahab became the king over Israel (Northern Kingdom) and he married Jezebel, the daughter of the king of Sidon. Ahab was weak and allowed Jezebel to introduce the worship of Baal (a word meaning false gods). Ahab came to the throne about 40 years after the death of Jeroboam, the king who had put the golden calf at Dan in the north and at Bethel in the south. After Jeroboam died, there was a continued moral decline in Israel. When Ahab became king, the Bible says in I Kings 16:30, *"He did evil above all that were before him."* He built an alter to Baal in Samaria, the capital city of Israel. The worship of Baal was often accompanied by drunken orgies and degrading rites. This was against the Lord God of Israel.

   Elijah appeared as God's man at this zero hour in Israel's history.

   The first thing Elijah did was pronounce God's judgment in the form of a drought (I Kings 17:1). Underline the verse. (The length of the drought is not given here but it lasted 3½ years as we shall see later.)

   (2) Elijah is Supernaturally Cared For - I Kings 17:2-7

   In spite of the drought, God cared for His prophet. Look at I Kings 17:4 _____

   God provided water and food.

   (3) The Widow of Zarephath - I Kings 17:8-16.

   When the brook of Cherith dried up, the Lord told Elijah to go to Zarephath to a widow to care for him. God supernaturally fed Elijah, the widow and her household all the days of the drought.

Underline I Kings 17:13-14. Now verse 15 _____

_____

Notice the plan of God here in this passage. *Give of what one has first, then the Lord takes care of the giver.*

(4) Elijah Raised the Widow's Dead Son - I Kings 17:17-24.

The supernatural power of God was again displayed in the prophet. Underline I Kings 17:21 and 23. Write verse 24 _____

_____

(5) Elijah Told to Meet King Ahab - I Kings 18:1-16.

The Lord told Elijah to go and meet Ahab "in the third year;" "there was a sore famine in Samaria" (I Kings 18:1-2).

The verses 3 through 16 are a story of a scared believer who had ministered to 100 prophets. His name was Obadiah (not the writer). Note verse 4: "when Jezebel destroyed the prophets of the Lord, Obadiah took a hundred prophets and hid them." Obadiah reluctantly arranged a meeting between Elijah and Ahab. Reread verses 14-16.

(6) Elijah Challenged Ahab at Mt. Carmel - I Kings 18:17-40.

The story is one you probably know. The power of God is at stake and Elijah challenged the prophets of Baal to pray down fire. They failed but Elijah did not. He prayed and God answered. Look at I Kings 18:36-39. *The prayer was one of the authentication of the power of God, and that Elijah was His prophet.*

Underline the seven "thats" in verses 36 and 37.

Write in verse 39 _____

_____

(7) Elijah Pronounced the End of the Drought - I Kings 18:41-46

The faith of Elijah is paramount. By faith he said "there is a sound of an abundance of rain" (verse 41). He went to the top of Carmel and prayed until there was a great rain.

(8) God Cared for Elijah in Depression - I Kings 19:1-18

After a victory one often falls into deep depression. Elijah was a man like all of us. After the victory on Mt. Carmel, he fled to the wilderness and wanted to die. Underline I Kings 19:4.

He was ministered to by an angel of the Lord (I Kings 19:4-7).

Elijah went to Mt. Horab, where he heard the voice of God while in a cave (I Kings 19:8-18).Elijah was told he had the support of 7,000 who had not bowed their knee to Baal. Of the 7,000, one was to be his companion and successor. Notice verses 16 and 18. The companion was Elisha (I Kings 19:19-21).

(9) Elijah's Message to Ahaziah, the Son of Ahab - II Kings 1:1-18

Ahaziah succeeded his father to the throne of Israel. He was injured (verse 2) and feared death. The Lord sent Elijah to tell Ahaziah that he would die (verse 4). Elijah had great faith and his prayers were heard by the Lord God. He prayed down fire to destroy those who would destroy him. (verses 9-12).

(10) The Translation of Elijah - II Kings 2:1-11

The prophet of fire, who successfully challenged the god of fire, ascended to heaven in a chariot of fire. Elisha requested "a double portion of thy spirit be upon me" (verse 9).

Write in verse 11 _____

_____

He is translated to glory without dying.

(11) Elijah is to Come Again - Malachi 4:5-6

Jesus confirmed this in Matthew 17:10-13. Also look up Luke

1:11-17; Matthew 11:14. (We shall cover this more in the New Testament section of this lesson.)

(12) Elisha was a prophet of miracles.

He took the mantle of Elijah and did all in the name of the Lord. We shall list the miracles and the Scripture. Look up each one in your Bible.

(a) He struck the Jordon and it divided (II Kings 2:14).

(b) He purified the water at Jericho (II Kings 2:19-22).

(c) He pronounced a curse on the lads at Bethel (II Kings 2:23-24).

(d) He foretold the success against Moab (II Kings 3:16-27).

(e) He filled vessels with oil for a widow (II Kings 4:1-7).

(f) He raised the dead boy at Shunam (II Kings 4:18-21, 32, 37).

(g) He took the poison out of the stew at Gilgal (II Kings 4:38-41).

(h) He fed 100 men on little food (II Kings 4:42-44).

(i) He healed Naaman of leprosy (II Kings 5:1-19).

(j) He transferred Naaman's leprosy to Gehazi (II Kings 5:20-27).

(k) He made an axhead float to the surface in the Jordon River (II Kings 6:1-7).

(l) He told Israel of the secret plans of Syria (II Kings 6:8-12).

(m) He prayed and his servant's eyes were opened (II Kings 6:13-17).

(n) He blinded the Syrian Army (II Kings 6:18-23).

(o) He promised food to Samaria and God provided (II Kings 7:1-20).

(p) He told Benhadad, king of Syria, he would die (II Kings 8:7-15).

(q) He foretold three victories of Israel over Syria (II Kings 13:14-19).

(r) After his death, Elisha raised a dead man (II Kings 13:20-21).

(13) *Elisha had* twice *the power of Elijah and he used that power in a merciful and beneficial way.*

Everything he performed was in the power of God. He performed twice as many miracles as did Elijah.

What a pair of giants for God!

5. **WHAT THE NEW TESTAMENT SAYS ABOUT ELIJAH AND ELISHA:**

(1) Elijah is mentioned in the New Testament more than any other prophet.

(Elisha is *not* mentioned.) We shall take only a few New Testament references.

(2) Elijah appeared at the transfiguration of our Lord (Matthew 17:1-13).

Jesus was transfigured (glorified) on the high mountain and there appeared Moses and Elijah with Him. They talked of the departure, exodus, of our Lord at Jerusalem (Luke 9:31).

At this scene there was Moses, whose task was the formation of the elect nation. Moses had passed through death.

We have Elijah, whose task was the reformation of the apostate nation. He was translated and did not taste death.

We have Peter, James and John—representatives in the flesh—not glorified, still alive.

The lesson here is that the transfiguration is a picture, a "Parousia," meaning "the coming of the Lord." When the disciples looked upon that scene and when we read it, it is a preview of the glorious return of Christ.

The two great representatives of Judaism, the Law and the Prophets, surrendered the seals of office to the Lamb of God.

Write in Matthew 17:5 _____

_____

Now verse 8 _____

_____

(3) **While at the transfiguration, Jesus spoke of Elijah coming again (Matthew 17:10-13).**

In verse 10 Jesus said, "Elijah truly shall first come and restore all things."

Then in verse 11 Jesus said, "Elijah has come already and they knew him not, but have done unto him what they wanted. Likewise shall the Son of man suffer of them."

Now you are wondering, aren't you?

In verse 13 a part of the clue is found, "Then the disciples understood that **He spake of John the Baptist.**"

John The Baptist came in a ministry completely in the spirit and power and likeness of Elijah (Luke 1:17).

(4) **Elijah shall appear, as recorded in Revelations 11:3-12.**

The two witnesses at the crisis hour for the world are identified in verse 6. Read and underline.

The shutting of heaven so that it rains not reveals Elijah. The turning of the water to blood is none other than Moses. *They have returned as "my two witnesses to prophecy a thousand two hundred and three score days"* (verse 3). That is 1,260 days, or 42 months, or 3½ years.

This should open a new study for you.

(5) **James 5:17-18 tells us so much.**

Elijah was of like passions. He prayed; it rained not for 3½ years. He prayed again and it rained.

6. **THE LESSONS YOU SHOULD LEARN FROM THIS STUDY:**

(1) An unknown became one of the greatest prophets in the Bible.

(2) Elijah had only what God gave him. He had no worldly goods, no formal education, not even a family as far as we know. God took Elijah and made him a "prophet of fire."

(3) *The Lord still needs people, willing to give all that God has given to them.*

(4) God's judgment has to be proclaimed by God's servants when a nation forgets the Lord.

(5) When a person does His will, God cares for him. He did for Elijah and Elisha.

(6) Elijah was translated like Enoch. Neither tasted death. Wouldn't it be great to experience a translation like theirs? We may. The time is short.

CAN YOU REMEMBER?

1. How many times is Elijah mentioned in the New Testament?
2. What does Baal mean?
3. Who was king and wife when Elijah appeared?
4. What was his first pronouncement? How long did the drought last? How do you know?
5. How many miracles did Elisha perform in our study?

YOUR NEXT ASSIGNMENT:

1. Read II Kings 16 throught 21; II Chronicles 28 through 32; Isaiah 36 through 39; Jeremiah 15:4; 26:18-19.

100

2. The next study will be on Hezekiah, the king to whom God gave an additional 15 years.
3. Review your study of Elijah and Elisha.
4. Mark your Bible where new truths are learned.

Lesson 24
"Hezekiah, God Added Fifteen Years"

(Where lines are provided, look up the Scripture and write it or its meaning in the space provided.

1. **THE MEANING OF THE NAME:**

   Hezekiah means "the might, or strength, of Jehovah."

2. **BASIC SCRIPTURES:**

   II Kings 16 through 21; II Chronicles 28 through 32; Isaiah 36 through 39; Jeremiah 15:4; 26:18-19.

3. **FAMILY BACKGROUND:**

   Hezekiah was the son of Ahaz, king of Judah, and Abijah, daughter of Zechariah. Abijah is also referred to in Scripture as Abi (II Kings 18:2 compared to II Chronicles 29:1).

   Hezekiah's father, King Ahaz, was the 11th king of Judah. He was a wicked king who took sacred things from the temple and made sacrifices to idols (II Chronicles 29:19-23). "He did not right in the sight of the Lord" (II Chronicles 28:1).

   You will notice that in both references to Hezekiah taking the kingship there is an unmistakable influence in his life. Notice both II Kings 18:2-3 and II Chronicles 29:1-2. Note that **both** Scriptures state:

   - "he was twenty and five years old when he began to reign"
   - "he reigned twenty and nine years in Jerusalem"
   - "his mother's name was Abi (Abijah), the daughter of Zachariah"
   - "and he did that which was right in the sight of the Lord, according to all that David, his father, had done"

   Ahaz was a sinful king. So the mother of Hezekiah, Abijah or Abi, had to counteract all the evil influence. You will note in Scripture, after the mention of his mother, that "he did that which was right." Here was a godly mother who clung to the meaning of her own name, "my Father is Jehovah," and the meaning of the name of her son, Hezekiah, 'the strength of Jehovah."

4. **WHAT THE OLD TESTAMENT SAYS ABOUT HEZEKIAH:**

   (1) He conducted a revival - II Kings 18:3-7; II Chronicles 29:3-30:13

   Hezekiah commenced his reign by repairing and cleansing the temple at Jerusalem (II Chronicles 29:3) _____

   _____

   He removed the "high places" of idol worship which had come into being under his father, Ahaz (II Kings 18:4) _____

   _____

   He made preparation for and established the passover, not only for Judah but for all Israel. He invited all Israel to come to Jerusalem (underline II Chronicles 30:1 and 5).

   (2) The Assyrian threat to Jerusalem - II Kings 18:13-37; II Chronicles 32:9-19; Isaiah 36

When the Assyrians came, as they always did to a new government, they came under Sennacherib and found the fenced cities of Judah. The Assyrians had conquered all in their path to the north and they were surprised and puzzled that Hezekiah would attempt to resist them. Sennacherib sent his spokesman, Rabshakeh, to ridicule and to try to terrorize Jerusalem, II Kings 18:17-37.

(3) Hezekiah sought a man of God, Isaiah - II Kings 19:1-7; Isaiah 37:1-4 and 14-20

When Hezekiah received the threat from Rabshakeh and from Sennacherib, he sent for the prophet Isaiah. The Lord answered through Isaiah. Underline Isaiah 37:6-7.

Then Sennacherib sent letters to Hezekiah demanding abject surrender (II Kings 19:14 and II Chronicles 32:17-19). Hezekiah, with Isaiah's encouragement, took the letters and "went up to the house of the Lord and spread it before the Lord."

(4) Hezekiah, a man of prayer - II Kings 19:14-19; II Chronicles 32:20; Isaiah 37:14-20

Note that this account of Hezekiah's reign is recorded **three** times in the Bible. It has to be important for God to give the same account three times.

Take the prayer in Isaiah 37:14-20. Write in verse 17 of this passage _____

_____

_____

The Lord God answered, again through the prophet Isaiah. Turn to Isaiah 37:33-35.

The Lord defended His people with an angel (Isaiah 37:36; also in II Kings 19:35 and II Chronicles 32:21-22). Write in Isaiah 37:36

_____

_____

Sennacherib was killed by his own sons (Isaiah 37:38).

(5) Hezekiah's illness and recovery - II Kings 20:1-11; Isaiah 38:1-8

Hezekiah became very "sick unto death" (II Kings 20:1). The Lord sent Isaiah to tell him: (complete the last part of verse 1). "Thus saith the Lord, _____

_____

Again Hezekiah prayed. He turned his face to the wall and cried out to God, and the Lord heard his prayer. Isaiah was not out of the middle court when the Lord told Isaiah to go back and tell Hezekiah he would be healed on the third day (II Kings 20:4-5).

(6) Hezekiah is given 15 additional years - II Kings 20:6-11; Isaiah 38:5-8

Hezekiah was the only man who ever knew exactly how long he would live.

At the time of his illness, Hezekiah had no son and no heir to the throne of Judah. He wanted to live because he must have loved life and for sure he wanted a son.

God gave him 15 additional years. Write in Isaiah 38:5 _____

_____

The sign which the Lord gave was the great sun dial of King Ahaz. Read II Kings 20:8-11 and Isaiah 38:7-8. It was on this sun dial that the shadow went back 10 degrees as a sign that the 15 years would be added to the life of Hezekiah. The repetition of the word "degrees" should be noted in both Scriptural accounts. This was a supernatural happening that only God could have done. (This is a great study within itself. Perhaps you can find more on the subject. Look at Isaiah 38:20 and Psalms 120 to 135. 15 Songs of Degrees.)

(7) **What happened during those 15 years? - II Kings 20:12-19; Isaiah 39:1-8. Then II Kings 21:1-15; II Chronicles 33:1-18**

(a) **First,** Merodach-baladan, the up-coming king of Babylon, was getting ready to destroy Assyria when he heard of Hezekiah's recovery. He sent letters and gifts by his messengers. Hezekiah was flattered and invited in the men of Babylon and showed them the treasures of his entire domain. Underline Isaiah 39:2. Isaiah, the prophet, pronounced God's judgment upon Hezekiah and Judah. Write in the words the Lord spoke through Isaiah in Isaiah 39:6 _____

_____

(b) **Secondly,** in that 15-year extension, the Lord gave to Hezekiah, his son, Manasseh. Manasseh was 12 years old when he began to reign, and he reigned for 55 years in Jerusalem. His slogan could have been, "he did that which was evil in the sight of the Lord" (II Kings 21:1-2).

Of all the kings, there were none as mean and as sinful as Manasseh.

Isaiah told Hezekiah in Isaiah 39:6-7 that Judah and Jerusalem would be carried away into Babylon. Also, the children that should come from his seed would become eunuchs in Babylon. (Daniel was one of those from the king's seed. See Daniel 1:1-4).

The prophecy of Isaiah came true because of the sin of Manasseh. Note II Kings 21:11 _____

_____

Now verse 13 _____

_____

Underline II Kings 23:26-27.
Underline II Kings 24:3-4.
The Lord describes His judgment in unique and blunt words in Jeremiah 15:1-4. Underline verses 1 through 3 and then write in verse 4 _____

_____

So, in the 15-year extension God gave to Hezekiah we see the reasons for God's judgment, through His prophets, upon Judah and Jerusalem. Hezekiah played into the hands of Babylon; his son, the meanest king ever to live, was further cause for the Babylonian captivity. **So the pride of Hezekiah before Merodach-baladan and the awful sinfulness of his son caused the judgment of the Lord.**

(8) **The death of Hezekiah - II Kings 20:20-21; II Chronicles 32:32-33**

In recording the death of Hezekiah in II Kings 20:20, mention is made of, "he made a pool, and a conduit, and brought water into the city." You will find a reference to that in II Chronicles 32:30 and Isaiah 36:2. That conduit, known today as Hezekiah's Tunnel, is what made Jerusalem great. The city was high, and water made it the ideal place. If you ever go to Israel, you will want to see Hezekiah's Tunnel and read from Scripture about its origin.

(9) **Hezekiah reigned during Isaiah's time - Isaiah 1:1**

In Isaiah 1:1 you find four kings mentioned. The vision Isaiah had from the Lord was "in the days of Uzziah, Jotham, Ahaz, and Hezekiah, kings of Judah."

105

Isaiah spoke, preached, prayed, prophesied to Judah during this period.

5. **WHAT THE NEW TESTAMENT SAYS ABOUT HEZEKIAH:**

   (1) Not one single word is mentioned about Hezekiah in the New Testament.

6. **THE LESSON YOU SHOULD LEARN FROM THIS STUDY:**

   (1). A good mother can often have more influence on her children than a wicked, apostate father such as Ahaz.

   (2). When God places a person in a position, he should honor the position and calling. Hezekiah did by starting a revival.

   (3). We should learn to clean up a mess and straighten out confusion instead of adding to it.

   (4). When in doubt, go to God and to God's servants. Hezekiah prayed and sent for Isaiah.

   (5). Pride can easily beset any one of us. Be on guard. The term "I" is the middle letter of PRIDE.

   (6). Sometimes God will grant our requests but "bring leanness to our souls" (Psalms 106:15). What we think is best may not be the best. God granted Hezekiah fifteen years, at his request, and he experienced "leanness of soul."

CAN YOU REMEMBER?

1. Who was Hezekiah's mother?

2. What did Hezekiah do when he became king?

3. When in danger, to whom did Hezekiah turn for help?

4. Hezekiah was the only man who knew _____

   _____

5. Hezekiah's son was _____

   His father was King _____

6. What were the two predominant things that resulted from Hezekiah's additional 15 years?

YOUR NEXT ASSIGNMENT:

1. Read all of Ezra, 10 chapters, and all of Nehemiah, 13 chapters; Isaiah 44:28 through 45:1-4 and 13.

2. Our next study will be on those two great men of God, Ezra and Nehemiah.

3. Review your study and notes on Hezekiah.

4. Mark your Bible where new truths are learned.

Lesson 25
"Ezra and Nehemiah"

(Where lines are provided, look up the Scripture and write it or its meaning in the space provided.)

1. **THE MEANING OF THE NAME:**
   Ezra means "help."
   Nehemiah means "Jehovah comforts."

2. **BASIC SCRIPTURES:**
   Ezra 1 through 10; Nehemiah 1 through 13; Isaiah 44:28 through 45:1-4 and 13.

3. **FAMILY BACKGROUND:**

   (1) Ezra was a great figure in Jewish history. He was a descendant of Israel's high priest, Aaron, as recorded in Ezra 7:1-5. He was a scribe, Ezra 7:6, which means he was an expert instructor in the Scriptures.

   Tradition has made him one of the great Jewish leaders in history. He is said to be the founder of the Great Synagogue, a group of Jewish scholars who recognized the Canon of Scripture and settled it as the Word of God. Out of the Babylonian captivity was born the Canon of Scripture. Until that time the Scriptures were diverse; how they were preserved is known only to God. Tradition tells us that Ezra and the men of the Great Synagogue placed together the Canon, meaning "rule," of the Old Testament. These Old Testament books are the ones we have in our Bible today. They are in the *Septuagent*.

   (2) Nehemiah was of the tribe of Judah (Nehemiah 2:3). He was born while his family was in exile (the Babylonian captivity), but grew up in an abiding faith in the God of Israel.

   Alexander Whyte, in his writings on Nehemiah, says, "A man with the counsel of God alone in his mind and in his heart. A reserved and resolute man. A man to take command of other men. A man in no haste or hurry. He will not begin until he has counted the cost. And then he will not stop till he has finished the work."

   This is only a thumbnail sketch of both men. You can grasp their character, however.

4. **WHAT THE OLD TESTAMENT SAYS ABOUT EZRA AND NEHEMIAH:**

   (1) Ezra

   (a) The Biblical account of Ezra does not begin until the seventh chapter of Ezra. Note in chapter 7:
   - Ezra was a descendant of Aaron, (Ezra 7:1-5)
   - He was a ready scribe in the law, (Ezra 7:6)
   - He went back to Jerusalem with a Bible in his hand. Write in Ezra 7:10

   _____

   - Note again the emphasis on "a scribe of the words of the commandments of the Lord . . ." (verse 11)
   - Again in verse 12, "a scribe of the law of God of heaven."
   - Ezra was sent by the king to inquire about the civil and religious conditions in Jerusalem and whether they con-

formed to the teaching of God's law. Write in verse 14 _____

_____

- Ezra was to take all that the king and the people gave for the building of the temple at Jerusalem (Ezra 7:15-26).

(b) Ezra was a good administrator.

In chapter 8 Ezra led a company of almost 2,000 (males only) to Jerusalem. This was in addition to the 50,000 who had gone with Zerubbabel eighty years before. Ezra organized the group and led them safely to Jerusalem.

(c) Ezra was a great intercessor (prayer warrior).

When he arrived in Jerusalem, he was grieved to discover the Jews, including some of the priests, had married gentile (heathen) wives (Ezra 9:1).

Ezra prayed first. Note Ezra 9:5 _____

_____

Separation took place and the Jews gave up their gentile wives. Notice Ezra 10:3 and 10-13.

(d) The Word read and taught by Ezra (Nehemiah 8:1-8).

When the temple was completed and the walls finished, the people gathered to hear the Word of the the Lord. They asked Ezra to read and to explain the Word. Look at Nehemiah 8:1, 3, 4, and underline these verses.

Write in Nehemiah 8:5 _____

_____

Also verse 8 _____

_____

(e) Ezra in act and deed, emphasized:
- Worship
- The importance of the Word of God
- Teaching the Word, as well as reading it
- The power of prayer
- Separation from the world
- Wisdom of God in everyday living

(f) Ezra died, according to Josephus, about the time of Eliashib's succession to the high priesthood.

(2) **Nehemiah**

(a) Nehemiah served in the high office of cupbearer in the Persian court, a position of honor and influence. Notice Nehemiah 1:11.

(b) Nehemiah heard from his brother of the condition in Jerusalem. The walls were in ruin and the gates were as they were left by the Babylonians. This news made Nehemiah weep, pray and fast (Nehemiah 1:2-4).

(c) From December to April (compare Nehemiah 1:1 with 2:1), four months, he prayed and fasted. The king noticed his appearance and knew Nehemiah had a "sorrow of heart" (Nehemiah 2:2). He requested that the king send him to Judah, "that I may build it" (Nehemiah 2:5). The king granted his request and commissioned him to do what God had placed on his heart (Nehemiah 2:6-9).

(d) Nehemiah, the wall builder (Nehemiah 2:11 to 6:19).

When Nehemiah reached Jerusalem, he made a secret survey of the ruined walls and encouraged the people to work (Nehemiah 2:11-20).

Underline Nehemiah 2:13 and 18 in your Bible.

He sectioned off the wall to different groups, all working at the same time (Nehemiah 3). He had so successfully organized the people that, in spite of opposition, the work was finished in 52 days (Nehemiah 6:15). Underline that verse.

Write in Nehemiah 4:6 _____

_____

(e) Nehemiah was a good organizer and leader, a man of prayer led by the Spirit. Write in Nehemiah 4:9 _____

_____

Here you see the practical working with the spiritual.

(f) After the Spiritual awakening, led by Ezra, the people made a covenant with Nehemiah to worship Jehovah (Nehemiah 9 and 10). Underline Nehemiah 9:36-37. Write in Nehemiah 9:38 _____

_____

In Nehemiah 10:1 you read, "Now those that sealed were Nehemiah, the Tirshatha (means the governor)," and then names of all who signed the covenant are listed.

(g) Nehemiah was, and is, a good example of a leader, led of God. All classes of people rallied to help rebuild the damaged walls. This was because of Nehemiah's sterling leadership qualities.

People will always follow a leader, especially a leader who is devoted to the Lord.

(h) Nehemiah put the Lord and Lord's house in proper focus. Notice Nehemiah 13:9-10. Now write in Nehemiah 13:11 _

_____

Underline Nehemiah 13:14.

(i) Nehemiah punished those who violated the Sabbath (Nehemiah 13:15-22).

Some of the Jews were buying from the merchants on the Sabbath. Nehemiah took strong action against both; the Jews for buying, the merchants for selling. Look at Nehemiah 13:17, 19, and 20.

Now write in Nehemiah 13:21 _____

_____

(3) Ezra and Nehemiah, with Zerubbabel, led the remnant out of captivity back to the land the Lord had promised to Abraham and his seed.

How and why?

God announced, through Isaiah, 175 years before, that Cyrus would open the gates of Babylon and proclaim to Jerusalem that the city and temple should be rebuilt. Look at Isaiah 44:28 _____

_____

Now underline Isaiah 45:1-4.

Cyrus was named by the Lord before he was born.

(4) The books of Ezra and Nehemiah deal only with the small remnant that voluntarily left Bablyon and went back to Jerusalem.

The book of Esther deals only with those Jews who remained in Babylon and did not return to their homeland. Now remember the next sentence. *Old Testament history closes after the account in Ezra, Nehemiah and Esther. The remainder of the Old Testament, in the main, is prophecy concerning Israel before, during and after the captivity. All of the prophets speak and shed light on all Scripture from Genesis through Esther.*

5. **WHAT THE NEW TESTAMENT SAYS ABOUT EZRA AND NE-HEMIAH:**

Neither are mentioned by name but they live by example throughout the New Testament era. They have influenced all Christianity by leading Israel back into Jerusalem and Judah, thus fulfilling the prophecy of the Lord God of Israel.

6. **THE LESSONS YOU SHOULD LEARN FROM THIS STUDY:**

   (1) We should be students, teachers of the Word. Ezra was a good example.

   (2) We should be ready to receive the call of God and go, do, and say what He may direct.

   (3) Ezra made good preparation for going to Jerusalem to hold a "revival."

   (4) When the Lord places a burden on our hearts, we should pray, seek His will and His way and then do it ourselves. Nehemiah did; he even looked different.

   (5) We should organize and pray and work. All three. We do one and two, but leave the third to "George."

   (6) Nehemiah humbly depended on the Lord and surmounted all of his obstacles and foes in building the wall. Again teaching us, "All things are possible with God" (Matthew 19:26).

CAN YOU REMEMBER?

1. Who was Ezra?
2. Who was Nehemiah?
3. Ezra is remembered as a _____.
4. How did Nehemiah get permission to go to Jerusalem?
5. How did Nehemiah accomplish his great task?
6. Why are these books so important to us?

YOUR NEXT ASSIGNMENT:

1. Read all 10 chapters of Esther.
2. The next study will be on "Esther, For Such A Time As This."
3. Review your study of Ezra and Nehemiah.
4. Mark your Bible where new truths are learned.

Lesson 26
"Esther, For Such A Time As This"

NOTES

(Where lines are provided, look up the Scripture and write it or its meaning in the space provided.)

1. **THE MEANING OF THE NAME:**
   Esther means "star."

2. **BASIC SCRIPTURES:**
   Esther 1 through 10.

3. **FAMILY BACKGROUND:**
   Esther was born the daughter of Abihail, a Benjamite. Her Hebrew name was *Hadasseh*, meaning "myrtle." Esther was left an orphan and was adopted by Mordecai, a Benjamite. See Esther 2:5-7. Mordecai was a palace official at Shushan, the Persian royal city. Abihail was the uncle of Mordecai, making Esther his cousin. This was one of the warmest relationships in Scripture. The love of Mordecai for Esther was as the love of a father for a daughter.

   Remember, this took place back in the land of captivity. The Persians were in control with Ahasuerus as king. He is Xerxes of secular history. The book of Esther deals with those who remained in Babylon. The Books of Ezra and Nehemiah deal with the remnant who returned to Jerusalem. Between Ezra chapters 6 and 7 the events of the Book of Esther took place.

4. **WHAT THE OLD TESTAMENT SAYS ABOUT ESTHER:**
   (1) The providence of God can be seen in the Book of Esther.

   Queen Vashti was ordered by her husband, Ahasuerus, to show her beauty to a host of drunk men at a feast. Vashti refused (Esther 1:12) and the king and his cohorts wrote a decree concerning wives honoring their husbands (Esther 1:15-18). Queen Vashti was set aside because she refused to expose herself to the king's company. This was an act of courage, but she did it and lost her position (Esther 1:19). This action left the position open and a decree was sent out to find young women, for the king to select the next queen.

   (2) Mordecai, the Jew, took Esther to the king's house to be among the young women, of which one was to be selected as queen.

   Esther did not reveal that she was a Jew. Mordecai told her not to reveal her background. Write in Esther 2:10 _____

   _____

   After awaiting a period of one year, Esther was taken before the king (Esther 2:16).

   (3) Esther became the queen (Esther 2:17).

   Write in Esther 2:17 _____

   _____

   She did not reveal, even then, that she was a Jewess (Esther 2:20). She came to the throne at a critical time.

(4) Haman, the Jew hater (Esther 3:10; 8:1, 9:10; 9:24).

Haman was promoted to be above all the servants of the king. By a decree from the king, all the servants were to bow down and revere Haman (Esther 3:1-2). Haman was an Agagite from Amalek. Naturally, he would hate the Jews, as did all Amalekites. Amalek was Esau's grandson.

Mordecai refused to bow down to Haman because he knew the law of God and obeyed that law. Look up Deuteronomy 5:7-10. Write in verse 9 of that passage _____

_____

Haman was mad because Mordecai would not revere him. Haman decided to kill all the Jews scattered throughout the empire (Esther 3:6); "Haman sought to destroy all the Jews that were throughout the whole kingdom."

Haman went to the king and secured his consent in writing, by the offer of a bribe. Underline Esther 3:8-9. The letter was sent to all 127 provinces, giving orders to kill all Jews. Underline Esther 3:13.

(5) Mordecai heard of the decree of the king concerning the Jews.

He sent a copy of the decree to Esther by one of her servants. Mordecai sent word to Esther to go to the king and make a request on behalf of her people (Esther 4:5-8). Esther sent word to Mordecai that she had to obey the rules of the king's court. She could not enter the king's quarters unless he called for her, or if the king held out his gold sceptre to one that stood in the inner court. She had not been called to the king's quarters for thirty days. Underline Esther 4:11. The message was given to Mordecai.

(6) Esther received the second message from Mordecai.

The message is the challenge of this Book. Notice Mordecai 4:14. Mordecai said, *"who knoweth whether thou art come to the kingdom for such a time as this?"*

Esther acted quickly. She sent word to Mordecai to gather all the Jews that were in Shushan and to fast and pray for her for three days and nights. She promised to do the same (Esther 4:16). Esther promised to go against the law of the king by entering into his presence. Notice her statement at the end of Esther 4:16, "If I perish, I perish."

(7) The courage of Esther was great.

She dressed in her royal apparel and stood in the inner court. Only the sceptre of the king could save her (Esther 5:1).

The king, on his throne, saw Esther and held out the golden sceptre. Esther touched it and went to the king (Esther 5:2). The Lord God of Israel was at work.

Note the first thing the king said to Esther (Esther 5:3) _____

_____

Esther made her request that the king and Haman attend her banquet that day and return for a second banquet on the next day. At that time she would tell the king her desires (Esther 5:4-8).

(8) Haman left the banquet feeling like a "big shot."

He had been the only guest of the king and queen. He and his wife prepared a gallows, 75 feet high, to hang Mordecai the next day (Esther 5:9-14).

But something happened that night. The king could not sleep. He had the servants read to him the record of events. In the reading, he learned of Mordecai saving his life (Esther 2:21-23). The king asked, "What honor hath been done unto Mordecai for this?" The answer was "nothing" (Esther 6:1-3).

Haman went back the next day and the king asked him the same question. Write in Esther 6:6 _____

Notice the pride of Haman. He just knew the king was referring to him.

Haman told the king what should be done (Esther 6:7-9). Then the shock came to Haman. Write in Esther 6:10 _____

_____

Haman went home and had to be taken by the king's servants to attend the second banquet of Esther.

(9) Esther was bold.

The future of the Jewish people depended on her. She made her request to the king to save her people (Esther 7:3-4). In response, the king wanted to know who would want to destroy her people.

The moment of truth had arrived. Esther had the opportunity and she said; (Esther 7:6) _____

_____

Haman was sentenced to die on the very gallows he had made for the Jew, Mordecai. Write in Esther 7:10 _____

_____

(10) Mordecai was brought to the king and honored, even though the king knew that he and Esther were Jews.

The king reversed the orders he had given through Haman. Mordecai was elevated to premier over the 127 provinces. Read Esther 8:1-16. Underline verses 15 and 16. Look at Esther 9:4 _____

_____

_____

Also Esther 10:3 _____

_____

(11) The Feast of Purim was instituted.

The Jews, then in Persia, celebrated their deliverance from the massacre planned by Haman. They called the celebration the "Feast of Purim." The word "purim" comes from "pur," meaning "lot." Haman had cast "pur" (lots), to ascertain a day for destroying the Jews. Underline Esther 9:21 and 24.

To this day, the Jews read the Book of Esther every year at the Feast of Purim. Look at Esther 9:32.

(12) Was God in all of this?

Yes, He was. Look up Proverbs 21:1 _____

_____

Also Isaiah 54:7 _____

_____

Now Proverbs 16:33 _____

_____

5. WHAT THE NEW TESTAMENT SAYS ABOUT ESTHER:

(1) Esther is not mentioned in the New Testament; however, she was used of God to save the people of Israel so that the Deliverer, Christ, might come as promised.

The providential care of God for His people is so evident throughout the Book of Esther.

The Jews in Persia were there by choice. After the Jewish remnant had gone back to Jerusalem, by proclamation of Cyrus (Ezra 1:2-4), the majority remained in Persia. They were God's people and

113

they believed in Jehovah, but their hearts were set on things of this world. God watched over them.

We have people like that in our churches. We have people like that in our nation.

6. **THE LESSONS YOU SHOULD LEARN FROM THIS STUDY:**

1. Esther obeyed Mordecai, her foster father. A lesson America and the world needs.

2. She was not ashamed to be a Jew. Are we ashamed of being Christians?

3. Esther had courage, even though she could have perished. We need that kind of courage.

4. Elevated to the high honor of being queen had no affect on Esther's love and loyalty for her people, the average Jew. We often forget our origin and our inheritance.

5. God used Esther as an instrument, within His own providence, for the working out of His purpose for His people. Are we available to God?

6. She was a national figure, declaring her case for her own people. We Christians should exert our Christian influence for the Lord and His church.

CAN YOU REMEMBER?

1. Name at least four characters in the Book of Esther.
2. Who was Esther?
3. What was Haman's other "name" or title?
4. How did God use Esther?
5. What happened to Mordecai?

(**A reminder:** The Old Testament *history* closes after the account of Ezra and Nehemiah and Esther. Ezra and Nehemiah deal with the small remnant who returned to Jerusalem and Judah. The Book of Esther deals with the Jews who remained in the land of captivity.

All of the prophets wrote in the main *prophecy* concerning Israel before, during, and after the captivity.

Another clarification might help in understanding God's Word. Israel, the Northern Kingdom, had been taken into captivity by Assyria about 745 B.C. The Babylonians took Jerusalem and Judah in about 606 B.C. The Babylonian Empire took the lead in the destruction of Ninevah, and absorbed the Assyrians. The Babylonians were then taken over by the Medo-Persian Empire.

So in the Books of Ezra, Nehemiah and Esther, we find that "all tribes" are mentioned over and over again. In Esther alone, the 127 provinces included the Jews from India to Ethiopia. The name Jew and Israelite became synonomous during the captivity period.)

YOUR NEXT ASSIGMENT:

1. Read Isaiah 1 through 12; 40 through 66 (only about 34 pages in your Bible); Matthew 8:17; 12:17; Romans 9:27; 10:16; 15:12.

2. The next study will be on "Isaiah, The Prince of Prophets."

3. Review your study of Esther.

4. Mark your Bible where new truths are learned.

Lesson 27
"Isaiah, The Prince of Prophets"

(Where lines are provided, look up the Scripture and write it or its meaning in the space provided.)

1. **THE MEANING OF THE NAME:**
   Isaiah means "salvation of Jehovah."

2. **BASIC SCRIPTURES:**
   Isaiah 1-12; 40-66; Matthew 12:17; Luke 24:44; Romans 9:27; 10:16; 15:12; I Peter 1:10-11.

3. **FAMILY BACKGROUND:**
   Little is known of Isaiah's background. We are told in Isaiah 1:1 that he was the son of Amoz. Tradition tells us that Amoz was a brother to King Amaziah, who was a brother to Uzziah, the king. In that event Isaiah was first cousin of King Uzziah. Perhaps this could shed light on the first part of chapter 6, later in our study.

   Isaiah was a man of the city. He lived all his life in the city. His ministry and labor were in the city. His ministry of over 50 years, from 750 B.C. to about 700 B.C., was in the city. His city was Jerusalem.

   Isaiah was an aristocrat. He was a man of culture and always seemed at home in the king's court. He grew up in a day of influence and prosperity. King Uzziah of Judah and Jereboam II of Israel (Northern Kingdom), brought the people to the highest heights of prosperity. With prosperity came vice. The history and the Book of Isaiah read like the lives of some Americans who have grown up knowing nothing but wealth and plenty. Isaiah lived in that atmosphere and saw his people plunge into sin. Isaiah did not dress as an aristocrat; he walked around in a garment of hair cloth like Elijah, calling people to repentance.

   Isaiah was a poetic genius as he declared the message of the Lord God. He was a great speaker and a perfectionist with words. *His figures of speech are from the Lord.* What a preacher!

   Isaiah had a wife (Isaiah 8:3), and was the father of two sons. His first son was named Shear-jashub (Isaiah 7:3), which means "a remnant shall return." His second son has the longest name in the Bible, Maher-shalal-hash-baz, which means "speed the spoil," meaning a "speedy doom for Judah's enemies."

   Isaiah was a man of boldness and integrity. He spoke with boldness, as need might have been, but with love and tenderness. He was a man who listened to the Lord.

   Isaiah preached to the background found in II Kings 15-20 and II Chronicles 26-33. He was a prophet of Judah but he also spoke concerning Israel as well as to the Gentile nations.

4. **WHAT THE OLD TESTAMENT SAYS ABOUT ISAIAH:**
   (1) Isaiah Was a Prophet of God (Isaiah 1:1; 2:1; 6:1).

   Isaiah says in Isaiah 1:1, what he *saw* in a *vision*. Write in verse 1:

   _____

   _____

   This verse is important because it presents what the Lord revealed

115

to Isaiah and the time frame in which Isaiah lived and preached. He saw a vision about Judah and Jerusalem during the days of the four kings. This was the first vision of the Lord to Isaiah. Notice the message begins with, "Hear, or listen, for the Lord has spoken." The message is to Judah and Jerusalem.

Notice that God always leaves a remnant in Isaiah 1:9. Underline the verse. The doctrine of the "remnant" is throughout Isaiah and the Bible. Look up: Isaiah 10:20-22, Isaiah 11:11-16, Isaiah 37:1-4, Isaiah 37:31-32, Isaiah 46:3.

Isaiah spoke God's great invitation, a word of grace, in Isaiah 1:18

_____

_____

_____

God spoke through Isaiah, the prophet, about the **near** and **distant** future of His people. He spoke of judgment in the first part of this first vision. Then the word of love in verses 18 and 19. Finally in verse 20, a *severe warning,* "for the mouth of the Lord has spoken it."

In Isaiah 2:1, again Isaiah "**saw** the **word** concerning Judah and Jerusalem." From this verse to the end of Isaiah 5 is the **second vision** given to Isaiah. (It is so difficult not to teach and write about each verse, but our subject is the man, Isaiah). Isaiah spoke what he saw. He was a prophet.

(2) The Confirmation and Commission of the Prophet, Isaiah. (Isaiah 6)

In the experiences of Isaiah 6, Isaiah gives us the vision and his account of the confirmation of his call as a prophet (one who speaks for God). Isaiah's call was from an unchanging God, who still calls and confirms the same today.

Look at Isaiah 6:1: "I saw also the Lord sitting upon a throne." Isaiah discovered that over and above the dead king, Uzziah, there was one true King of the nation Israel. Isaiah *saw* the temple filled with the "glory of God." "His train filled the temple," the Shekinah Glory of God.

Around the throne were the seraphim (celestial-angels of the Lord), crying, "Holy, holy, holy," always referring to the three of the Godhead; God the Father, God the Son, God the Holy Spirit. (Look up Colossians 2:9.)

First, the vision of the King. Then the detailed call of the man, Isaiah. Note the first words of the call in Isaiah 6:5 _____

_____

He saw himself first as a sinful being of unclean lips. **When we see Jesus, as Isaiah saw Him, we then know we are unclean.**

In verses 6 and 7, one of the seraphim took a coal of fire and touched his lips and said, "Lo, this has touched thy lips and your iniquity is taken away and your sin purged." Isaiah was being prepared for the great work of God. There is a cleansing accomplished at once by divine grace in our lives. *Then there is the progressive, daily cleansing by the glowing coal of Jesus Christ touching us in prayer, Bible study, worship.*

In verse 8 Isaiah heard the voice of the Lord saying, "_____

_____."

Note Isaiah volunteered, "Here am I, send me."

In the commission, verses 9 through 13, the Lord said to Isaiah, "Go, tell, until." Isaiah was sent to people who would not listen, but the Lord warned them through Isaiah. Not all was in vain because out of his preaching a "tenth" (verse 13), also referred to as "holy seed" in verse 13, a remnant would respond. Why would

Isaiah be sent to such people? Turn to John 12:36-41. John 12:40 is identical to Isaiah 6:10. Underline John 12:41.

Just as an oak tree or turpentine tree cut down still has life in its roots, so Israel will have life in "the tenth," the remnant.

So, the man Isaiah—called, confirmed, commissioned—became the "prince of prophets."

(3) As a Prophet, Isaiah Prophesied of Things to Come to Pass in His Own Time (Isaiah 7:1-12 is one example.)

In this passage King Pekah of Israel (Northern Kingdom) and King Rezin of Syria formed a consipiracy to dethrone Ahaz and overrun his kingdom in the South, Judah. This confrontation is recorded in II Chronicles 28. Ahaz, instead of turning to God, sought help from Tiglath-Pileser, king of Assyria. God sent Isaiah to prophecy what was about to take place. Notice Isaiah 7:3-4 and underline. In essence, Isaiah said to Ahaz, "Do not be afraid of Pekah, of Israel (Ephraim), or Rezin, of Syria; they are but smoking firebrands, or the ends of burned out logs." Ahaz had already purposed in his heart to obtain help from his own desire.

The Lord spoke again through Isaiah to Ahaz and said in Isaiah 7:11 _____

_____

.

Ahaz responded by saying that he would not test the Lord. It was then that Isaiah looked beyond King Ahaz and delivered the Messianic prophecy of Isaiah 7:14. " _____

_____

_____ ."

Here Isaiah predicted the immediate future of Judah and the distant future of a coming Messiah. Notice Isaiah 7:13. The message is to the "house of David." Tiglath-Pileser came and took the Northern Kingdom and Syria and the cities of Judah. Had it not been for the intervention of God, he would have taken Jerusalem. Ahaz did not listen to the prophet, Isaiah.

Again in Isaiah 36 and 37, Isaiah told Hezekiah not to be afraid of Assyria. In Isaiah 37:21-38, what Isaiah said came to pass with 185,000 Assyrians killed by one angel of the Lord God. The Lord, through Isaiah, said so, and it came to pass.

(4) He Saw and Predicted the Distant Future.

Isaiah saw the first coming of Christ in Isaiah 7:14, 9:6-7 and 61:1. Isaiah saw the second coming of Christ in Isaiah 11:1 and 61:2b. Isaiah saw the death of Christ on the cross in chapter 53. Underline Isaiah 53:2-5 Write in verse 6: _____

_____

Underline Isaiah 53:7-9. *Also read of the crucifixion of Jesus in Isaiah 50:6-9 and Isaiah 52:13-15.*

Isaiah saw the glorious Kingdom of Christ (Isaiah 59:20-21 and Isaiah 65:17-25). He saw and proclaimed not only the Kingdom of Christ, but also a new heaven and a new earth in Isaiah 66:22.

5. **WHAT THE NEW TESTAMENT SAYS ABOUT ISAIAH:**

(1) Jesus authenticated the writings of the prophets.

Write in Luke 24:44 _____

_____

(2) Paul quotes Isaiah concerning Israel.

Write in Romans 9:27 _____

Underline Romans 10:16. Write in Romans 15:12.

_____

_____

- (3) **Peter said the prophets prophesied of the grace to come.**

  Underline Peter 1:10-11.

- (4) **Matthew wrote of the fullfillment of Isaiah's prophesy in Matthew 12:17-21, a direct quote from Isaiah 42:1-4.**

  It came to pass word for word.

- (5) **There are 21 references to Esaias, the Greek for Isaiah, in the New Testament.**

  Look up as many as you can find.

  Scores of references are made about "the Prophets" in the New Testament. Isaiah was one of them.

NOTE: _There is so much about this great man, Isaiah. I encourage you to read the Book of Isaiah with Jesus in your mind as you read. You will find that Isaiah wrote so much about Him, and what is yet to come to pass in the future._

6. **THE LESSONS YOU SHOULD LEARN FROM THIS STUDY:**

   - (1) God can use an instrument yielded to Him.
   - (2) Our station, our position in life, makes no difference. God can use us.
   - (3) What the Lord says, through His prophets, is a fact; we are to believe Him.
   - (4) The fact that Isaiah's prophecies came to pass in reference to Judah, Israel and the Gentile nations, **means that all of the prophetic statements about the second coming of Christ and His Kingdom shall also come to pass.**

     Isaiah answered God's call and was commissioned to do a job for the Lord. We should learn to "Go, tell, until."

DO YOU REMEMBER?

1. What does Isaiah mean?
2. Name his two sons.
3. Who was Isaiah?
4. What is your impression of this prophet?
5. What kings did he serve under? There were four.

YOUR NEXT ASSIGNMENT:

1. Read Jeremiah 1; 14-20; 26-45; Matthew 16:13-16; Matthew 2:17; 27:9; Hebrews 8:8-12.
2. Read all you can on Jeremiah, our next study.
3. Review your study of Isaiah.
4. Mark your Bible where new truths are learned.

Lesson 28 "Jeremiah, the Prophet"

(Where lines are provided, look up the Scripture and write it or its meaning in the space provided.)

1. **THE MEANING OF THE NAME:**

   Jeremiah means "whom Jehovah has appointed."

2. **BASIC SCRIPTURES:**

   Jeremiah 1; 14-20; 26-45; Matthew 16:13-16; Matthew 2:17; 27:9; Hebrews 8:8-12.

3. **FAMILY BACKGROUND:**

   Jeremiah was born to Hilkiah, who was the son of Ithamar of Anathoth. (Do not confuse this Hilkiah with the son of Shallum in I Chronicles 6:4 and verses 13-15.) Anathoth was a tiny village about three miles north of Jerusalem.

   He was born a priest (Jeremiah 1:1) _____

   _____

   He grew up in the midst of the priestly office. He was living during the days of the prophets Nahum and Zephaniah. His background, temperament and ability qualified him in a unique way for the work God had for him.

   His ministry began in the 13th year of the reign of Josiah, about 60 years after the death of Isaiah. After the death of Josiah, the kingdom of Judah was headed for the Babylonian captivity. Jeremiah remained in the land of Judah ministering to the poor remnant until they went into Egypt. Jeremiah went with them to Egypt because he was compelled to go (Jeremiah 43:5-7). His love for his nation, its struggles, its downfall, gives us something of the times in which Jeremiah lived and spoke the Word of the Lord.(Historical background is in II Kings 22-25).

4. **WHAT THE OLD TESTAMENT SAYS ABOUT JEREMIAH:**

   (1) His Call to be a Prophet.

   The Word of the Lord spoke loud in the ears of Jeremiah. Underline Jeremiah 1:4.

   He was chosen by the Lord before he was born to be a prophet to the nations. Write in Jeremiah 1:5 _____

   _____

   Notice the striking words of the call: "I formed thee, I knew thee, sanctified thee, ordained thee."

   (2) Jeremiah's Response to God's Call.

   Jeremiah responded like most of us would respond. Notice Jeremiah 1:6, "Ah, Lord God, I cannot speak: for I am a child." Jeremiah felt his inexperience and his weakness as a young man.

   But the Lord had called and He said to Jeremiah (Jeremiah 1:7) _

   _____

   Moses said the same thing in his call, and God's attitude was one

119

of anger. In the case of Jeremiah, He was tender, "Say not, I am a child."

Then the Lord gave Jeremiah encouragement and strength in Jeremiah 1:8. Underline the verse.

(3) His Commission from the Lord.

The Lord gave Jeremiah a job to do and He commissioned him to a difficult task. ·

First, He touched Jeremiah's mouth with His hand and said, "Behold, I have put my words in thy mouth" (Jeremiah 1:9).

Then the hard task is given in Jeremiah 1:10 _____

_____

Underline Jeremiah 1:17 and 19. God gave assurance in face of opposition.

(4) Jeremiah's Preaching Opposed.

Jeremiah was given the task of being an "overseer of nations and kingdoms, to root up, to break down, to destroy, to rebuild and to establish" (Jeremiah 1:10). Jeremiah had a heart of sympathy for his nation like no other spokesman for God. Yet, he knew he had to deliver the message of the Lord and, as usual, most people did not want to hear that message.

The men of his home village of Anathoth were among the first to oppose him and threatened to kill him if he did not quit prophesying. Look at Jeremiah 11:18-23 and underline verse 20, which are the words of Jeremiah. The Lord's answer and judgment are in verse 22 _____

_____

The opposition to his preaching in Judah, telling them they were out of the will of God, caused more hostility throughout the land toward the prophet. Again he cried for judgment in Jeremiah 18:18-23. Underline verse 20.

Again, and again, Jeremiah preached the judgment of God upon Judah, the leaders, and religious leaders. For this, he had the courage of the Lord. Look at chapter 20:1-6. He was placed in stocks by the son of the priest and governor in the house of the Lord. Notice his boldness in Jeremiah 20:4 and 6. We could go on with illustrations of his boldness in preaching, but there is much we must learn from Jeremiah.

(5) Jeremiah's Grief and Lamentation.

Jeremiah was more introspective than the other prophets, always looking within himself. He loved his nation, his people; yet God told him what to do, and at times his declaration hurt him as much, if not more, than the people. All of us who preach and teach can understand his feelings. When he preached the judgment, his heart often would break. Look at Jeremiah 9:1 _____

_____

In Jeremiah 20:7-8 Jeremiah cried, even wanted to quit. Underline verse 7-8. But he could not. The Word of God was in him. Write in Jeremiah 20:9 _____

_____

His nature was tender. His distress and sorrow for Judah were felt deeply and he lamented (cried) over what he had to see and do. He wondered why he had been born. Look at Jeremiah 20:14-18. Also Jeremiah 15:10 _____

_____

Jeremiah was forbidden to marry because of the terrible times and judgments of God. Look up Jeremiah 16:1-4 and write in verse 2

He lived a lonely life with no love, comfort or encouragement of a wife and family. He gave up his friends in that tiny community of Anathoth. He gave up his own personal liberty. He was a man of sorrow and is known as "The Weeping Prophet" more than any other title. We should think of him as "God's Bold Giant With a Heart of Love."

Yes, Jeremiah suffered for being a prophet of God. He had to keep on preaching in face of trial because the "Word of the Lord was in him." Look up Jeremiah 15:15-16. Underline verse 15 and write in verse 16 _____

_____

Notice "the word was unto me the joy and rejoicing of my heart." Digest that verse!

The "Book of Lamentations" expands on Jeremiah's grief and heartbreak as well as his hope. Read Lamentations 3.

(6)   Jeremiah's Messages of Hope.

Remember Jeremiah was "to root up, to break down, to destroy, to rebuild, and establish" (Jeremiah 1:10). In his preaching of the judgment of God upon Israel, Judah, and the Gentile nations (which comprises most of his book), there had to be a message of "rebuilding and establishing" faith.

One of his messages of hope is found in Jeremiah 18:1-10, which is entitled "The Potter and the Vessel." This was a message to all Israel. Read Jeremiah 18:1-5, and write in verse 6 _____

_____

"He is the Potter, I am the clay. Mold me and make me after Thy will." Does the song sound familiar?

The message of hope is that Israel was chosen as an honorable vessel by the Lord God, but she constantly went against God and His Word. As a result, she was divided, scattered and headed for captivity. The Lord sent a message by Jeremiah to Israel, a message of hope. That message is in verses 6 and 8.

Another message of hope is in Jeremiah 31:31-34. This is the message of the "New Covenant." Jeremiah became a prophet of hope. The Lord told him to announce a "New Covenant" to the whole house of Israel. The "New Covenant" would supersede the law of Moses. The "New Covenant" provided exactly what the Old Covenant of law demanded. Jeremiah 31:33-34 provides:

- **knowledge** — "I will put my law in their mind"
- **obedience** — "and write it in their hearts"
- **consecration** — "I will be to them a God and they shall be my people"
- **fellowship** — "All shall know me"
- **cleansing** — "For I will remember their sins no more"

Finally, another message of hope is in Jeremiah 32:6-15. Here the message of hope is delivered by action on Jeremiah's part. He bought a plot of ground in his home community, a sign of faith in his own prediction of the restoration of Judah (verse 15), and a sure sign to Judah of that coming restoration. The plot was to be in the hands of Babylon, yet he bought it. Look at Jeremiah 32:17: "there is nothing too hard for thee." (For Jeremiah's Messianic Prophecies, see "Through The Bible In One Year," Basic Study, Lesson No. 19.)

5. **WHAT THE NEW TESTAMENT SAYS ABOUT JEREMIAH:**

(1)   Jeremiah must have had a spirit like that of Elijah, John the

Baptist or Jesus.

Read Matthew 16:13-16. Write in verse 14 _____

_____

Then Peter's great confession is in verse 16. Underline.

(2) **In the New Testament, Jeremiah is called Jeremy and Jeremias.**

Notice Matthew 2:17-18 refers to Jeremy, the prophet.

(3) **The New Covenant given to Jeremiah is repeated and explained in Hebrews 8:7-13.**

Write in Hebrews 8:6 _____

_____

The New Covenant was brought about by the redemptive work of Christ. It was a covenant of grace brought about by the Son of David, Jesus. Turn to Jeremiah 33:15-18. Underline verse 15. While you are at Jeremiah 33, underline verse 3.

Read and re-read Jeremiah 31:31-34 and Hebrews 8:7-13. Remember the words "covenant" and "testament" mean the same. Now read Hebrews 9:14-15.

6. **THE LESSONS YOU SHOULD LEARN FROM THIS STUDY:**

(1) Jeremiah teaches us the Divine judgment on nations.

(2) We must learn to be faithful even when we cannot be successful.

(3) We should expect some persecution and criticism from the world. "His grace is sufficient."

(4) God will faithfully keep His promises to Israel and to us.

(5) All of us, great or small, have hours and days of grief, discouragement and tears. God can use us better after we surrender all to Him.

(6) Jeremiah must have had a character and a nature much like our Lord. His compassion, his words of love, heartbreak, judgment and future events make him much like Jesus. "Some say you are Isaiah, Jeremiah, etc.," were the words in Matthew 16:13-16.

DO YOU REMEMBER?

1. Jeremiah was both _____ and _____

2. What was Jeremiah called to do?

3. What response did he get from the people?

4. What type of nature did Jeremiah have as he preached and saw the results?

5. Was all his preaching about messages of doom?

6. What hope did he give to Israel?

YOUR NEXT ASSIGMENT:

1. Read II Kings 24 and 25; Daniel 1-5.

2. The next subject will be Nebuchadnezzar, the king of Babylon.

3. Review your study of Jeremiah.

4. Mark your Bible where new truths are learned.

Lesson 29
"Nebuchadnezzar"

(Where lines are provided, look up the Scripture and write it or its meaning in the space provided.)

1. **THE MEANING OF THE NAME:**
   Nebuchadnezzar means "defend the boundary" or "Nebo, defend the boundary."

2. **BASIC SCRIPTURES:**
   II Kings 24 and 25; Daniel 1 through 5.

3. **FAMILY BACKGROUND:**
   Nebuchadnezzar was the son of Nabopolassar, the king of Babylon. The father had a successful campaign against the Assyrians and founded the Babylonian Empire. Names are sometimes confusing to a student of the Bible. Geography changed so rapidly, as it still does, and the names of places become meaningless. In the case of Babylon (since that is where the captivity took place), we should know about the area where Nebuchadnezzar reigned. Babylonia was a region of western Asia with Babylon as its capital. It is sometimes called Shinar (Genesis 10:10 and 11:2), and sometimes the land of the Chaldeans. Abraham was the Ur of the Chaldees.

   Nebuchadnezzar was by far the most famous of all the kings of the East. His was the first "worldwide empire" the then-known world had ever seen.

   Why would Nebuchadnezzar be in a study such as this? Because he was a character of Scripture. He was a great king in his day. *He is remembered for his bad deeds and nothing else*. The Lord God of Israel had a sovereign plan in the life of Nebuchadnezzar.

   Yet we shall see the *good* as well as the bad about this king.

4. **WHAT THE OLD TESTAMENT SAYS ABOUT NEBUCHADNEZZAR:**

   (1) Nebuchadnezzar Took Judah and Jerusalem Into Captivity for Seventy Years. (II Kings 24:1-2; 10-16; II Kings 25:1-9)
   This was in direct fulfillment of the words of Isaiah, the prophet, in II Kings 20:17-18 and of the prophecy of Jeremiah in Jeremiah 25:9-11. Notice in verse 9, the Lord called Nebuchadnezzar "my servant."

   Write in Jeremiah 25:11 _____

   _____

   Read II Chronicles 36:6, 7, 10, 19-21. Underline these verses.

   Among his captives were Daniel with three others who were eunuchs, all highly learned, and of the royal seed (Daniel 1:1-4).

   (2) The First Test of Nebuchadnezzar With the Servants of God.
   The king commanded the four Hebrews to eat and drink from his table. They refused, knowing that some of the food was forbidden by the law of God. After ten days of only bread (pulse) and water, the four Hebrews looked better and were fatter in flesh than the ones who ate the king's food and drink. Look at Daniel 1:15 and 20. Instead of being mad and consumed with power, Nebuchadnezzar saw in them a unique wisdom because they could understand dreams and visions.

(3) The Dream of Nebuchadnezzar.

The great dream of the king in Daniel 2, was interpreted by Daniel. In the interpretation, Nebuchadnezzar was told of the destruction of his own kingdom.

His reaction is what is important. Notice Daniel 2:46-49. Write in Daniel 2:47 _____

_____

(4) The Image of Gold and the King's Reaction.

The king, Nebuchadnezzar, ruled babylon and built it into a great place. He made an image of gold on the plain of Dura and called for the people to worship the image of himself. This was self deification. The word "worship" is used three times in Daniel 3:5-7.

Three Hebrews, Daniel excluded, refused to bow down and worship the image of Nebuchadnezzar. They were Shadrach, Meshach, and Abed-nego. The king placed them in a furnace seven times hotter than usual.

Again Nebuchadnezzar learned a lesson about the Lord God. Notice his words in Daniel 3:25 _____

_____

Then again in Daniel 3:28 _____

_____

(5) The Testimony of Nebuchadnezzar.

The Testimony of the king in Daniel 4:1-3 belongs chronologically at the conclusion of chapter 4. The entire chapter contains the testimony of a Gentile king relating how he came to the knowledge of the true God, Jehovah.

This chapter was a Babylonian state document. It was a confession of his sin and pride. It was a confession of his faith in Jehovah God.

Notice Daniel 4:2-3 _____

_____

This testimony came from Nebuchadnezzar after he went through the agony described in chapter 4.

(6) The Sovereignty of God.

In Nebuchadnezzar's dream in Daniel 4, Daniel told him the meaning of the dream. He was told of the power of God and that God could rule. Write in Daniel 4:17 _____

_____

That is the sovereignty of God in the lives of men and nations.

Daniel restated that same thing in the interpretation of the dream in Daniel 4:25. Write in the last part of that verse: "till thou know

_____

_____ ."

The vision was fulfilled in Nebuchadnezzar's life. Underline Daniel 4:31.

Write in the last part of verse 32: "until thou shalt know

_____

_____ ."

After he lived as a beast of the field for seven years eating grass, his body wet from dew each night, his hair long like eagle's feathers, his nails like bird's claws, after this we see the true spirit of the man.

124

(7) From Judgment to Mercy.

Nebuchadnezzar was judged by the Lord. He was a very cruel man. We have seen one or two of his actions already.

In Jeremiah 29:22 the prophet names two men, Jews, whom Nebuchadnezzar roasted in the flames.

In II Kings 25:7 he put out Zedekiah's eyes after he slew Zedekiah's sons.

Nebuchadnezzar brought misery to the world. He uprooted people and deported them.

Nebuchadnezzar was a proud and arrogant man. He built the greatest city on the face of the earth.

But judgment was pronounced upon him and God did exactly what He said He would do. The judgment was harsh, but the king learned a tremendous lesson. The Lord chastens those who know Him and acknowledge Him. The Lord always acts in His own timing. In this case, judgment came 12 months after Daniel told Nebuchadnezzar the meaning of the dream. Notice Daniel 4:29 and underline.

With judgment in the past one can see the great mercy of the Lord in Nebuchadnezzar's actions and words.

A king honored and praised God. Write in all of Daniel 4:34

_____

_____

He first looked up. A beast looks down. He looked up and "blessed the most High."

Underline verse 35.

Write in verse 37 _____

_____

5. **WHAT THE NEW TESTAMENT SAYS ABOUT NEBUCHAD-NEZZAR:**

   (1) There is no reference to Nebuchadnezzar by name in the New Testament. But there is much teaching in the life of this famous king that is applicable today. (We shall discuss under #6.)

   (2) There is a great deal of teaching in the form of "examples" or "types" or "pictures" in the study of this king. Some of these examples are easy to identify;

   Babylon - the kingdoms of this world

   Nebuchadnezzar - seven years madness

   Tree - a man (Psalms 1:3); Nation (Matthew 24:32-33)

   Roots - new life

   Seven Years - trial, tribulation

6. **THE LESSONS YOU SHOULD LEAR FROM THIS STUDY:**

   (1) "That the most High rules in the kingdom of men, and giveth it to whom-soever He will, and setteth up over it the basest of men," (Daniel 4:17, 25 and 32)

   (2) Nebuchadnezzar took every lesson from Daniel and God with a deep sense of humility. He was not angry at the Jew, Daniel, for telling him what he should do.

   (3) Most of us, in modern day Christendom have a preconceived notion or we have been taught that Nebuchadnezzar was a very bad man, dead and probably suffering the torment of Hades. Now, that is what most people think. But , what does the Bible say? You have seen in this lesson his sins, his judgment and his confession of the Lord God.

   (4) Daniel had Nebuchadnezzar falling prostrate at his feet. He fell on his face and worshipped Daniel, yet Daniel stayed in his place and did not take advantage of the king. How could Daniel have such

strength? Through prayer, regular prayer, secret prayer.

(5) Our lives, our leaders, our nation, our pastors, our teachers are important to our Lord, and He still directs in the affairs of men, great or small. "He is the same yesterday, today and forever."

(6) After a severe period of trial we should "look up" and praise Him just like Nebuchadnezzar did after seven years.

DO YOU REMEMBER?

1. What is another name for Babylonia?
2. Who prophesied the 70 year captivity?
3. What made Nebuchadnezzar a great king in his day?
4. How did Daniel have control over the king?
5. Has your opinion of Nebuchadnezzar changed at all?
6. What was the most severe judgment Nebuchadnezzar received?

YOUR NEXT ASSIGNMENT:

1. Read the 12 chapters of Daniel; Matthew 24:15; Mark 13:14; Hebrews 11:33-34.
2. Our next study will be Daniel. This lesson we looked at the king of Daniel's day. This lesson and the next go together. Don't miss either one.
3. Review your notes on Nebuchadnezzar.
4. Mark your Bible where new truths are learned.

Lesson 30
"Daniel"

(Where lines are provided, please look up the Scripture and write it or its meaning in the space provided.)

1. **THE MEANING OF THE NAME:**
    Daniel means "God is my judge."

2. **BASIC SCRIPTURES:**
    Daniel 1 through 12; Matthew 24:15; Mark 13:14; Hebrews 11:33-34.

3. **FAMILY BACKGROUND:**
    Daniel was of noble, if not royal, blood (Daniel 1:3). We know nothing of his parents, only that Daniel was of the tribe of Judah.

    At about age 20, Daniel was taken from Jerusalem to Babylon by Nebuchadnezzar, king of Babylon. Daniel was young but had wisdom beyond his years. His aptitude was high in all subjects, especially science.

    Daniel had a spotless character. He was referred to three times as "the greatly beloved one" in Daniel 9:23, 10:11 and 19.

    Daniel was indeed a prophetic statesman of his day. Jeremiah was a contemporary of Daniel in his later ministry. Daniel pondered the words of Jeremiah 25:8-13, concerning the 70 years of captivity. (Notice Daniel 9:2.)

    Daniel, then Ezekiel — both Jews and both prophets — were taken captive to Babylon. They were the prophets of God during their captivity. Even though Daniel was in captivity, there was "a note of birth, and breeding, and aristocracy about his whole character," says Alexander Whyte, the great English preacher.

4. **WHAT THE OLD TESTAMENT SAYS ABOUT DANIEL:**

    (1) Prophecy Fulfilled.
    The prophecy of the 70 years of captivity of Judah was foretold by Jeremiah in Jeremiah 25:8-13. Notice Jeremiah 25:11 _____

    _____

    Now turn to Daniel 9:2 _____

    _____

    Read and underline II Chronicles 36:21.

    Daniel was taken in the first deportation to Babylon in the third year of Jehoiakim, king of Judah (Daniel 1:1). Deportation was completed the fourth year (Jeremiah 25:1).

    (2) Descendants of Hezekiah.
    Isaiah said in Isaiah 39:5-7 that the "sons that shall issue from thee, which thou shalt beget, shall they take away, and they shall be eunuchs in the palace of the king of Babylon." Note also verse 6 of the same passage in Isaiah 39 _____

    _____

    (3) Hebrew Names Changed.
    Four Hebrews, including Daniel, who met the qualifications of Nebuchadnezzar in Daniel 1:3-4, were taken and made eunuchs. They were placed under the prince of eunuchs, who changed their

Hebrew names. The purpose in changing their names to Babylonish names was to wean them away from their land, their faith in the Lord God and to get them to adopt the religion and habits of Babylon.

The names were changed (Daniel 1:7) as follows:

- **Daniel,** meaning "God is my judge" to Belteshazzar, meaning "whom Baal favors"
- **Hananiah,** meaning "beloved of the Lord" to Shadrach, meaning "illumined by the sun god"
- **Mishael,** meaning "who is as God" to Meshach, meaning "who is Ishtar"
- **Azariah,** meaning "the Lord is my help" to Abed-nego, meaning "slave of the god of wisdom"

Now you have Belteshazzar, who was Daniel. (Do not confuse the name with Belshazzar of Daniel 5). You also have the three famous names of Shadrach, Meshach and Abed-nego. Do not forget, these were their Babylonish names.

Changing a man's name does not always change his character. These four Hebrews were deeply rooted in their own faith and they did not change.

(4) God's Representative in Babylon.

It was God's purpose to make the descendants of Abraham, the Hebrew nation, the leading nation of the world. Their disobedience and idolatry prevented that and the earthly reign was transferred from Israel to Babylon.

God raised up Daniel to speak for Him in the courts of Babylon. Daniel spoke a supernatural language and, thereby, impressed not only the Babylonians but also his own people. The only hope for the Hebrews in captivity was this man, Daniel. He spoke in such miraculous fashion, with the power of God, so that even the Jews in captivity realized that the Lord God of Israel was still their God and they were His people.

What Daniel said, by the inspiration of God, was prophecy. Daniel was different. All the other prophets, such as Isaiah and Jeremiah, were to go to the people and proclaim the Word of the Lord. Daniel was to record what was revealed to him through visions. Look up Daniel 12:4 and 9 and underline these scriptures in your Bible.

(5) The Miracles and Prophecies of Daniel.

We are not able to go into a verse by verse study during this lesson. We will only point out some of the miraculous prophecies of Daniel. (For a study of the Book of Daniel, see Through The Bible In One Year, Vol. 1, Basic Study, Lesson 21.)

(a) Daniel and the three Hebrews refused to defile themselves by eating the king's meat and wine. They ate only bread and water and appeard fairer and fatter than the others (Daniel 1:5-16). What was the outcome? Notice Daniel 1:17 _____

_____

Note Daniel 1:20, "In all matters of wisdom and understanding they were ten times better than the astrologers."

This was a miracle of the Lord!

(b) The Meaning of Nebuchadnezzar's Dream (Daniel 2).

The king had a dream which was a summation of the entire course of the "Times of the Gentiles." None of the astrologers and magicians could interpret the dream. They sent for Daniel.

Daniel and his three companions prayed (Daniel 2:17-18).

God answered and revealed the meaning of the dream to Daniel in a night vision. Underline Daniel 2:19-22. Daniel gave a testimony of the power of God to the king (Daniel

2:28). Notice, "what shall be in the latter days," also in verse 29, "what shall come to pass hereafter," said twice.

Then Daniel sets forth the meaning of the dream. He names the world powers from Babylon on to the kingdom of heaven pictured in the dream as the coming of the "Stone cut out without hands," which is Jesus Christ coming in the days of the ten kings (Daniel 2:44-45). **A miracle of God.**

(c) Daniel's Vision (Daniel 7).

We go to Daniel 7 where the Lord reveals to Daniel in a dream-vision, a message concerning the same world powers.

This was God's way of writing prophecy. All these world powers have come and have fallen. The prophecy of the man of sin (Daniel 7:24-25) and the prophecy of the kingdom of our Lord is again emphasized (Daniel 7:27). (It would take 200 typewritten pages to detail these prophecies. Our study is Daniel and how God used him.)

Another miracle of God!

(d) Daniel Interprets the Tree Vision of the King (Daniel 4).

The dream of the king was one to be interpreted by Daniel. It could have spelled doom for Daniel, but he was faithful to the Lord. He had to tell Nebuchadnezzar that God still ruled over men and nations. Underline the king's description in Daniel 4:17. Now underline Daniel's interpretation of the same words at the close of verse 25, and also verse 32. **Another miracle of God!**

(e) Belshazzar and the Handwriting on the Wall (Daniel 5).

The grandson of Nebuchadnezzar, named Belshazzar, witnessed God's handwriting on the wall. Again Daniel witnessed to the power of God and told what the writing meant. The meaning is in verses 25-28. That night Belshazzar was killed and Darius took the kingdom (verses 30-31).

Another miracle of God!

(f) Daniel In the Lions' Den (Daniel 6).

The story is popular but the real test in the Scripture is the faith of Daniel.

Daniel refused to bow down to a decree from man. Note Daniel 6:7. Because he refused, he was placed in a den of lions, but not harmed. Darius acknowledged God (verse 26).

Another miracle of God!

(g) The 70 Weeks of Daniel (Daniel 9).

This is detailed in "Through The Bible In One Year," Vol 1, Basic Study.

What was predicted and what has come to pass in reference to chapter 9 is **another miracle of God!**

(h) Israel in the Latter Days (Daniel 10-12).

The three chapters go together. They speak of the vision of the glory of God and what God said to Daniel in Daniel 10:14

_____

These chapters were a vision and a prophecy. Daniel was able to declare the Word of the Lord and interpret the future from Darius to the man of sin yet to come. Daniel wrote about the endtime, just like John in Revelation.

Another miracle of God!

5. **WHAT THE NEW TESTAMENT SAYS ABOUT DANIEL:**

(1) The Lord Jesus spoke of Daniel in Matthew 24:15 _____

_____

Jesus referred to Daniel 9:27 and 11:31 in that verse.

(2) Paul describes the man of sin in II Thessalonians 2:3 _____

_____

Paul uses the same imagery as Daniel in Daniel 7:8.

(3) In Hebrews 11:33 you find a reference to Daniel. Note verse 33 _

_____

(4) Also in Hebrews 11:34, the first part refers to the three Hebrews in the fire.

6. **THE LESSONS YOU SHOULD LEARN FROM THIS STUDY:**

(1) Daniel was taken to Babylon at about 19 or 20 years of age. He lived there through the third year of Cyrus. He must have lived there no less than 72 years. It could have been longer. All of his life he spoke for God in a land of captivity.

(2) The secret of Daniel's victorious life was prayer.

(3) All that God told Daniel to say came to pass except what is yet to come to pass (the man of sin and the end time). All the prophecies were fulfilled in history. Remember, Daniel nor any other prophet could foresee this age of the church. The seventieth week of Daniel is yet future.

(4) Daniel was a man whom God could use to outline the ages to come. He spoke miraculously for God.

(5) If Jesus authenticated the words of Daniel, we should never doubt his prophecy.

(6) Daniel 4:17, 25, and 32 say, "That the living may know that the most High ruleth in the kingdom of men, and giveth it to whomsoever He will." This declaration of God is still true.

DO YOU REMEMBER?

1. Who went with Daniel into captivity?
2. Why were the Hebrew names changed?
3. In what sense was Daniel different from the other prophets?
4. Name four miracles of God through Daniel.
5. How long was Daniel in Babylon?
6. Do you now see the importance of the last lesson on Nebuchadnezzar?

YOUR NEXT ASSIGNMENT:

1. Read Jonah 1 through 4; II Kings 14:25; Matthew 12:38-41; Luke 11:29-32.
2. Our study next lesson will be Jonah, a character of great controversy.
3. Review your notes on Daniel.
4. Mark you Bible where new truths are learned.

Lesson 31
"Jonah"

NOTES

(Where lines are provided, please look up the Scripture and write it or its meaning in the space provided.)

1. **THE MEANING OF THE NAME:**

   Jonah means "dove."

2. **BASIC SCRIPTURES:**

   Jonah 1 through 4; II Kings 14:25; Matthew 12:38-41; Luke 11:29-32.

3. **FAMILY BACKGROUND:**

   Jonah was the son of Amittai. He came from Gath-hepher, a village in Galilee. The village was about three miles from Nazareth, the hometown of Jesus. Jonah was a real character, a real person. He was a good example of the carnality of man wanting his own way, pouting, disobedient.

4. **WHAT THE OLD TESTAMENT SAYS ABOUT JONAH:**

   (1) Jonah Was a Prophet (II Kings 14:25).

   In this verse the identity of Jonah is confirmed. He is said to be the son of Amittai. He is called a prophet and he came from Gath-hepher. This identifies Jonah as being the same person as is mentioned in Jonah 1:1.

   King Jeroboam II of Israel was the greatest king and reigned the longest time over the northern kingdom. His recaptured territories reached as far as Hamath, about 200 miles north of Samaria, the capital city of the northern kingdom of Israel. His recapturing the territory was a direct fulfillment of a prophecy by "Jonah, the son of Amittai, the prophet which was of Gath-hepher."

   The prophet of II Kings 14:25 is the same person as Jonah, who is mentioned in the book bearing his name. Turn to that little-noticed reference in II Kings 14:25 and underline the last half of the verse.

   This reference in II Kings gives the approximate time of Jonah's ministry. He ministered during a part of the reign of Joash and Jeroboam II, between 800 and 850 B.C.

   With this one verse from II Kings 14 we should recognize that Jeroboam was a real person. Jonah was a real person and a prophet. Gath-hepher was a real place. *Why would anyone question such things as real people and places?*

   Jonah is a book in the Bible, a character in Scripture, interpreted by some as myth, legend, parable, fiction and allegory. There has been much controversy surrounding this little book and Jonah himself.

   We proclaim, based only upon the Word of God, that Jonah was a real person and a real prophet. The narrative of the book is *actual* and *factual*. If it is only fictional, it contains no authentic significance at all. The literal interpretation of the book is imperative because the integrity of the Lord Jesus Christ is at stake.

   (2) The Disobedient Servant (chapter 1).

   Jonah was a servant of God. The Lord gave explicit instructions to the prophet in Jonah 1:2 _____

   _____

   Notice the words *"arise, go."* He was told to go to Nineveh, the

Gentile capital city of Assyria. Jonah was a *Jewish* preacher, commissioned by the Lord to go in person and preach to the Gentiles.

Jonah went the opposite direction to Tarshish. Three times in the first 10 verses we read of Jonah fleeing "from the presence of the Lord" (twice in verse 3 and in verse 10). Jonah was fleeing from his duty as a spokesman for God.

A great storm was sent by the Lord. The sailors were afraid. Jonah went down into the ship and went to sleep. What a lot of "going down" for Jonah.

In Jonah 1:3 - "he went down to Joppa"

        1:3 - "he went down into the ship"

        1:5 - "Jonah was gone down into the sides of the ship"

Jonah knew the reason for the storm and he told the sailors in verses 9 and 10. The sailors tried to reach land but all was in vain. They took Jonah and cast him overboard (verse 15).

Remember, the sailors knew who he was. (Read Jonah 1:9 and 10 again.)

Look at Jonah 1:17 _____

_____

No miracle in Scripture has caused more argument. The natural man will not accept the supernatural until he accepts the Supernatural One, Jesus Christ.

(3) The Praying Servant (chapter 2).

Jonah was swallowed by a great fish, a special fish "the Lord had prepared." Immediately, Jonah began to pray. The entire prayer was one of praise and thanksgiving and total rededication.

Underline Jonah 2:1.

The climax of the prayer is Jonah 2:9 _____

_____

"The Lord spake unto the fish, and it vomited out Jonah upon the dry land" (Jonah 2:10).

(4) The Recommissioned Servant (chapter 3).

The most encouraging words which a person away from God can hear are, "and the word of the Lord came unto Jonah the *second time*."

The Lord re-stated more in detail what Jonah was to do in Jonah 3:2 _____

_____

So again, Jonah was to *"arise, go, preach."*

Three times the Lord spoke about Nineveh as "that great city." It was three days journey walking through it (Jonah 3:3).

When Jonah was in the city one day's journey, he began to preach, "Yet 40 days and Nineveh shall be overthrown." The people believed God. Even the king sent out a proclamation that all his people should pray and turn from their evil way (verse 5-8).

The results are in Jonah 3:10 _____

_____

God gave to His disobedient servant a second chance, and he preached and the great city turned to God.

The question always in the minds of most students is: How did it happen? We turn to the New Testament and quote Jesus, "For as Jonah was a *sign* unto the Ninevites," (Luke 11:30) (we shall cover this verse under the New Testament section), and from this we know Jonah was a *sign*. What kind of a sign?

Recall in chapter 1, during the storm, Jonah told the sailors who he was and that he had "fled from the presence of the Lord." The boat took a beating (Jonah 1:4). They made it back to port and what a story they had to tell all the people. Then, all the people near the seashore and in the shops saw Jonah. The people of the city knew of him and his survival. It reached their ears before Jonah arrived.

Thus, Jonah was a sign to the Ninevites.

(5) The Angry, Perplexed, Learning Servant (chapter 4).

The first three verses express Jonah's feelings (Jonah 4:1) _____

_____

Underline verse 2.

Write in verse 3 _____

_____

Why was Jonah so angry? Why did he want to die? Why did he want Nineveh destroyed?

Because Jonah knew that if Nineveh repented and turned to God, then Israel would be in danger. Jonah did not want God to spare Nineveh. Assyria was the rising world power destined to destroy Israel. Isaiah foretold the Assyrian invasion 20 to 30 years before (Isaiah 7:17). If Nineveh (the Assyrian capital) were destroyed, Israel would be saved.

Jonah was so displeased, since Nineveh was to be spared, he prayed for his life to be taken (Jonah 4:3, 8, and 9). The gracious response of God gives the climax of the book (verse 10 and 11). God's *compassion* for a people such as the Gentiles in Nineveh and His *patience* with a stubborn, angry preacher are the real lessons to be learned.

Jonah learned the watchcare of the Lord, the love of the Lord for all people, the grace of God toward him and toward Nineveh.

The servant, Jonah, finally learned the lesson of serving the Lord. A called servant cannot run from the presence of the Lord. A servant of the Lord must pray, arise and go, regardless of personal feelings and desires.

5. **WHAT THE NEW TESTAMENT SAYS ABOUT JONAH:**

(1) Jesus foretold his death and resurrection to the scribes and Pharisees by the *sign* of the prophet Jonah. Turn to Matthew 12:38-41. Write in verse 39 and 40 _____

_____

Notice in verse 41, Jesus spoke of "the preaching of Jonah." Jesus was "the greater than Jonah."

(2) The sign of Jonah (Luke 11:29-32).

Jesus gave us the reason Jonah had such power. Note verse 30 __

_____

The only sign Jesus would give to the people was the sign of Jonah. That sign pointed to Jesus, "So also shall the Son of man be to this generation." In verse 32 Jesus said, "for they repented at the preaching of Jonah; and, behold, a greater than Jonah is here."

6. **THE LESSONS YOU SHOULD LEARN FROM JONAH:**

(1) Learn the truth of Paul's words in Romans 3:29. Look it up.

(2) God's purpose of grace can not be frustrated. If Jonah had not gone to Nineveh, would God have destroyed the city? God would not have been limited by Jonah nor Jonah's refusal. God could have had another man ready, yes, even another fish ready.

(3) God is gracious. The Word of the Lord comes to us the second, third and fourth time, and on and on He deals with us. He does not give up on us (Philippians 1:6).

(4) This is the one book of the Old Testament which gives us a sign, a

133

type, a forecast of the resurrection of Jesus Christ. Paul said, "The Jews require a sign, and the Greeks seek after wisdom; but we preach Christ" (I Corinthians 1:22-23).

(5) Jonah came out of the fish after three days and three nights, just as Jesus came out of the tomb. Just as Jonah was a sign to Gentile Nineveh, so shall the Son of Man be. After the resurrection, the Gospel was then taken to the Gentiles.

(6) Jesus authenticated Jonah, the man, and Jonah, the book.

DO YOU REMEMBER?

1. What identifying remarks do you recall about Jonah?
2. Why was Jonah really afraid?
3. Nineveh was the capital of _____ .
4. How was Jonah a sign to Nineveh?
5. Can you identify with Jonah? (Running from the Lord, praying when in trouble, pouting when you do not get your own way.)
6. Why must we accept the facts of Jonah? Do we have Scriptural grounds for accepting the facts of Jonah?

YOUR NEXT ASSIGNMENT:

1. Read Zechariah 1-14; Matthew 24 and 25; Revelation 19:7-21.
2. The next lesson will be on the prophet Zechariah, a man who wrote much about Jesus and the endtime.
3. Review your notes on Jonah.
4. Mark your Bible where new truths have been learned.

Lesson 32 "Zechariah, the Prophet"

GREAT CHARACTERS OF THE BIBLE

(Where lines are provided, please look up the Scripture and write it or its meaning in the space provided).

1. **THE MEANING OF THE NAME:**

   Zechariah means "whom Jehovah remembers."

2. **BASIC SCRIPTURES:**

   Zechariah 1-14; Matthew 24 and 25; Revelation 19:7-21.

3. **FAMILY BACKGROUND:**

   Zechariah was both a prophet and a priest. His is one of the common names in the Old Testament. We find 27 other people in the Old Testament bearing the same name. This Zechariah was the writing prophet who wrote the book bearing his name, which is next to the last book of the Old Testament.

   Zechariah was the son of Berechiah, the son of Iddo, a prophet and a priest (Nehemiah 12:4). This means that Zechariah was of the family of Aaron, the high priest.

   Zechariah was contemporary with Haggai. When the Bible is opened to this prophecy, one finds the people of Israel at a most critical period of their history. After 70 years of captivity in Babylon, they were granted permission to return to their own land and rebuild their beloved city of Jerusalem. Only a minority, a remnant of about 50,000 people, returned under Zerubbabel, the governor, and Joshua, the high priest. This remnant was filled with enthusiasm. Within seven months they built the altar of burnt offerings and were offering sacrifices to the Lord (Ezra 3:1-6).

   In the second year of their return to Jerusalem they started to rebuild the temple. At that time the foundations were laid (Ezra 3:8-13). Then, bitter opposition on the part of the Samaritans developed and disrupted the work (Ezra 4:1-23). The building of the temple stopped and the people became complacent. They did not care.

   God raised up a prophet named Haggai with the message needed at that time. His message was to exhort the people to rebuild the temple (Haggai 1:2-4, 8 and 2:3-4). His preaching brought about a revival. In the midst of that revival, God raised up *another* prophet to give *further* messages to the people in Jerusalem. The name of that prophet was *Zechariah*.

   The book of Zechariah was one of the three prophetic writings of the Old Testament which was after the captivity. His preaching and prophetic utterances were in the nature of encouragement. Haggai was to arouse the people to the outward task of building the temple. Zechariah sought to lead the people in an inward change. The inward change was necessary to get the people to respond to finishing the temple of the Lord.

   This background is necessary to comprehend the life and preaching of Zechariah.

4. **WHAT THE OLD TESTAMENT SAYS ABOUT ZECHARIAH:**

Copyrighted© unauthorized reproduction prohibited by law.

(1) Zechariah Warned the People (Zechariah 1:1-6).

Zechariah was used of God to warn the people to return to the Lord because His Word is eternal. Write in Zechariah 1:3 _____

_____

(2) Zechariah Received 10 Visions concerning Jerusalem (Zechariah 1:7 and 6:15).

The meaning of all 10 of the night visions can be summarized in the statement of the Lord in Zechariah 1:14 _____

_____

The summary continues in Zechariah 1:15 _____

_____

The summary of the Lord climaxes in Zechariah 1:16 _____

_____

Thus, we find that in all of the night visions given to Zechariah the Lord had one great unifying thought in all 10 visions. That one great thought is given in three phrases, "I am jealous for Jerusalem with a great jealousy; I am displeased with the nations that are at ease and they helped forward the afflicition (on Israel); I am returned to Jerusalem with mercies: my house shall be built in it, saith the Lord of hosts." (For an account of the 10 visions, see "Through The Bible In One Year," Volume 1, Basic Study, page 107.)

(3) Zechariah's Answer Concerning Rituals (chapters 7 and 8).

In these two chapters there are four messages. The Lord spoke through the prophet Zechariah concerning the "fasts" the people had been observing during the 70 year captivity.

God's answer was direct. Their fast was a religious form; they should have listened to the former prophets. Notice Zechariah 7:5-7 and underline verses 5 and 6.

The people were told of the purpose of God again. Israel was to be blessed (Zechariah 8:1-8).

The people were told by the Lord, through Zechariah, to heed the words of the prophets "in these days" (Zechariah 8:9). The prophets they were to heed were Haggai, Zechariah and Malachi. They would *then* speak and do justly (Zechariah 8:16-17). Then all of their *fasts* would become *feasts* of joy and gladness. Notice Zechariah 8:19 and underline.

(4) Zechariah Foretells the Coming of Jesus Christ (Zechariah 9-14).

(a) The first "burden" is in chapters 9 through 11.

A "burden" in Scripture is a heavy message containing the judgment of God. It is heavy for the prophet to declare. You find that term at the beginning of chapter 9 and chapter 12.

The first "burden," or prophecy, contained judgment upon the cities surrounding Palestine (Zechariah 9:1-8.).

From predictions of judgment, Zechariah turned to the great theme and prediction of a coming King.

In Zechariah 9:9 _____

_____

Notice, *"Thy* King cometh," not *"a* king." He was the Messiah King of Israel. This verse was the triumphal entry into Jerusalem by our Lord. (Compare Zechariah 9:9 with Matthew 21:5.)

This verse 9 is *a prophecy of the first coming of Jesus Christ.*

In this prophecy of Zechariah, as in all Old Testament revelation, there is no clear distinction drawn between the *two comings* of the Messiah. The first and second advents (comings) of Christ are seen in the Old Testament like two great mountain peaks on the horizon. From a distance they seem to almost touch each other. When closer, an extensive valley separates the two mountains. The valley between the two comings of Christ was never revealed to the prophets. In that valley, between the two comings of Christ, is the present church age. *The prophets never saw this period of time.*

So in verse 9, the Messiah came the first time — righteous, possessing salvation as a Savior should, lowly, riding upon an ass.

But in verse 10 is pictured *His second coming* in power and glory. Write in verse 10 _____

_____

Jesus shall speak peace, have dominion to the ends of the earth and He shall establish peace on the earth. There can be no real peace until He comes the second time.

In Zechariah 11:7-14 the Lord Jesus Christ was rejected at His first coming. Zechariah depicted in graphic terms the rejection of Christ.

In Zechariah 11:11 the "poor of the flock" was the "remnant according to the election of grace" (Romans 11:5) — those Jews who believed on Him at His first coming. They had "waited on me and knew it was the Word of the Lord."

Write in verse 12 _____

_____

Underline verse 13 and mark in your Bible margin, "Matthew 27:3-10." The terms *"Beauty and Bands"* mean "grace of the Lord" for Beauty. Bands means "union of Judah and Israel."

(b) The second "burden" is in Zechariah 12-14.

These chapters form one prophecy of the second coming of Christ and the establishment of His kingdom upon the earth.

In Zechariah 12:1-9 the siege of Jerusalem by the nations of the earth is described. This is called the last battle, Armageddon. Underline Zechariah 12:2, 8, and 9.

In verse 10 we see the grace of God and the revelation of Christ to the house of David. Write in verse 10 _____

_____

A summary of the last battle is given in Zechariah 14:1-3. Underline verse 2.

The actual second coming of Christ is in Zechariah 14:4 ____

_____

Underline that verse in your Bible. Notice He will touch down on the Mount of Olives, the same place from which He ascended into glory. He shall reign over the earth (verse 9) _

_____

The remainder of Zechariah 14:16-21 is a description of the kingdom of our Lord.

5. **WHAT THE NEW TESTAMENT SAYS ABOUT ZECHARIAH:**

(1) Zechariah is not named in the New Testament; however, his prophecies are referred to often.

(2) Compare Zechariah 9:9 with Matthew 21:4-5 _____

_____

(3) Compare Zechariah 11:12 with Matthew 26:15 _____

_____

Also underline Matthew 27:9-10 in your Bible.

(4) Matthew 24 and 25 gives the Olivet discourse. Read the two chapters after reading Zechariah 12-14.

(5) Revelation 19 and 20 give an account of the same period which Zechariah predicted almost 500 years before.

Also Revelation 16:14-15 gives an account of the battle of Armageddon.

6. **THE LESSONS YOU SHOULD LEARN FROM ZECHARIAH:**

(1) The night visions of Zechariah set forth one great fact, "I am jealous for Jerusalem," said the Lord.

(2) Since the Lord God had selected a nation, a tribe, a family from whom His Son was to come, He was displeased with the nations that afflicted Israel.

(3) We should never let "rituals" take the place of true worship of the Lord.

(4) Zechariah saw the first and second coming of our Lord with specific detail. He was a foreteller, a seer, a prophet of the Lord.

(5) Since His first coming fulfilled to the letter the prophecies of Zechariah, Isaiah and others, we should know that the details of His second coming shall be fulfilled in like manner.

(6) The prophets saw both the first and second comings of Christ, but they never saw the age in between, the church age in which we live.

DO YOU REMEMBER?

1. Who was Zechariah's contemporary?
2. What was Zechariah's great job in dealing with the remnant in Jerusalem?
3. What did the ten visions of Zechariah mean?
4. Do you remember the meaning of Zechariah 12:10?
5. Where will Jesus actually return to the earth?
6. What impression did Zechariah make on you?

YOUR NEXT ASSIGNMENT:

1. Read Matthew 9 and 10; Mark 2 and 3; Luke 5 and 6; Acts 1.
2. The next study will be on Matthew, one of the 12 Apostles. Read all you can find about him.
3. Review your study of Zechariah.
4. Mark your Bible where new truths are learned.

Lesson 33
"Matthew"

(Where lines are provided, look up the Scripture and write it or its meaning in the space provided.)

NOTE: The teacher and pupil will see a change in the format as we approach the characters of the New Testament. In the Old Testament character study, No. 4 in each outline was, "What the Old Testament Says About the Character." In the New Testament character study, No. 4 will be "What the New Testament says about the Character." No. 5 will be "The Use of the Old Testament By, or in Reference To, the Character."

1. **THE MEANING OF THE NAME:**

Matthew means "gift of Jehovah."

2. **BASIC SCRIPTURES:**

Matthew 9 and 10; Mark 2 and 3; Luke 5 and 6; Acts 1.

3. **FAMILY BACKGROUND:**

Matthew was the son of Alphaeus. Matthew was a "publican," which means, "a Jewish tax collector for the Ancient Romans." Mark and Luke speak of him as Levi as you will see in Mark 2:14 _____

_____

and in Luke 5:27 (underline in your Bible).

A "publican" was a person the Jews hated. The low esteem they had for a person in the position can be found in the phrase, "publicans and sinners" (see Matthew 9:11 and 11:19).

"Levi" indicates that he was from the tribe of Levi, but this man degraded the priestly name. Some believe the Lord changed his name to Matthew, while others believe that Matthew selected the name himself, since the name means "the gift of God." He is called Matthew from the time of his call to follow Christ.

4. **WHAT THE NEW TESTAMENT SAYS ABOUT MATTHEW:**

(1) Matthew's Call to Discipleship.

While sitting at the place where he collected taxes, Matthew saw Jesus pass by and Jesus said *two words* to the publican, "follow me." Look up Matthew 9:9 _____

_____

Also Luke 5:27 _____

_____

Without hesitation, Matthew forsook all and followed Christ.

(2) Matthew Celebrated With a Feast.

To celebrate his new life in Christ, Matthew opened his home to a great feast for publicans and others. Matthew does not tell us it was in his home, but Mark and Luke state the place (Mark 2:15 and Luke 5:29). Underline both verses in your Bible.

Notice that all three writers indicate that Jesus was there eating with the publicans and sinners. This was one way Matthew could tell the world he had accepted the Messiah; a way to introduce Jesus to his old friends known as publicans and sinners.

The everpresent Scribes and Pharisees were there to criticize and condemn the Master and disciples for eating with such a group. The response of Jesus is one of the great statements of the Lord in the first three Gospels (Matthew 9:12, Mark 2:17 and Luke 5:31-32).

(3) Matthew was Appointed An Apostle.

The 12 disciples were instructed by Jesus and "sent forth." The word "apostle" means "one sent forth." The original apostles were ones who had seen Jesus and had witnessed His resurrection. Write in Matthew 10:1-2. _____

_____

A "disciple" means "a learner, a pupil." So, the apostles were disciples. The term is used for all who have accepted Christ and become "learners or pupils" of His teaching.

(4) Matthew Became the Author of the Gospel of Matthew.

Matthew is the "book of the generation of Jesus Christ, the son of David, the son of Abraham" (Matthew 1:10). This connects Jesus with two of the most important of the Old Testament covenants: the Davidic Covenant of Kingship (II Samuel 7:8-16) and the Abrahamic Covenant of promise (Genesis 12:1-9 and 15:1-18).

(5) The Unique Features of the Book of Matthew.

(a) Matthew presents Christ as the Messiah-King. Look at Matthew 2:2 _____

_____

_____

Underline Matthew 21:4-5 and 25:34.

(b) Matthew wrote primarily to the Jews.

From their own Scriptures, the Old Testament, they believed that their Messiah-King would come through the line of Abraham. Matthew, therefore, gave the genealogy from Abraham to Joseph, the husband of Mary. He summarized the genealogy in Matthew 1:17, confirming 42 generations from Abraham to Christ. List the three groups of 14 generations in Matthew 1:17 _____

_____

(c) Matthew presented the "kingdom of heaven."

The term, "kingdom of heaven," can be found 32 times in Matthew. The word "kingdom," used 55 times in Matthew, sets forth the prevailing theme Matthew presented to the Jews.

John the Baptist was the first to use the expression, "the kingdom of heaven is at hand" (Matthew 3:2).

When Jesus began His ministry, He began with the very same announcement. Write His words in Matthew 4:17 _____

_____

Since neither John nor Jesus attempted to explain the meaning of the term, it is reasonable to assume that the hearers knew its meaning. They understood the term to be a summation of all the Old Testament prophecies concerning a king to be over a visible kingdom. The King-Messiah would reign from the throne of David. They understood the meaning in Matthew 1:20-23 and Luke 1:32-33. How could they have understood such statements? They had read Isaiah, Jeremiah, Micah and all the prophets. (We will cover this in the next section of the lesson.)

Matthew wrote of a "King in His kingdom." Jesus came as the King of the Jews. The King was crucified and the kingdom rejected. When He comes again, He will reign from the throne of David and over the house of Jacob.

The Kingdom of Heaven and the church are not the same.

The kingdom of heaven is yet future. When the Lord Jesus comes again, all who are Christians will enter that kingdom, not as subjects, but we shall *reign* with Christ as King in His kingdom.

In Matthew 13, the kingdom of heaven is mentioned 12 times. Find the 12 and underline them in your Bible.

(d) Matthew recorded the instructions to the 12 apostles (Matthew 10).

Only in Matthew will one find our Lord's instructions to the 12. He wrote 42 verses on the subject. Mark gave only seven verses to the subject; Luke, only six verses.

Notice in Matthew 10:1, "He called the twelve disciples."

In verse 2 they are called "apostles." Notice they are named two by two and sent forth. Look at Matthew 10:2-5 and list the six sets of two apostles:

_____   _____

_____   _____

_____   _____

_____   _____

_____   _____

_____   _____

In verse 6, they were to preach to _____

_____

(e) Only Matthew recorded the first mention of the church.

All the Gospel writers penned Peter's confession. Only Matthew recorded Jesus' words to the apostle Peter, in reference to the church. Turn to Matthew 16:17-18 and underline. Mark in your Bible "First mention of the church." Now write in verse 18 _____

_____

Briefly, Jesus did *not* mean that the church was to be built on Simon Peter. The actual translation of verse 18 is "Thou art Petros (a stone) and upon this Petra (a mighty rock, Christ) I will build my church." The Lord founded the church on Himself, the Rock of our salvation.

Peter is careful to tell us the same thing in I Peter 2:3-8. Read that passage and write in verse 6 _____

_____

(f) Matthew was present at the Ascension of the Lord.

In Acts 1 Jesus instructed the disciples about the power of the Holy Spirit when He would come upon them. They witnessed Jesus ascending in the clouds and heard the instruction that Jesus would return in like manner (Acts 1:1-11).

In Acts 1:13 you will find Matthew listed as one being in the upper room, awaiting the day of Pentecost.

Underline Acts 1:8 and 13.

5. **THE USE OF THE OLD TESTAMENT BY MATTHEW:**

(1) Matthew quotes the Old Testament about 100 times in his writing. We shall observe only a few.

(2) Matthew 1:23 is a fulfillment of Isaiah 7:14 _____

141

_____

(3) Matthew 2:5 is a fulfillment of Micah 5:2 _____

_____

(4) Matthew 2:15 is a fulfillment of Hosea 11:1 _____

_____

(5) Matthew 3:3 is a fulfillment of Isaiah 40:3 _____

_____

(6) Matthew 12:18-21 is a fulfillment of Isaiah 42:1-4. Write in Isaiah 42:1. _____

_____

_____

(7) Matthew 13:35 is a fulfillment of Psalms 78:2 _____

_____

(8) Matthew 21:4-5 is a fulfillment of Zechariah 9:9 _____

_____

(9) Matthew 24:21-22 is a fullfillment of Daniel 12:1 _____

_____

(10) Matthew 26:15 is a fulfillment of Zechariah 11:12 _____

_____

(11) Matthew 26 and 27 fulfills Isaiah 53. Compare for yourself.

(12) Matthew was a brilliant Jew who knew how to keep orderly writings. His thorough treatment of the ministry of Jesus is one of the most beautiful works ever recorded.

Matthew is to the New Testament what Genesis is to the Old and New Testaments. Read Matthew often.

6. **THE LESSONS YOU SHOULD LEARN FROM MATTHEW:**
   (1) When the Lord calls, we should respond as Matthew did.
   (2) Even those hated individuals in society are valuable in the hands of the Lord.
   (3) It is good to offer Christian hospitality.
   (4) The meal was used in the days of Jesus to win and witness. Matthew opened his home to publicans and sinners.
   (5) We are all disciples if we are believers. However, we must be in a position to learn and to expose ourselves to learning. Remember, a disciple is a learner.
   (6) Jesus is coming back, and we who know Him shall reign with Him.

DO YOU REMEMBER?

1. Who was Matthew?
2. What was he called, and why?
3. He was a Jew. To whom primarily, did he write his book?
4. What is the major theme through his book?
5. When did Matthew last see the Lord Jesus?
6. Matthew presents Christ as _____

YOUR NEXT ASSIGNMENT:

1. Read Acts 12 and 13; Acts 15:36-41; Colossians 4:10-11; II Timothy 4:9-11, and I Peter 5:13.
2. The next study will be on Mark.
3. Review your notes on Matthew.
4. Mark your Bible where new truths are learned.

Lesson 34
"Mark"

(Where lines are provided, look up the Scripture and write it or its meaning in the space provided.)

1. **THE MEANING OF THE NAME:**

   Mark means "a large hammer."

2. **BASIC SCRIPTURES:**

   Acts 12 and 13; Acts 15:36-41; Colossians 4:10-11; II Timothy 4:9-11; I Peter 5:13.

3. **FAMILY BACKGROUND:**

   Mark, known as John Mark, wrote primarily to the Roman mind, while Matthew, you recall, wrote to the Hebrew mind.

   Mark was his Roman surname, while John was his Hebrew name. He was the son of one of the Mary's in Jerusalem. She must have been a widow of some means. Her brother Barnabas, Mark's uncle, was a wealthy Levite from Cyprus. Barnabas was a great influence in young Mark's life. Peter and Paul also had great influence on him.

   Mark, an associate of the apostles, is mentioned in the writings of Paul and Luke.

4. **WHAT THE NEW TESTAMENT SAYS ABOUT MARK:**

   (1) Mark's Home, A Place of Prayer (Acts 12:12).

   The first mention of Mark by name is in connection with that remarkable prayer meeting in his home. Herod had just beheaded James (Acts 12:2) and had arrested Peter. Members of the faith gathered at the home of Mary, the mother of John Mark, to pray for Peter. The Lord answered their prayer. Look up Acts 12:2 _____

   _____

   (2) Mark Accompanied Barnabas and Paul (Acts 12:25).

   Barnabas and Paul had been in Antioch and had gone to Jerusalem to take a gift for the relief of the brethren in Jerusalem (Acts 11:27-30). When the mission had been completed, they took Mark with them and returned to Antioch. Underline Acts 12:25.

   Barnabas and Paul were separated by the Holy Spirit to go on the first missionary journey. They took John Mark (called only John) with them to help with their preaching and teaching. Write in Acts 13:5 _____

   _____

   The three reached Perga, and *there* Mark turned away from the two leaders and returned to Jerusalem. It is intimated from Paul's reaction that Mark had become afraid of facing the great challenge of reaching the heathen world. Notice Acts 13:13 _____

   _____

   (3) The Division of Paul and Barnabas Over Mark (Acts 15:36-40).

   Whatever the reason for Mark's conduct in going back to Jerusalem, Paul disapproved of it so much that he refused to take Mark with him when a second journey was proposed. Write in Acts

15:37 _____

_____

Also Acts 15:38 _____

_____

This caused such a contention between Paul and Barnabas, that they separated. Barnabas took Mark and they went to Cyprus. Underline Acts 15:39.

Paul selected Silas (Silvanus), to accompany him.

(4) **The Years of Silence and Mark's Restoration (Colossians 4:10).**

Almost 20 years elapse before Mark is mentioned again in Scripture. What happened to Mark during those years? Tradition tells us that Mark had a remarkable ministry in Egypt, founding the first Christian church in Alexandria.

After the period of silence, Mark is next mentioned in Scripture in Colossians 4:10 and Philemon 24. Paul was in prison in Rome, where he penned the two letters. In both, Paul mentions Mark. He was still alive and with Paul. It appears from these Scriptures that what had happened to divide Paul from Barnabas had been forgiven and forgotten. The impact of Paul's statement to Colosse is found in Colossians 4:11: "These only are my fellow workers unto the kingdom of God which have been a comfort unto me." Only three Jewish Christians in Rome remained loyal to Paul. One was Mark, who was restored to a position of full honor.

(5) **Paul's Request for Mark To Be With Him (II Timothy 4:9-11).**

In Paul's last letter, written from prison in Rome, Paul wished for Mark to be sent to him. Look at II Timothy 4:11 _____

_____

Mark befriended Paul before in Rome. Paul needed Mark. Paul was facing martyrdom.

(6) **Peter Referred to Mark as a Son (I Peter 5:13).**

Peter called Mark, "my son," indicating that Mark was one of Peter's converts. Write in I Peter 5:13 _____

_____

Mark had been restored in the eyes of Paul, and had grown more dear to Peter.

(7) **Mark Was the Author of the Book of Mark.**

The book of Mark has long been considered a writing influenced by the apostle Peter.

Dr. J. Vernon McGee says, "The Epistle to the Romans had preceded Mark and it was in circulation in Rome." Mark had access to this Epistle. On the human plane it is well to keep in mind:

- First — that Mark had the *facts* of the Gospel from Peter.
- Second — He had the *explanation* of the Gospel from Paul.

Mark then authored the Gospel of Mark under the inspiration of the Holy Spirit and with the training and help and experience of being with Peter and Paul. Many of the things written in Mark were facts related to him by the apostle Peter.

(8) **Unique Features of the Book of Mark.**

(a) Mark presents Christ as Servant.

The theme of the book is Mark 10:45 _____

_____

From this verse we see that he was God's Servant to give Himself for us.

(b) Mark's Beginning of his Book.

Notice verse 1, "The beginning of the Gospel of Jesus Christ." Mark did not go back to the beginning of Jesus, only "the beginning of the Gospel."

(c) The Omissions in the Gospel of Mark.

Since Mark presents Christ as Servant, we should note the omissions:

- nothing about His virgin birth. No reference to His birth at all, befitting a servant.
- no record of Jesus as the boy in the temple is given.
- no Sermon on the Mount. A servant has no kingdom.
- no divine titles are used for Jesus. Mark calls Him, "Master."
- no long detailed accounts. Mark wrote only facts.
- no statement that His work was finished. A servant could not make such a statement. (As the Son of God He did — John 19:30)
- no complete record of parables. Matthew recorded 14, while Mark only four.

Those are some of the omissions.

(d) Look at some of the works of Jesus as Servant:

- taught with authority (1:22)
- demons were cast out (1:23-27)
- fever healed (1:29-30) (Peter's mother-in-law)
- different diseases healed (1:32-34)
- lepers made whole (1:40-45)
- palsied man made to walk (2:1-12)
- withered hand cured (3:1-5)
- multitudes healed (3:6-12)
- storm at sea calmed (4:35-41)
- maniac's mind restored (5:1-15)
- woman's hemorrhage stopped (5:21-34)
- Jarius' daughter brought back to life (5:35-43)
- five thousand fed (6:32-44)
- he walked on the sea (6:45-51)
- all that touched Him were made whole (6:53-56)
- deaf and dumb heard and spoke (7:31-37)
- four thousand fed (8:1-9)
- blind man healed (8:22-26)

These miracles of Jesus, the Servant, *were proof* of His mission from God the Father. With these works came massive opposition against Him from the Scribes and Pharisees (Mark 7:1-5). His answer is in Mark 7:6-23.

(e) The Servant Rejected.

Even though Jesus was presented as a Servant in Mark, He knew He would have to die.

Notice Mark 8:31. "The Son of Man must suffer . . . be killed and after three days rise again."

He presented Himself to Jerusalem on a donkey. In Matthew you read, "Behold Your King." Not in Mark. Read Mark 11:9-10. Only a reference to the "kingdom of our father David."

(f) The Sacrifice of the Servant.

Mark 14 through 16 records the trial, agony, prayer, crucifixion, burial and resurrection of Jesus. The Lord spoke of the cross often after chapter 8.

Underline Mark 10:32-34.

Look up Mark 14:24-25 _____

_____

Finally, the last verse of Mark tells us that the servant is "still working with us" (Mark 16:20).

5. **THE USE OF THE OLD TESTAMENT BY MARK:**

 (1) Mark did not use as many Old Testament references as Matthew; however, he knew and taught from the Old Testament. We shall list only a few. These references are given to make you search the Scripture and realize that Scripture teaches Scripture.

 (2) Mark 1:3 is a fulfillment of Isaiah 40:3 _____

 _____

 (3) Mark 7:6 is a fulfillment of Isaiah 29:13 _____

 _____

 (4) Mark 11:9-10 refers to Zechariah 9:9, but note the Servant is not called King.

 (5) Mark 12:35-36, Jesus affirms Psalms 110:1 _____

 _____

 (6) Mark 13:14 is a fulfillment of Daniel 9:27 _____

 _____

 (7) Mark 15:23 compares with Psalm 69:21 _____

 _____

 (8) Mark 15:24 is a fulfillment of Psalm 22:18 _____

 _____

 (9) Mark 15:34 is a fulfillment of Psalm 22:1 _____

 _____

 (The main reason some of the lessons are designed in this fashion is to make you search the Scriptures.)

6. **THE LESSONS YOU SHOULD LEARN FROM MARK:**

 (1) The reward of a good mother. Mary, the mother of Mark, had a great influence in Mark's life. Her home was open for the work of the Lord.

 (2) Mark lived and worked among Christians. Friends we select do make a difference in life.

 (3) Mark used his God-given talent of helping the apostles and writing what he heard from them. We have that record in the Word of God.

 (4) When the Lord places us in the background — in total silence as was Mark — He uses us mightily.

 (5) The ministry of letter writing is a ministry all of us can perform for the Lord. Mark wrote and has blessed lives through the ages.

 (6) The life of Christ was truly a life of service. He was depicted by Mark as the Servant.

DO YOU REMEMBER?

1. Who were the three men most influential in the life of Mark?
2. Was Mark an apostle?
3. What caused the division between Paul and Barnabas?
4. Scripture is silent in reference to Mark for about 20 years. What does tradition say about his ministry?
5. What most impressed you about Mark as you studied this lesson?
6. After only two lessons on New Testament characters, do you see the value of learning the Old Testament as well as the New?

YOUR NEXT ASSIGNMENT:

1. Read Luke 1:1-4; Colossians 4:14; II Timothy 4:11; Philemon 24; also the "we" section of Acts — Acts 16:10-17; 20:5 to 21:17; 27:1 to 28:16.
2. The next study will be on Luke — the person, not the book.
3. Review your notes on Mark.
4. Mark your Bible where new truths are learned.

Lesson 35
"Luke, the Physician"

(Where lines are provided, look up the Scripture and write it or its meaning in the space provided.)

1. **THE MEANING OF THE NAME:**

   Luke means "luminous" or "giver of light."

2. **BASIC SCRIPTURES:**

   Luke 1:1-4; Colossians 4:14; II Timothy 4:11; Philemon 24; also the "we" section of Acts (where Luke includes himself by using "we" or "us"). That section is Acts 16:10-17; 20:5 to 21:17; 27:1 to 28:16. Also Acts 1:1.

3. **FAMILY BACKGROUND:**

   We know less about Luke than any of the other New Testament writers. Nothing is written of his parents nor his home life. We do know that he was a brilliant man, possessing a quality of beauty, culture, rhetoric and philosophy. This is evident from his writings.

   He *should not* be identified with the Lucius of Acts 13:1, nor with the Lucius of Romans 16:21.

   Luke wrote the third Gospel and the Book of Acts. He wrote to the Greek mind.

4. **WHAT THE NEW TESTAMENT SAYS ABOUT LUKE:**

   (1) Luke Was the Author of Luke and Acts.

   We know that Luke wrote the Books of Luke and Acts. In Acts 1:1 Luke mentions the same person he addressed in Luke 1:3. Write in Acts 1:1 _____

   _____

   _____

   Notice Theophilus is mentioned. He is the same person mentioned in Luke 1:3. This man, Theophilus, was a man of high rank in Rome and a convert to Christ. His name is most meaningful, "Theo," meaning God and "Philus," meaning friend. Theophilus, then, was a "friend of God."

   In writing the Gospel of Luke, he gave his reasons for writing the Gospel (Luke 1:1-4). Notice in these verses:

   - "many have taken in hand" (many have written).
   - "to set forth in order a declaration" (systematic writing).
   - "those things believed among us" (the Gospel).
   - "they delivered them to us" (the writings or beliefs were delivered, or told, to Luke).
   - "were eyewitnesses and ministers of the Word" (Luke received from the Apostles words and writings).
   - "It seemed good to me also, having had perfect understanding of all things from the very first" (actually in Greek).
   - "from above" (Luke affirmed that what he was about to write was confirmed by inspiration; therefore, it was perfect understanding).
   - "to write unto thee in order, that thou might know the certainty of those things wherein thou hast been instructed" (the

writing is not necessarily in chronological order but a systematic presentation of facts).

The first four verses present the fact that Luke wrote his book from the record and testimony of eyewitnesses. This was confirmed by the inspiration of God. "All Scripture is given by the inspiration of God" (II Timothy 3:16).

In writing the book of Acts, Luke refers to "the former Treatise, of all that Jesus began to do and teach." Luke was referring to his Gospel of Luke.

(2) **Luke Was a Companion of Paul (Acts 16:10-17).**

In this verse we find the beginning of what is called the "we section of Acts." For the first time, Luke includes himself in the travels and ministry of Paul. At Troas Luke joined Paul. From Traos Luke went with Paul to Philippi. Underline Acts 16:12.

Scripture indicates that Luke could have remained at Philippi because in Acts 20:6 he says, "And *we* sailed from Philippi." Luke remained with Paul from this point. You will notice the word "we" in all of chapter 21. Notice especially 21:17 _____

_____

Luke was in Caesarea by the Sea during Paul's stay in prison for two years.

In Acts 27:1 they set out for Rome. They arrived in Rome by the Appian way, and there Paul was held under guard. Scripture indicates that Luke was with Paul until he was martyred.

(3) **Luke Was a Physician (Colossians 4:14).**

In the Gospel of Luke approximately 50 words are medical terms. McGee says, "Luke used more medical terms than Hippocrates."

In Colossians 4:14 Paul says _____

_____

Luke, the beloved physician, was with Paul as he wrote the Epistle to the Colossian church.

(4) **Luke Was a Fellow laborer With Paul (Philemon 24).**

Paul classified Luke as a "fellow laborer" and confirmed his presence in Rome. Philemon was a prison Epistle.

(5) **"Only Luke Is With Me" (II Timothy 4:11).**

One of the most precious chapters in Scripture is the fourth chapter of II Timothy. It was Paul's last words before facing death.

Everyone seemed to depart and left Paul on his own. In II Timothy 4:16, Paul indicated this fact: _____

_____

But as Paul was to stand in Nero's palace and be judged, he said these words, "Only Luke is with me." From the Mamertine Prison — cold, damp, dark — Paul penned that glorious chapter in II Timothy.

(6) **The Gospel of Luke.**

(a) Luke presents Christ as "the Son of Man." Look up Luke 19:10 _____

_____

_____

Luke presents Jesus as the human, divine One. John presents Jesus as the divine-human One. Both authors present both God and Man, the God-Man.

(b) Luke traces the genealogy of Jesus to Adam (Luke 3:23-38).

Luke presents the genealogy of Mary. Matthew presents the genealogy of Joseph.

There is no discrepancy in Luke 3:23. Joseph was *not* the son of Heli, but the son of Jacob, as shown in Matthew 1:16. Jewish custom taught the fact that when a woman was in the line of descendants, her husband's name was included as the descendant. Therefore, "Joseph, the husband of Mary," in Matthew, was named in Luke as the "son of Heli." Heli was the father of Mary. Joseph, by custom, was called a "son."

(c) Luke Established the Manhood of Jesus (Luke 2).

Luke wrote about the forerunner of Jesus, John the Baptist, and the announcement of the virgin birth of Jesus in chapter 1. *Then* as "great with child," "she should be delivered," "she gave birth to her first born son," "a babe," "eight days for the circumcising of the child." All of these physical references are in Luke 2:5-21.

Jesus grew as a natural, human lad (Luke 2:40) _____

_____

When He was 12 years old He went with His parents to Jerusalem. This was the age for the preparation of the "Bar Mitzvah" — meaning "a son of the commandment, or law." His humanity is the main emphasis of Luke (Luke 2:42).

(d) The Manhood of Jesus Took Nothing From His Deity.

Luke records the wonderful miracles of Jesus. Luke records 23 parables; 18 of them are found nowhere else. Luke took nothing away from His divine nature. He only emphasized Jesus as a man to give us a better understanding of His feelings, agony, pain and heartbreak. Luke presents more on the prayer life of Jesus than any other writer. (See "Through The Bible In One Year," Basic Study, p. 131.)

(7) **The Acts of the Apostles**

(a) The Outline of the Acts of the Apostles

Dr. W.A. Criswell, in his book, "Acts, An Exposition, Volume 1" says, "Just as the Lord outlined for John, the Revelation, so in the Book of Acts we see the Lord's outline for this book. His followers are to be witnesses unto Him in Jerusalem, and in all Judea, in Samaria, and to the uttermost parts of the earth. Luke follows that outline in the writing of the book."

So in Acts 1 through 7 the Gospel was confined to Jerusalem.

In Acts 8 through 12 the Gospel spreads to Judea and Samaria and to the Gentiles, such as Cornelius, and Greek idolators in Antioch.

In Acts 13 and on, the gospel is preached in Rome and to the uttermost parts of the world.

Write in Acts 1:8 _____

_____

(b) There is no ending to the book of Acts.

The history and the facts written by Luke have no formal ending. The book stops at the end of chapter 28, but that is not the end of the Acts of the Holy Spirit. It has no ending because God is not through. He is still working in us and through us to preach the Gospel to every part of the world. Jesus declared this in John 14:12 _____

_____

Jesus continues His work from glory as he presides over us in teaching and preaching His Word. He presides over His church as we minister to others.

(c) Jesus gave us the gift of the Holy Spirit.

The Holy Spirit came in power after Jesus ascended back into heaven. He had promised us the power of the Holy Spirit as a gift from Him and God the father after the days of His flesh. Look up and underline:

- Luke 24:49
- John 14:16
- John 14:17
- John 14:26
- John 15:26
- John 16:6-7
- John 16:12-14

5. **THE USE OF THE OLD TESTAMENT BY LUKE:**

   (1) Luke quoted the Old Testament as a scholar. He was a brilliant man and knew the Scriptures of the Old Testament. We shall list only a few from Luke, and then Acts.

   (2) Luke 1:31 is a fulfillment of Isaiah 7:14 _____

   _____

   (3) Luke 1:32 is a fulfillment of Isaiah 9:6-7. Underline in your Bible.

   (4) Luke 2:4 is a fulfillment of Micah 5:2 _____

   _____

   (5) Luke 4:18 is a fulfillment of Isaiah 61:1. Underline in your Bible.

   (6) Acts 2:17-18 is a fulfillment of Joel 2:28-29 _____

   _____

   (7) Acts 2:19-20 is yet to be fulfilled as told in Joel 2:30-31. Underline in your Bible.

   (8) Acts 4:11 is a fulfillment of Psalm 118:22 _____

   _____

   (9) Acts chapter 7 speaks of the full history of Israel from Abraham in Haran to the time Stephen spoke. He just quoted the Old Testament. Luke quotes Stephen, the first martyr.

   (10) Acts 8:32 speaks of the power of the Scripture, Isaiah 53:7-8, to save the Ethiopian eunuch.

   (11) In Acts 13:16-41 Paul uses Israel's past in brief to point the Jews to Christ; then verses 42-43 to Gentiles. The Old Testament was the basis for the sermon.

6. **THE LESSONS YOU SHOULD LEARN FROM LUKE:**

   (1) Luke was a man who never mentioned himself by name in his own writings. He must have had little or no pride. This is a quality for a Christian.

   (2) He was a student of the Scriptures and believed them. We should learn from him the value of remembering and writing.

   (3) Luke was inspired by the Holy Spirit ("from the very first" is "from above" in Luke 1:3). All of us are indwelt by the Holy Spirit if we believe; therefore, we can do anything He wants us to accomplish.

   (4) Luke was loyal. What a blessing it is to have a friend who has "staying power." Paul wrote "only Luke is with me."

   (5) The Acts of the Holy Spirit did not end with Acts 28.

   (6) The Holy Spirit is the Ascension gift sent into our hearts by the promise of the Father in the name of Jesus, the Son.

DO YOU REMEMBER?

1. On what authority did Luke write the Gospel of Luke?

2. Was Luke appealing to (writing to) a certain type of mind? Name the type.

3. How do we know he wrote "The Acts of the Apostles?"

4. Where did he get his outline for the Book of Acts?

5. Can you give that outline?

6. Where did Luke accompany Paul? Name two or three places.

YOUR NEXT ASSIGNMENT:

1. Read John 1 through 7; John 20-21; Mark 1:19-20; Matthew 20:20. The word "believe" occurs over 100 times in the Gospel of John. Underline all you can find.

2. The next study will be on the Apostle John. He wrote five books in our New Testament: The Gospel of John; I, II, III John and Revelation.

3. Review your study on Luke.

4. Mark your Bible where new truths are learned.

Lesson 36
"The Apostle John"

(Where lines are provided, look up the Scripture and write it or its meaning in the space provided.)

1. **THE MEANING OF THE NAME:**

    John means "whom Jehovah loves."

2. **BASIC SCRIPTURES:**

    John 1 through 7; John 20-21; Mark 1:19-20; Matthew 20:20; Revelation 1:1-10.

3. **FAMILY BACKGROUND:**

    There were as many boys named John in the ancient days as there are John's today. This John was the son of Zebedee and Salome. He was the younger brother of James. John came from a family of fishermen in Galilee. Zebedee was prosperous and had servants (Mark 1:16-20). John and James were given a "nickname" by Jesus "The Sons of Thunder" (Mark 3:17).

    John was a Jewish Christian. He became "the disciple whom Jesus loved." The original meaning of his name corresponded with his experience.

4. **WHAT THE NEW TESTAMENT SAYS ABOUT JOHN:**

    (1) John Was One of the First Disciples of Jesus (Matthew 4:18-22).

    Jesus began selecting the disciples at the beginning of His public ministry. He selected Simon Peter and Andrew first. The next two were James and John. Both teams selected were brothers.

    (2) John Was Made an Apostle (Matthew 10:1-6).

    The 12 were *first* learners, or pupils, known as disciples. A disciple is a learner, a student. In Matthew 10:1-6 the Lord Jesus called the 12 disciples and gave them power.

    In Matthew 10:2 notice the change in title _____

    _____

    An apostle was one selected by the Lord and was an eyewitness to the resurrection of Christ (Acts 1:21-22). The word "apostle" means "a messenger, one sent forth with orders."

    (3) John and James Were Men of Zeal and Courage (Luke 9:51-56).

    Where did John and James get that name, "The Sons of Thunder?" While they were still with Jesus, they showed a great degree of boldness and a ready temper.

    On the occasion in Luke 9:51-56, Jesus and the disciples were refused entrance to a Samaritan village. That infuriated James and John and their reaction was to act immediately. Notice Luke 9:54

    _____

    With the spirit of grace, the Lord rebuked them with words of patience and love. Underline Luke 9:55-56.

    You find another reaction of John in the same chapter, Luke 9:49-50, and again Jesus corrected him.

    (4) The Ambition of John and James (Matthew 20:20-28).

GREAT CHARACTERS OF THE BIBLE

NOTES

These two boys were eager and full of zeal. Their mother went with her two sons and asked for a place of honor for James and John. Notice Matthew 20:21 _____

_____

Again, the response of Jesus softened them. Jesus used the example of James and John to teach all 12 the meaning of service and of following Him.

Note the reaction of the 10 in Matthew 20:24 and underline.

Jesus' answer is worth memorizing. Underline it in Matthew 20:28. You will recall that this verse was the central message of Mark. It is also found in Mark 10:45.

Their zeal and pride were softened by the grace of the Lord Jesus. Those defects became an element of strength and glory. They were tough. Jesus needed this quality tempered by His grace and example.

(5) John Was the Beloved Disciple of the Lord.

John became a loving person. His writings are filled with the subject of "love."

He became the disciple whom Jesus loved in a special way. Look at John 13:23 _____

_____

Underline John 19:26 and 20:2.

Look up John 21:7 _____

_____

Now, John 21:20 _____

_____

(6) John Was One of Three Special Apostles of Jesus.

All of us have heard the names of the three in messages or lessons. Jesus selected the three — Peter, James and John — to be with Him on certain occasions:

- at the raising of Jairus' daughter (Mark 5:37)
- at the transfiguration (Matthew 17:1)
- at the agony in Gethsemane (Matthew 26:37 and Mark 14:33)

Look up these Scriptures and underline the names of the trio.

(7) John Witnessed the Risen Christ (John 20:19-30).

With the other disciples, John saw the risen Christ as He came and stood in their midst (John 20:19). Thomas was not present at that time, but a week later Jesus appeared to them again. Jesus allowed doubting Thomas to touch Him. See John 20:27 _____

_____

John went to Galilee, as the Lord had directed them, and again saw the risen Lord (John 21:1-2 and Matthew 28:10-16).

John was in the upper room after the ascension of Jesus and His promise of the Holy Spirit (Acts 1:13).

(8) John Became Active in Missionary Work (Acts 3:1-11).

The Lord Jesus told them to preach the Gospel. John teamed up with Peter and they began their ministry. They went to the temple to pray, and healed a lame man at the gate (Acts 3:1-11).

Peter preached the Gospel; John and Peter were imprisoned (Acts 3:12 through 4:4).

Notice Acts 4:13 _____

_____

Peter and John were sent to Samaria to preach (Acts 8:14) _____

John stayed in Jerusalem during the persecution of the early church and was there during the Jerusalem Council. Compare Acts 15:6 with Galatians 2:1-9. John was a pillar of strength.

(9)   John Wrote the Fourth Gospel — The Book of John.

(a)   The other three Gospels are called Synoptic Gospels, meaning "a like view," while John reveals the Diety of Jesus, the inward heart of our Lord.

(b)   The theme of the Gospel as written by John can be seen in the first 14 verses. Only John presents Jesus in the following manner:

"In the beginning was the Word (Jesus), and the Word(Jesus) was with God, and the Word (Jesus), was God" (John 1:1).

"In Him was life, and the life was the light of men." (John 1:4).

Write in and memorize John 1:12 _____

_____

"And the Word (Jesus) was made flesh and dwelt among us, and we beheld His glory, the glory as of the only begotten of the Father, full of grace and truth" (John 1:14).

(c)   John uses the word "believe" over 100 times in this book.

(d)   John wrote this Gospel and tells why in John 20:30-31 _____

_____

(e)   No genealogy of Christ is given because none is needed to present Jesus as the manifestation of God in the flesh. Look at John 1:18 _____

_____

Underline John 16:28.

(10)   John Wrote the Epistles of I, II, III John.

(a)   *In I John,* the Apostle states the reason and purpose of the Epistle in John 5:13 _____

_____

This is the book of assurance. One can "know" from this book he is a child of God. The word "know" appears 38 times. Underline them.

The cleansing verse for all Christians is I John 1:9 _____

_____

John wrote this book for four reasons:

- "that your joy may be full" (I John 1:4)
- "that ye sin not" (I John 2:1)
- "to guard against false leaders" (I John 2:26)
- "that ye may know" (I John 5:13)

(b)   In II John, the Apostle wrote the brief Epistle of 13 verses to encourage us to walk in truth and love (verses 1-6) and to guard the doctrine of Christ (verses 7-13). Notice especially verse 9 _____

_____

The word "doctrine" means "a teaching, a truth" of God.

There is a warning in the book concerning false teachers (verses 7 and 10).

(c)   *In III John* the Apostle wrote to a man he loved in the Lord. Gaius was walking in the truth. John states a great word of encouragement for Gaius and for us in verse 2 _____

155

(11) John Wrote The Revelation of Jesus Christ.

    (a)   In the Revelation, five times the writer says that he is John:

- Revelation 1:1
- Revelation 21:2
- Revelation 1:4
- Revelation 22:8
- Revelation 1:9

    (b)   John wrote the Revelation just as it was outlined by the glorified Lord in Revelation 1:19. (For a detailed study of Revelation, two lessons are given in "Through The Bible In One Year," Vol. 1, Basic Study).

    (c)   In the terrible war that destroyed Jerusalem in A.D. 70, John went to Asia Minor, and was for twenty five years, the pastor of the church in Ephesus.

        All external evidence of history supports the Scriptural evidence in reference to John.

        John was on the Isle of Patmos in exile for preaching the Word of God. The Roman Emperor Domitian sentenced him to Patmos where John penned The Revelation of Jesus Christ. Irenaeus, who died in A.D. 190, was the pupil of Polycarp, who was a convert of John. Polycarp was pastor in Smyrna when The Revelation was written. Irenaeus stated that he had heard Polycarp talk about John and the writing of The Revelation during the last part of the reign of Emperor Domitian.

5. **THE USE OF THE OLD TESTAMENT BY JOHN:**

    (1)   John was an apostle. He became a missionary and later a pastor. He knew the Scripture — the Old Testament — and quoted it and preached it. We give only a few references to show, once again, that Scripture teaches and explains Scripture.

    (2)   John 1:21 refers back to Malachi 3:1 _____

    (3)   John 1:23 is a fulfillment of Isaiah 40:3 _____

    (4)   John 3:14-16 is a fulfillment of Numbers 21:8-9 _____

    (5)   John 8:28 and 12:49-50 speak of Deuteronomy 18:15 and 18. Please underline the two verses in Deuteronomy.

    (6)   John 12:12-15 is a fulfillment of Zechariah 9:9 _____

    (7)   John 12:38 is a fulfillment of Isaiah 53:1. Underline in your Bible.

    (8)   John 12:39-41 is a fulfillment of Isaiah 6:10 _____

    (9)   John 19:24 is a fulfillment of Psalm 22:18 _____

    (10)   John 7:42 refers back to Micah 5:2. Look up and underline.

6. **THE LESSONS YOU SHOULD LEARN FROM JOHN:**

    (1)   John and James were tempered, softened, by the grace of the Lord Jesus. We can be changed by His grace.

    (2)   The "Sons of Thunder" became different men. John became the one "whom the Lord loved." James gave his life for the cause of Christ (Acts 12:2).

    (3)   The Bible is the truth of God, the Word of God, because the words of the Bible witness to Jesus. John states that Jesus is the "Word made flesh."

    (4)   We have Jesus, the living Word, and the Bible, the written Word. Both witness to the saving grace of God, in Christ.

(5) Ambition is fine if it is controlled by the Lord Jesus, the One who should control our lives.

(6) Obedience to the commands and teachings of Jesus was paramount in John's life. Obedience is a necessity in the church today. We must return to the Word, the Bible, and the Word, the Lord Jesus.

DO YOU REMEMBER?

1. Why were John and James called "the Sons of Thunder?"
2. They were made apostles. What is an apostle?
3. How did John and James show ambition to the Lord?
4. In the famed trio of the Lord, which ones were named?
5. John was known as " _____."
6. John wrote five books of the New Testament. Name them.

YOUR NEXT ASSIGNMENT:

1. Read Matthew 3; Luke 1 and 3; John 1; Isaiah 40:3-5; Malachi 3:1 and 4:5-6.
2. The next lesson will be on John, the Baptist.
3. Review your notes on John, the apostle.
4. Mark your Bible where new truths are learned.

Lesson 37
"John, the Baptist"

GREAT CHARACTERS OF THE BIBLE

(Where lines are provided, look up the Scripture and write it or its meaning in the space provided.)

1. **THE MEANING OF THE NAME:**

   John means "whom Jehovah loves."

2. **BASIC SCRIPTURES:**

   Matthew 3; Luke 1 and 3; John 1; Isaiah 40:3-5; Malachi 3:1 and 4:5-6.

3. **FAMILY BACKGROUND:**

   John the Baptist was born to Zacharias and Elisabeth, both being descendants of Aaron. He was of full priestly descent. Look at Luke 1:5

   _____

   They lived in the hill country of Judea (Luke 1:39). John's mother, Elisabeth, was a cousin to Mary, the mother of Jesus. John the Baptist was born into a godly home and was nurtured in an atmosphere of love for the Lord God (Luke 1:6).

4. **WHAT THE NEW TESTAMENT SAYS ABOUT JOHN THE BAPTIST:**

   (1) The Angel Gabriel, Divinely Proclaimed His Birth (Luke 1:11-19).

   (a) While Zacharias the priest was in the temple at Jerusalem fulfilling his priestly duties by offering incense upon the alter, the angel Gabriel appeared at his side. Write in Luke 1:11 __

   _____

   (b) The angel announced to Zacharias that he would have a son and even told him what to name the child, Luke 1:13 _____

   _____

   (c) Elisabeth was barren and both she and Zacharias were old (Luke 1:7).

   (d) Doubting what he had heard, Zacharias asked the angel, "Whereby shall I know this? I am old and my wife stricken in years'" (Luke 1:18).

   (e) Then the angel identified himself to Zacharias. Look up Luke 1:19 _____

   _____

   (2) Zacharias Doubted the Words of Gabriel (Luke 1:20).

   Because Zacharias doubted, he was stricken dumb and did not speak again until John was born and named. With Gabriel pronouncing the birth of John, it would seem that Zacharias would have believed that God would divinely perform all that was promised. The lack of faith on the part of Zacharias caused him to suffer some nine months of speechlessness.

   Write in Luke 1:20 _____

   _____

   When Zacharias came out of the temple, he could not speak to the people. He departed to his own house (Luke 1:23).

(3) Elisabeth Conceived (Luke 1:24).

After conception, Elisabeth hid herself for five months. God had removed the reproach (barren condition).

Her cousin, Mary, the mother of Jesus, visited with Elisabeth. Mary had been told by Gabriel about her cousin's conception (Luke 1:36).

(4) The Birth of John the Baptist (Luke 1:57-59).

John was one of the miracle babies of the Bible. As with Sarah in the Old Testament, God reversed the natural aging process of the bodies of both Zacharias and Elisabeth.

The time had come and Elisabeth gave birth to a son (Luke 1:57).

As usual, neighbors and relatives rejoiced with her and at the circumcision on the eighth day, they tried to name the boy after his father (Luke 1:59).

(5) Zacharias Named the Son, John (Luke 1:60-64).

Elisabeth would not accept the suggestion of friends to name the child after his father. She said, "his name shall be called John" (Luke 1:60).

Signs were made to Zacharias as to what the name should be. He wrote on a writing table exactly what Gabriel had told him. Look at Luke 1:63 _____

_____

After this Zacharias began to speak again. He praised God and began to prophesy (Luke 1:67-79). Underline verses 76 and 78.

John grew up in seclusion in the wilderness west of the Dead Sea (Luke 1:80). Notice, he was there "until the day of his showing to Israel."

(6) John the Baptist Began to Preach (Luke 3:2-3; Matthew 3:1).

(a) John preached fearlessly. He was the first authentic prophet to appear in Israel for about four centuries. He identified himself along with a call to repentance. Look at Matthew 3:2-3 and write in verse 3 _____

_____

(b) He proclaimed a new era, a new age called the kingdom of heaven. He came to prepare the people for the reception of Christ and to point out Christ in the person of Jesus (Matthew 3:2, 6; John 1:15).

(c) He announced Jesus as the manifestation of God (John 1:16-18).

Look up John 1:18 _____

_____

Underline verse 16 in your Bible.

At the same time the people asked if John were the Messiah. John answers courageously in John 1:19-23. Write in verse 20 _____

_____

He was to bear witness to the Light. He was not that Light (John 1:7-8).

(7) John Baptized Jesus in the River Jordon (Matthew 3:13-17).

(a) Jesus came to the river Jordon and John recognized Jesus. How did John recognize Him? He was one of the crowd. There is a key to this when all four Gospel writers are compared on the subject.

(b) In an unrecorded encounter, John was told of the sign which would distinguish Jesus as the Messiah. Turn to John 1:33-34; John said, *"And I knew Him not:* but He that sent me to baptize with water, the same said unto me, upon whom thou shalt see the Spirit descending, and remaining on Him, the same is He which baptizeth with the Holy Ghost. And I saw and bare record that this is the Son of God."

(c) With this word in his heart, John went about denouncing the Scribes and Pharisees as a generation of vipers and baptizing unto repentance the ones who would believe. Suddenly, John saw Jesus and said, "I have need to be baptized of thee and comest thou to me?" At the insistance of Jesus, John baptized Him and immediately the predicted sign was given. John saw "the Spirit of God descending like a dove and lighting upon Him: and lo a voice from Heaven saying, This is my beloved Son in whom I am well pleased" (Matthew 3:14-17).

John had said, "I knew Him not," (verse 31). Now, he knew, "saw, and bore record that this was the Son of God" (John 1:34).

(d) At the baptism of Jesus, the Trinity is manifested for the first time (Matthew 3:16-17).

- Jesus the Son is present in the water.
- The Holy Spirit descended like a dove.
- God the Father spoke from heaven.

(8) John's Message Before and After His Encounter With Jesus (Matthew 3:2; John 1:29).

Before, John preached, "Repent and be baptized" (Matthew 3:2).

After, John preached, "Behold the Lamb of God which taketh away the sin of the world" (John 1:29).

To a devout Jew, this term "Lamb of God" would bring to mind the entire sacrificial system. Thousands of lambs had been slain and their blood had only "covered" the sin. John used the familiar wording to get the Jew's attention. "The Lamb of God," in His shedding of blood, would settle the forgiveness of sin and atonement once and for all.

John had one supreme conviction. Look it up in John 3:30 _____

_____

(9) A Close Look at John the Baptist (John 3:31-34).

John did not desire glory for himself. This Scripture is factual in reference to that question.

John performed no miracles (John 10:41). All he said about Jesus was true. John was an ordinary man made extraordinary by his willingness to be led by the Spirit of God.

Yes, he was ordained before his birth to be the forerunner of Jesus Christ. Yet he was every inch a man, rugged, fearless, with a one-track mind. He never sealed his lips in reference to the Messiah. His life matched his message.

(10) The Supreme Tribute to John the Baptist (Matthew 11:9-13).

Jesus Himself said in Matthew 11:11 _____

_____

_____

_____

Jesus selected John the Baptist from all who had preceded him by giving to John such a great honor. Then Jesus paid tribute to his prophetic ministry in verse 9. Jesus said of John the Baptist, "A prophet? Yea, and more than a prophet."

Read the parallel Scriptures in Luke 7:24-29.

(11) The Death of John the Baptist (Mark 6:14-29).

The vindictiveness of Herodias caused John's death. Herod had taken his brother's wife and John the Baptist spoke to the subject in Mark 6:18 _____

Herodias had persuaded her daughter, who had pleased Herod by her dancing, to ask for the head of John the Baptist. Underline Mark 6:26 in your Bible. (Being sorry is not enough).

Herod granted the request and the head of John the Baptist was brought and presented to the daughter who gave it to Herodias (Mark 6:28).

In verse 27, note that John was in prison and there was killed. In verse 29, John's followers took his body and buried it in a tomb. When one remembers that *John's public ministry was confined to less than one year,* the extraordinary influence of the man can be realized. His ministry touched every part of society, from king to peasant. Never had a prophet had such influence as John. Jesus honored him as the greatest born of woman.

5. **THE USE OF THE OLD TESTAMENT IN REFERENCE TO JOHN THE BAPTIST:**

    (1) Luke 1:17 is a reference to Malachi 4:5 _____

        _____

    (2) Read Matthew 17:10-13, and compare with Malachi 3:1. Now write in Matthew 17:12-13 _____

        _____

    (3) Matthew 3:3 is a fulfillment of Isaiah 40:3 _____

        _____

    (4) Luke 3:5-6 is a fulfillment of Isaiah 40:4-5. Read and underline in your Bible.

    (5) John 1:29 refers back to Isaiah 53, especially verse 7 _____

        _____

    (6) John 1:21, "Art thou that prophet?" His answer goes back to Deuteronomy 18:15 _____

        _____

There are many other references to the Old Testament. We list only a few.

6. **THE LESSONS WE SHOULD LEARN FROM JOHN THE BAPTIST:**

    (1) John, rough and rugged in appearance, had convictions of such depth as to command the attention of the nation.

    (2) He supported and preached the Messiah. The greatest thing a Christian can do is support the cause of Christ and stay true to His teaching.

    (3) "He must increase and I must decrease" should be our soul's desire.

    (4) The role of the Christian and the role of the church should be attracting the lost to Jesus, not to ourselves. If they can see Christ in us, in our church, they will respond.

    (5) The greatness of John the Baptist was in his message. He prepared people to meet Jesus. The lesson is plain.

    (6) John was sincere. He had that quality. His motives rang true. The world spots a phony.

DO YOU REMEMBER?

1. What was unusual about the birth of John the Baptist?
2. Who named him?
3. When he began his ministry, who did he quote from the Old Testament?
4. What did Jesus say about John the Baptist?
5. He was likened to another Old Testament character. Can you name him?

6. How long was his ministry?

YOUR NEXT ASSIGNMENT:
1. Read Matthew 1 and 2; Luke 1 and 2; Mark 6; John 19:25-27; Acts 1:14.
2. The next study will be on Mary, the mother of Jesus.
3. Review your study of John the Baptist.
4. Mark your Bible where new truths are learned.

Lesson 38
"Mary, the Mother of Jesus"

(Where lines are provided, look up the Scripture and write it or its meaning in the space provided.)

1. **THE MEANING OF THE NAME:**

   Mary is the Greek form of Miriam meaning "bitterness, sorrow." (Mary certainly had many bitter experiences.)

2. **BASIC SCRIPTURES:**

   Matthew 1 and 2; Luke 1 and 2; Mark 6; John 19:25-27; Acts 1:14.

3. **FAMILY BACKGROUND:**

   All of the authentic material we have about Mary comes from Scripture and this is sufficient because so many myths have surrounded her name. God must have protected her and her name by giving to us only what is in His Word.

   Mary was of the tribe of Judah, and the line of David. In the genealogy of Joseph in Matthew, she is mentioned in Matthew 1:16: "Jacob begat Joseph, the husband of Mary, of whom was born Jesus, who is called the Christ." In Matthew 1:17, the 42 generations are given from Abraham to Christ.

   In Luke the genealogy of Mary is given, beginning at Luke 3:23 and continuing back to Adam. Notice in Luke 3:23, "Jesus, the son of Joseph which was the son of Heli, etc." Joseph was the *son-in-law* of Heli, the father of Mary. It is not said that Heli *begat* Joseph. Heli was a descendant of David. (In Matthew it is not said that Joseph *begat* Jesus.)

   Mary lived in Nazareth, a city of Galilee. We know nothing else of her home life or background.

4. **WHAT THE NEW TESTAMENT SAYS ABOUT MARY, THE MOTHER OF JESUS:**

   (1) Mary Was A Virgin (Luke 1:26; Matthew 1:23).

   (a) Mary, the mother of Jesus, was in Nazareth in the sixth month after the conception of John the Baptist. The angel Gabriel was sent from God to a *virgin* engaged to a man whose name was Joseph (Luke 1:26-27).

   (b) Matthew confirms the same fact. Look at Matthew 1:18, 23, 24, 25. All of these verses proclaim that Mary was a virgin. Write in Matthew 1:25 _____

   _____

   (c) Mary had known no man. She said so in Luke 1:34 _____

   _____

   (d) Paul confirms her purity in Galatians 4:4 _____

   _____

   The virgin birth is one of the cardinal doctrines of Christianity.

   (2) Mary, the Mother of Jesus Was Highly Honored (Luke 1:28 and 30).

(a) Gabriel, employed by God for distinguished service, announced to her that she was highly favored among women (Luke 1:28).

(b) Gabriel subsided her fears. She had found favor with God. Underline Luke 1:30.

(c) Mary was never made an object of worship in Scripture. She was descended from Adam through David. Look at Romans 1:3 _____

_____

In all of our Lord's words to Mary, he never intimated that she should be worshipped. Look at John 2:3-4 as just one example (other examples follow).

(3) Chosen to Be the Mother of Jesus (Luke 1:31-33, 35).

(a) Gabriel announced the conception and His name. Look at Luke 1:31 _____

_____

Matthew 1:21 is a parallel verse. Underline the verse.

(b) The announcement identified the Messiah (Luke 1:32, 33, 35).

Notice in verse 32: • "He shall be great . . ."
• "He shall be called the Son of the Highest . . ."
• "The Lord God shall give unto Him the throne of His father David . . ."

In verse 33: • "He shall reign over the house of Jacob forever . . ."
• "of His kingdom there shall be no end"

In verse 35: • "The Holy Ghost shall come upon thee (Mary) . . ."
• "the power of the Highest shall overshadow thee . . ."
• "that Holy thing which shall be born of thee shall be called the Son of God."

(c) Mary's humility and submission to such a miracle is found in Luke 1:38, "Behold the handmaid of the Lord, *be it unto me according to thy word.*"

Augustine said, "Mary first conceived Christ in her heart by faith, before she conceived in the womb."

Mary willingly yielded her body to the Lord God and the Holy Spirit took Diety and humanity and caused the conception, not of man, but of God.

(4) Mary's Song of Praise, the Magnificat (Luke 1:46-56).

(a) While visiting her cousin Elisabeth, Mary uttered a song of praise and thanksgiving to God. This section of Scripture is called the "Magnificat," which means, "song of praise." This expression by Mary is among the finest productions of poetic and prophetic literature.

Mary's inward joy and her faith in the Messiah to come can be found in her words. Notice especially Luke 1:46-47 _____

_____

Then verse 55 _____

_____

(b) Mary returned to Nazareth just before the birth of John the Baptist. She had gone to her cousin Elisabeth in her sixth

166

month and remained three months. The forerunner of Mary's Child was about to be born. Look at Luke 1:56 _____

_____

(5) Joseph's Revelation in a Dream (Matthew 1:18-21).

Poor Joseph did not want to hurt Mary and thought it might be good to put her away from him. But an angel directed him to marry her and to call the child, Jesus. Underline Matthew 1:20-21. (We will consider Joseph in detail next lesson.)

(6) The Birth of Jesus (Luke 2:1-20).

(a) A familiar story, so familiar we often miss the significance of such a birth.

Instead of remaining in Nazareth, Mary went with Joseph to Bethlehem to pay the tax. Joseph, being of Davidic descent, obeyed the instructions of Augustus. They "went *up* from Galilee, *out* of the city of Nazareth, *into* Judea, *unto* the city of David called Bethlehem" (Luke 2:4). This was about eighty miles.

(b) There Jesus, the Messiah, was born (Luke 2:7). This was no accident. Micah had foretold the place where the Messiah would be born.

A virgin had a Son!

(c) A scene of pure worship is in the remainder of Luke 2.

- the angels of the Lord, Luke 2:13-14
- the shepherds, verse 8
- Simeon, verses 25-35
- Anna, verses 36-38

There is no petition, no confession, only adoration.

(d) Simeon had been told he would see the Messiah before his death (Luke 2:26). When Mary and Joseph presented Jesus to the Lord God in the temple, Simeon was there, sent by the Spirit. Simeon took Jesus in his arms and rejoiced over the Messiah. Notice Luke 2:30 _____

_____

Simeon foretold to Mary that she would have great sorrow because of what would happen to Jesus, Luke 2:35 _____

_____

Mary's reaction to all of the miraculous things can be found in one verse, Luke 2:19 _____

_____

(e) Was Mary sinless? Read Luke 2:22-24; Leviticus 12:8. Underline the offerings "then she shall be clean."

(7) The Flight to Egypt (Matthew 2:13-21).

Being warned by an angel in a dream, Joseph took Mary and Jesus to Egypt because Herod had sought to destroy Jesus. They remained in Egypt until Herod's death. They went back into the land of Israel and to Nazareth which was to be the home of Jesus. (Only Matthew records this account in the life of Jesus.)

(8) Mary's Service to the Master (Luke 2:40-52).

(a) Jesus grew and was strong in spirit and wisdom and the grace of God was upon Him (Luke 2:40).

(b) Mary and Joseph took Him to God's house (Luke 2:41-50).

While in the temple, Jesus tarried and Joseph and Mary did not realize He was not with them. He was asking questions and listening to the doctors of law. Notice verse 47 _____

_____

167

When they found Him, He answered, giving to us His only words recorded until He began His public ministry. Write in verse 49 _____

_____

(c) Mary did not understand all He said, but she kept all these sayings in her heart (verse 51).

(d) She nurtured Him, raised Him, loved Him. All of this is summed up in verse 52 _____

_____

(9) Mary's Family (Matthew 13:55-56; Mark 6:3).

Jesus was her first born. Later she had four sons and several daughters by Joseph. Look at Mark 6:3 _____

_____

Some would teach the perpetual virginity of Mary, saying that the children named were cousins of Jesus, the sons of the wife of Alphaeus, also a Mary. We reject this theory and believe the Scripture as it is written. The children named were the natural children of Mary and Joseph, after the birth of Jesus who was by the Holy Spirit.

(10) Mary, a Follower of Her Son (John 2:1-10; Mark 3:31-35).

(a) At the beginning of the public ministry of Jesus, Mary appears in the Scripture. She was at the marriage in Cana. She tried to direct His actions, and thus, heard from Him a respectful but firm rebuke. Underline John 2:3-5.

(b) Similar truths are mentioned in Mark 3:31-35; Matthew 12:46-50.

Mary was now subject to Him, as the Son of God. She believed in His Messiahship. He was God in the flesh. His brothers did not believe in Him during His public ministry. As a result of His death and resurrection, His brothers became believers. They were in the Upper Room before Pentecost (John 7:5; Acts 1:13-14).

(c) Mary's deepest agony was as she stood at the foot of the Cross. She had followed Him on that last journey to Jerusalem. She witnessed His crucifixion.

Jesus spoke to her in the hour of His suffering. Look at John 19:26-27 and underline in your Bible.

The beloved disciple, John, took her to his home.

(11) Mary's Sorrow (Luke 2:34-35).

Simeon had predicted great sorrow for Mary because of all that would happen to her Son. She saw all of these things come in the life of Christ. She had to give Him to God, let Him be the Messiah. Simeon's prediction had come to pass.

(12) The Last Mention of Mary (Acts 1:14).

Mary was gathered in the Upper Room with the Apostles praying. This is the last mention of Mary in Scripture. We do not know the time nor the manner of her death.

5. **THE USE OF THE OLD TESTAMENT IN REFERENCE TO MARY, THE MOTHER OF JESUS:**

(1) Luke 1:31 is a fulfillment of Isaiah 7:14 _____

_____

(2) Luke 1:32 is a fulfillment of Isaiah 9:6-7. Underline in your Bible.

(3) Luke 2:4 is a fulfillment of Micah 5:2 _____

_____

(4) Matthew 1:23 and 25; Luke 1:55 is a fulfillment of the promised

168

Seed of women in Genesis 3:15 on to Seth, Shem, Abraham, Isaac, Jacob, Judah and David. Look at Galatians 3:16 _____

_____

(5) Luke 1:55 is a fulfillment of Genesis 17:19 _____

_____

All that we have studied in past lessons come to fruition in this lesson. All of the Old Testament speaks of the Redeemer, Seed, King, Immanuel and on and on we could quote names.

6. **THE LESSONS WE SHOULD LEARN FROM MARY, THE MOTHER OF JESUS:**

   (1) Her name, meaning "bitterness," came to pass as she suffered great sorrow because of all that happened to her Son. A mother, to some degree, suffers the same thing but it should keep them closer to the Lord, like Mary.

   (2) Mary was submissive to the Holy Spirit. We should always be in a like spirit.

   (3) We may not understand all things in reference to children but it is good to "ponder them in our hearts" and trust the Lord.

   (4) The Seed promised in Genesis was the Seed of woman, not man. We, therefore, must believe in the virgin birth of Jesus.

   (5) Mary never magnified herself, only her Lord. We should not magnify anyone but Jesus.

   (6) Mary was born of the Adamic race. She was honored by God and became the Saviour's mother. She acknowledged her need in the Magnificat, "My spirit hath rejoiced in God *my* Saviour." We understand her better because of her need and her sufferings.

DO YOU REMEMBER?

1. Which Gospel gives the genealogy of Mary?
2. Jesus was the Seed of _____
3. What is the Magnificat?
4. Was Mary sinless? How do you know?
5. Who made the announcement for God?
6. What do you remember the most about Mary?

YOUR NEXT ASSIGNMENT:

1. Read Matthew 1 and 2; Luke 1 through 4; John 1 and 6.
2. The next lesson will be on Joseph, the husband of Mary, foster father of Jesus.
3. Review your study of Mary, the mother of Jesus.
4. Mark your Bible where new truths are learned.

Lesson 39

The Two Josephs In the Life of Christ

"Joseph, The Husband of Mary; Joseph, of Arimathaea"

(Where lines are provided, look up the Scripture and write it or its meaning in the space provided.)

1. **THE MEANING OF THE NAME:**

   Joseph means "may God add."

2. **BASIC SCRIPTURES:**

   Matthew 1 and 2; Luke 1 through 4; John 1 and 6; Matthew 27:57-60; John 19:38-42.

3. **FAMILY BACKGROUND:**

   "It is unique that two Josephs were associated with Christ, one at His birth and the other at His death. Both of these men gave Jesus their best," says Dr. Herbert Lockyer in *All the Men of the Bible*. We shall take a brief look at both of these men in this lesson.

   Joseph, the husband of Mary, was a descendant of David (Matthew 1:20). He was a resident of Nazareth and a carpenter by trade.

   Joseph of Arimathaea, was a Jew of wealth and a member of the Sanhedrin, known as the Council. We know nothing of this Joseph except what is given to us in these brief Scriptures.

4. **WHAT THE NEW TESTAMENT SAYS ABOUT JOSEPH, THE HUSBAND OF MARY:**

   (1) Joseph, the Husband of Mary, the Mother of Jesus (Matthew 1:16; Luke 3:23).

   Most men would resent a title such as the one given to Joseph. He was known as "the husband of Mary" in both accounts of Scripture. Joseph is often referred to as the "forgotten man" in the story of the birth of Jesus. He was an important person in the birth and life of our Lord.

   Write in Matthew 1:16 _____

   _____

   Underline in your Bible Luke 3:23.

   (2) Joseph Was a Just Man (Matthew 1:19).

   When Mary was engaged to Joseph, she was carrying in her womb the Christ child. This was difficult for Joseph to comprehend.

Joseph was a just and reasonable man. He could not make Mary a public example and he was of a mind to put her away privately.

Joseph was a man of like feeling with all men. Can you imagine his shock, his feeling, when Mary, whom he trusted with all his heart confessed that she was expecting a child? Not Joseph's Child! Joseph and Mary decided that she should go to Hebron to see Elisabeth, her cousin (Compare Matthew 1:19 and Luke 1:39-56). There in the home of Elisabeth, expecting the birth of John the Baptist, Mary found encouragement. Zacharias could not speak at all so the two women had a good time talking.

(3)   The Dream of Joseph (Matthew 1:20-21).

While Mary was in Hebron (Joshua 21:11), Joseph was alone. He had not acted hastily. He had been patient. The Lord was faithful to Joseph. He sent an angel to Joseph in a dream. Notice the dream in Matthew 1:20-23:

- "Joseph, thou son of David," he was identified, verse 20.
- "fear not to take unto thee Mary thy wife," doubt erased, verse 20.
- "for that which is conceived in her is of the Holy Ghost," the miracle begins to unfold in Joseph's mind, verse 20.
- "she shall bring forth a Son, and *thou* shalt call His name Jesus: for he shall save His people from their sins," now Joseph knew that Mary was carrying the Messiah, verse 21.

(4)   The Fulfillment of Prophecy (Matthew 1:22-23).

How and why did Joseph understand the words of the angel in verses 20 and 21? Because he knew the Old Testament. He knew the prophecy of a coming Messiah.

In the same dream, the confirmation was given by the angel of the Lord. The angel had only to mention the words of Isaiah 7:14 and Joseph knew he was going to be a part of the life of the Messiah.

(5)   The Obedience of Joseph (Matthew 1:24-25).

Can't you see Joseph after that dream? He had heard an angel give him the Word of God. Mary was innocent. She was to be the mother of a Son, Jesus.

Assuming that Mary was still in Hebron, as most commentators believe, Joseph made his way to tell Mary the good news.

He took her as his wife. Write in Matthew 1:24 _____

_____

He was obedient to the instructions of the Lord. Write in Matthew 1:25 _____

_____

Notice the last phrase, "and he called His name Jesus."

(6)   He Protected His Family — Joseph's Second Dream (Matthew 2:13-15).

Herod plotted to kill the young Christ Child. Read the account in Matthew 2:1-12 which leads up to the critical verses. Being warned of God, Joseph and Mary did not return to Herod's land, but departed to go another way. The angel appeared to Joseph the second time. Notice verse 13 and write in, "Arise, and take the young child _____

_____

In verse 14, Joseph did exactly what the angel had instructed him to do. They remained in Egypt until Herod died.

This was another prophecy fulfilled (verse 15).

(7)   Joseph Was a Carpenter (Matthew 13:55; Mark 6:3).

Joseph was a carpenter in Nazareth. He taught Jesus the trade, it would seem. Look at Mark 6:3 and write in the verse and remember it _____

_____

In this verse you have Jesus identified in three ways:

- He was a carpenter
- He was the Son of Mary
- He was the brother of four brothers and He also had sisters. Naturally, these would be half-brothers and half-sisters.

(8) Joseph Cared For Jesus (Luke 2:51-52).

Jesus was subject to His parents. As a foster father, Joseph taught Him a trade, took Him to worship, and caused Him to grow in wisdom and stature.

(9) Joseph Disappears From the Scene.

Joseph could have lived into the beginning of the ministry of Jesus. Look at John 6:42 _____

_____

Joseph disappears and is not mentioned any more in Scripture. He was not at the crucifixion of Christ; therefore, it is inferred that he died prior to the death of Christ.

Some scholars say that since Mary was a widow, Jesus commended her to John, the apostle whom Jesus loved (John 19:26-27). Had Joseph been alive, Jesus would not have concerned Himself with the care of Mary.

4. **(CONTINUED) WHAT THE NEW TESTAMENT SAYS ABOUT JOSEPH OF ARIMATHAEA:**

(1) He Was A Secret Disciple (John 19:38).

This Joseph was of the Sanhedrin and rich. He was a follower of Jesus, secretly, "for fear of the Jews." Underline John 19:38. Notice in the next verse, another one "at the first came to Jesus by night." The person was Nicodemus. In John 3 you find the account. Here he is a changed man.

(2) He Did Not Agree With the Crucifixion (Luke 23:50-51).

Joseph was a part of the Sanhedrin, the council, and he was a just and good man. He never consented to what they had done to Jesus. Underline Luke 23:50.

(3) He Begged For the Body of Jesus (Matthew 27:57-58).

Joseph wanted to care for the body of Jesus. Joseph, who had not acknowledged Christ during His life, now does so in His death. It was common for friends to purchase the crucified bodies. Bodies not claimed were cast out as refuse.

Write in Matthew 27:58 _____

_____

(4) He Gave Jesus His Own Tomb (John 19:39-42).

John sheds light on Matthew's writing concerning the care of the body and placing Him in the tomb. In John 19:39-42, Nicodemus brought the material to prepare the body of Jesus. Look at John 19:39 and underline in your Bible.

Write in the next verse, 40 _____

_____

Underline verse 41. Notice, the garden was near the place of crucifixion. In the garden was a new tomb (sepulchre).

In verse 42, "they laid Jesus there."

Matthew 27:60 adds to the scene. Write in _____

_____

All four of the Gospel writers include this Joseph in their writings.

5. **THE USE OF THE OLD TESTAMENT IN REFERENCE TO THE TWO JOSEPHS:**
   (1) There is no reference by name to either Joseph in the Old Testament, however, both helped fulfill the prophecies of the Old Testament.
   (2) First, Joseph, the Husband of Mary:
       (a) Matthew 1:22-23 is a fulfillment of Isaiah 7:14 _____

       _____

       (b) Matthew 2:15 is a fulfillment of Hosea 11:1 _____

       _____

   (3) Second, Joseph of Arimathaea
       (a) Matthew 27:60 is a fulfillment of Isaiah 53:9 _____

       _____

       (b) Compare Matthew 27:60 to Daniel 6:17.

6. **THE LESSONS YOU SHOULD LEARN FROM BOTH JOSEPHS:**
   (1) The Lord rewards patience if we wait on Him as did Joseph, the husband of Mary.
   (2) Christ came as the Son of Man but He was never the son of a man.
   (3) We should care for our loved ones by protecting and providing for them.
   (4) The "forgotten man" had a great influence in the life of our Lord. Our influence for Christ can be just as real.
   (5) Joseph of Arimathaea was a secret disciple until the death of Christ. Jesus is alive; therefore, our belief in Him should never be secret.
   (6) Both men gave their best to Jesus. We should give our best to Him in all areas of life.

DO YOU REMEMBER?

1. What was Joseph's reaction to Mary's conception?
2. What changed Joseph's mind about Mary?
3. How did God protect Jesus from Herod?
4. How did Joseph influence Jesus in His young life?
5. What stands out in your mind about Joseph of Arimathaea?
6. Who helped in the preparation of the body of Christ for burial?

YOUR NEXT ASSIGNMENT:
1. Read Luke 10:38-41; John 11; John 12:1-3; also Matthew 26:6-13; Mark 14:3-9.
2. The next lesson will be Mary and Martha of Bethany.
3. Review your notes on the two Josephs in the life of Christ.
4. Mark in your Bible where new truths are learned.

Lesson 40
"Martha and Mary of Bethany"

(Where lines are provided, look up the Scripture and write it or its meaning in the space provided.)

1. **THE MEANING OF THE NAMES:**
   Martha means "lady, mistress."
   Mary means "bitterness, sorrow."

2. **BASIC SCRIPTURES:**
   Matthew 26:6-13; Mark 14:3-9; Luke 10:38-41; John 11; John 12:1-3.

3. **FAMILY BACKGROUND:**
   Martha and Mary seem to belong together in every study written by an expositor. Each had their own ministry, however; and one does not belittle the other. Most people will refer to them as "Mary and Martha," where as, Jesus placed Martha first, then Mary, then Lazarus.

   They lived in Bethany, a village one mile east of the summit of the Mount of Olives. The house in Bethany was a favorite place of Jesus.

   Some expositors have made Martha the daughter, wife or near relative of Simon, the leper. On the death of Simon, the house became hers since she was older than Mary or Lazarus. There is strong evidence to confirm this pattern in the Scripture (Matthew 26:6; Mark 14:3).

   Three people resided at the house in Bethany. Martha, Mary and Lazarus. We study only Martha and Mary in this lesson. In the next lesson Lazarus will be the subject of our study.

4. **WHAT THE NEW TESTAMENT SAYS ABOUT MARTHA AND MARY:**

   (1) Martha Received Jesus In Her House (Luke 10:38).

   Martha had the gift of hospitality. The Scripture intimates that the house belonged to Martha. The reception was a gracious and warm experience for the Master. It should be remembered that after Jesus left His home in Nazareth, He never returned for a period of rest and relaxation. He did go back to Nazareth to teach and was rejected. He even stated, "a prophet is not without honor, save in his own country, *and in his own house*" (Matthew 13:57).

   It was to this house in Bethany that He came because He loved the three who lived there. He found warm, loving hospitality in the home. There He could rest.

   (2) Martha Also Sat at Jesus' Feet (Luke 10:39).

   Martha too often has been revealed as a jealous and worldly minded person while Mary has been praised for her humility at the feet of Jesus.

   In this verse (Luke 10:39), the word "also" is very important. Both Martha and Mary sat at His feet and learned from the Master Teacher.

   There is every indication that Martha and Mary shared in all of the experiences together. Underline the word "also" in verse 39.

   (3) Mary Helped Prepare and Receive Jesus (Luke 10:40).

   Martha was the head of the house and was anxious to serve practically as well as spiritually. She was preparing the food for the Master and in her words she reveals something about Mary, often overlooked. Look at verse 40, "Lord dost thou not care that my sister hath *left* me to serve alone?"

This suggests that Mary had helped in the preparation and reception of Jesus. While Mary spent time at His feet, so had Martha learned at His feet and was inspired to practical service for Him. However, *doing* had become more important than *being* to Martha, "But Martha was cumbered about much serving." The word "cumbered" means "distracted." She wanted to be at His feet too, but was distracted because she had to prepare the meal.

(4) A Typical Family Complaint (Luke 10:40).

In the last part of verse 40, you read a typical family complaint. Martha said, (and I paraphrase), "Lord, I have everything to do and I can not hear all you are saying. We must give you a good meal and Mary has left me to do it all. Tell her to help me."

Sound familiar?

Both sisters loved the Lord and were sincere believers. Martha spoke her words to Jesus, not Mary.

(5) The Answer of Jesus (Luke 10:41-42).

(a) Write in verse 41 _____

_____

Jesus was gentle in His answer. He took Martha's question and used it to teach some of His truths. He taught, "You are anxious (careful) and troubled about many things."

(b) Martha and Mary understood His Words. Look at Luke 12:22

_____

Luke 12:26 _____

_____

(c) To paraphrase the statement Jesus made to Martha might help one understand: "Martha, Martha, you are busy with a large meal when one dish would be enough. My disciples have told me to eat, but I have meat (food) to eat which is the will of Him that sent me."

Turn to John 4:31-32 and 34. Write in your impression _____

_____

_____

Write in Luke 10:42 _____

_____

(d) Martha was anxious and troubled about many things, when really only one thing was needed; food for the soul should be more important than food for the body. This was "the good part which shall not be taken away from her" (Luke 10:42).

(6) The Second Reception of Jesus By Martha and Mary (John 11:20-29).

The second time we read of Jesus being received in Bethany, Martha and Mary had sent for Him. Their brother was sick and they needed the Master. (We will cover Lazarus in the next lesson. Now, only Martha and Mary.)

When Jesus decided to go to Bethany, notice the actions of the two women. First, Martha, then Mary.

John 11:20 _____

_____

Then John 11:28-29 _____

Jesus loved Martha, Mary and Lazarus (John 11:5).

(7) **Jesus Proclaimed a Fundamental Truth to Martha (John 11:25-26).**

It was to Martha that Jesus presented one of the most outstanding statements in the Bible as to His deity, power and authority.

John 11:25 _____

In verse 26, Jesus extended the invitation to "whosoever liveth and believeth in me shall never die." That included Martha and Mary and you and me. "Whosoever" includes everyone.

(8) **Martha's Confession of Faith (John 11:27-29).**

Jesus had asked Martha in verse 26, "Believest thou this?"

Martha then declared her remarkable confession of faith in verse 27: "Yes, Lord: I believe that thou art the Christ, the Son of God, which should come into the world."

Martha immediately called Mary "secretly," and said "The Master is come, and calleth for thee."

Mary's response is given in verse 29 _____

(9) **The Last Visit of Jesus With Martha and Mary (John 12:1-7).**

(a) Six days before the Passover, Jesus returned to Bethany. A supper was prepared for Him. Notice John 12:2 _____

Take notice, "There *they* made Him supper; and *Martha* served," indicating that Mary had helped prepare the meal. Martha, as usual, did the serving.

This is the last mention of Martha.

(b) On this occasion, Mary anointed Jesus with ointment of spikenard, a perfumed ointment in that day. It was very expensive, valued at about $132.00 (1975 dollar value).

Write in John 12:3 _____

(c) Judas Iscariot was at the supper. As usual, his true personality and greed became apparent. Look at John 12:5 _____

The response of Jesus is given in John but a more detailed statement is given in Matthew 26:12 _____

(d) Then Jesus announced that wherever the Gospel shall be preached in the world, Mary would be remembered for her act of love and devotion (Matthew 26:13). Jesus was to leave Bethany and make His triumphal entry into Jerusalem the very next day (John 12:12).

(e) Martha and Mary knew what was about to happen. Their home was quiet on that last night. Martha said nothing; Mary said nothing. Only the few words of Judas and the response of Jesus made up the conversation for the evening.

5. **THE USE OF THE OLD TESTAMENT IN REFERENCE TO MARTHA AND MARY:**

(1) There is no reference to Martha and Mary by name in the Old Testament. The basic truths they believed and lived by were truths from the Old Testament.

(2) Compare the "one thing needful in Luke 10:42 with David's state-

177

ment in Psalms 27:4 _____

_____

(3) Jesus proclaimed the great truth of John 11:25. The Old Testament saints of God believed as Martha. Look at Job 19:25-26 _____

_____

Also Daniel 12:2 _____

_____

(4) In John 12:3, Mary anoints Jesus. The name Christ means "the anointed." Look at Isaiah 61:1 _____

_____

6. **THE LESSONS YOU SHOULD LEARN FROM MARTHA AND MARY:**
   (1) The happy person is one who has both of their characteristics; Martha the practical, and Mary the spiritual.
   (2) The church requires both types. The Martha's and the Mary's are necessary in the work of the Lord.
   (3) Serving and obeying the Lord are duties of every Christian. Martha and Mary did both.
   (4) Martha and Mary sat at His feet and learned of Him. We should do so through prayer, Bible study and worship.
   (5) Mary gave the best she had to the Lord because she knew that He faced crucifixion. We should always give our best because He has overcome death and the grave so that we might believe in Him and live.
   (6) Rejoice! He is the resurrection and the life. We therefore have everlasting life if we believe in Jesus.

DO YOU REMEMBER?
1. Why did Jesus like to go to Bethany?
2. What was the distinct difference between Martha and Mary, in your own words?
3. Does one woman belittle the other in their actions?
4. What significant truth did Jesus reveal to Martha?
5. What was Martha's response?
6. When did Jesus last visit them?

YOUR NEXT ASSIGNMENT:
1. Read John 11; 12:1-17.
2. The next subject will be Lazarus, the only man who died twice, physically.
3. Review your notes on Martha and Mary.
4. Mark your Bible where new truths are learned.

Lesson 41
"Lazarus, Whom Jesus Raised"

(Where lines are provided, look up the Scripture and write it or its meaning in the space provided.)

1 **THE MEANING OF THE NAME:**

Lazarus means "God has helped"

2. **BASIC SCRIPTURES:**

John 11; 12:1-17.

3. **FAMILY BACKGROUND:**

Lazarus was a brother to Martha and Mary of Bethany. He was one of that household where Jesus loved to go and rest and fellowship. Jesus loved all three in the family; Martha, Mary and Lazarus.

Alexander Whyte says in his writings on Bible Characters:

> "Lazarus of Bethany comes as near to Jesus of Nazareth, both in character, and in his services, and in his unparalleled experience, as mortal man can ever come. Lazarus' name is never to be read in the New Testament till the appointed time comes when he is to fall sick, to die, and to be raised from the dead for the glory of God. *Nor is his voice ever heard.* Lazarus loved silence. He sought obscurity. He liked to be overlooked. He revelled in neglect. Let Martha sweat and scold; let Mary sit still and listen; and let Lazarus only be of some use to them."

As one can see, Lazarus was one who just wanted to serve and cared not for praise.

It is amazing that only John records the story of this one whom Jesus loved. What is given in the book of John is uniquely his and the Holy Spirit gives to John, the *apostle whom Jesus loved,* the inspiration and authority to write about this *man of Bethany whom Jesus loved.*

4. **WHAT THE NEW TESTAMENT SAYS ABOUT LAZARUS:**

(1) Lazarus, of Bethany, Was Sick (John 11:1-3).

Mary is specifically identified in verse 2 as the one who anointed Jesus with the ointment. There were so many women with the name, John made sure she was identified.

Lazarus, the brother of Martha and Mary, was sick enough for the sisters to become concerned. His sisters knew where Jesus was and their first thought was of Him. They sent a special message to Jesus and the message of verse 3 was only eight words, "Lord, behold, he whom thou lovest is sick." Jesus was "beyond Jordon" (John 10:40).

(2) "This Is For The Glory of God" (John 11:4).

One of the most striking statements made by Jesus is found here in verse 4. Write in the verse and underline it in your Bible _____

_____

Notice that the words of Jesus are emphatic. The "sickness was not unto death, but for the glory of God, that the Son of God might be glorified thereby."

The Lord can do His greatest work when the ones who love Jesus are ill. Never get the impression from His teaching that sickness is all bad. Far from it; for sickness can be for the glory of God.

Jesus was to do something startling in the life of Lazarus, "for the glory of God."

(3) **Jesus Delayed His Return to Bethany (John 11:6-16).**

  (a) By delaying His return to Lazarus in Bethany, Jesus had the opportunity of doing more for Lazarus than for any other in His ministry. Had He gone immediately and cured Lazarus, He would have done no more than He had done for many others. He purposely waited two days so that He could perform a great and startling miracle.

  (b) When Jesus said in verse 7, "Let us go into Judea again," His disciples reminded Him of the danger He had encountered before (verse 8). The words of the disciples caused Jesus to teach a truth to them and to us. Read verses 9-10. In essence, Jesus said, "If a man walks according to how he feels in his heart and according to what he can see, he only falls into the snares of this world. One must walk in the light of the truth of God."

Jesus knew what was about to happen to Him. He also knew that what He was about to do for Lazarus would bring the wrath of the Sanhedrin.

  (c) "Lazarus sleepeth" (verse 11).

To such a statement, the disciples thought it well for Lazarus to sleep because it would do him good. But Jesus was speaking of death. They should have known the meaning of the words of Jesus. Paul referred to physical death as sleep in I Thessalonians 4:13-14.

  (d) Jesus had to declare, "Lazarus is dead" (verse 14).

The amazing statement of death was followed by the words of verse 15, "I am glad for your sakes that I was not there, to the intent ye may believe."

Jesus waited until He knew that the miracle He was about to perform would be greater proof of His power than anything the disciples had ever seen.

Underline verse 15 in your Bible.

  (e) Thomas made a bold statement (verse 16).

Thomas, or Didymus which means "twin," said "Let us also go that we may die with Him." Knowing the malice of the Jews against Christ, Thomas expressed a willingness to die with Christ. Thomas did *not* mean they would die with Lazarus. He only had concern for the Master and this was his way of expressing such love.

(4) **Jesus Arrived Near Bethany (John 11:17-37).**

  (a) Jesus did not go into Bethany at first (verse 30).

When Jesus arrived near Bethany, He found that Lazarus had been in the grave four days (verse 17).

When Martha heard of His coming, she went to meet Him while Mary stayed in the house (verse 20). She immediately declared her faith in God and the power of Jesus (verses 21-22). She met Him with faith and simple trust.

  (b) Martha's statement of faith (verses 23-27).

Jesus, loving Martha, said, "Thy brother shall rise again" (verse 23).

Jesus then declared one of His greatest statements. Write in verse 25 _____

_____

Jesus then said, "Believest thou this?" (verse 26).

Martha said, "I believe Thou art the Christ, the Son of God, which should come into the world" (verse 27). If she believed Him to be the Christ, there would be no difficulty in her believing that He was the Resurrection and the Life.

   (c)   Martha called Mary secretly (verses 28-35).

She was secret in her call to Mary because there were Jews in the house mourning with Mary. They were no friends of Jesus. Mary hastened to Jesus and fell at His feet (verses 29, 31, 32). Her usual position was "at His feet." Jesus was inwardly, deeply moved by the grief of Martha and Mary. Verse 33 says, "He groaned in the spirit."

The shortest verse in the Bible expresses how Jesus felt. Write in verse 35 _____

_____

(5) Jesus At the Grave Raised Lazarus From the Dead (John 11:38-44).

   (a)   This would be the last miracle of Jesus to awaken the Jews before He went to Jerusalem. He was to recall Lazarus back from glory after only four days. Perhaps Jesus wept because of that fact.

   (b)   Lazarus physically had begun to smell. Read and underline verse 39.

   (c)   "Believe and see the glory of God" (verse 40).

Again, Jesus had to remind Martha that belief and faith were imperative. Underline verse 40.

Then the stone was rolled away from the grave (verse 41).

   (d)   Jesus prayed so all could hear (verses 41-42).

Notice the prayer was said with a voice to be understood, so that people standing by the grave might believe.

   (e)   It happened! Lazarus came out of the grave (verses 43-44). Jesus said three words, "Lazarus, come forth."

Write in verse 44 _____

_____

Notice that Lazarus was bound with graveclothes. Compare with John 20:5-7.

(6) Many Jews Were Saved (John 11:45-46).

Write in verse 45 _____

_____

The word spread to the Pharisees that Jesus had raised Lazarus.

(7) The Plot to Put Jesus to Death (John 11:47-57).

The word "council" means Sanhedrin. They plotted to put Jesus to death because He was a threat to their followers. Raising Lazarus was too much for them to take.

Write in verse 53 _____

_____

(8) Lazarus Attended A Supper In Bethany (John 12:2, 9, 17, 18).

   (a)   The resurrected Lazarus sat at the table with Jesus at the supper. Martha, as usual, served (verse 2).

   (b)   The appearance of Lazarus caused excitement and many Jews went to Bethany to see, not only Jesus, but Lazarus (verse 9).

   (c)   Read and underline verses 10 and 11. The chief priests considered putting Lazarus to death again because many Jews believed in Jesus. These two verses are seldom mentioned.

   (d)   Many were saved because the people who saw Lazarus come out of the grave gave testimony of Jesus. Many people met Him as He entered Jerusalem to face trial and crucifixion (verses 17-18).

5. **THE USE OF THE OLD TESTAMENT IN REFERENCE TO LAZARUS:**

   (1) In John 11:11, Jesus used the term "sleepeth" for physical death. This was a term familiar to the disciples taken from the Old Testament. Look up II Samuel 7:12 _____
   _____

   I Kings 1:21 _____
   _____

   I Kings 2:10 _____
   _____

   Deuteronomy 31:16; underline "Behold thou shalt sleep." Psalm 13:3 _____
   _____

   (2) John 11:24 refers back to Job 19:25-26 _____
   _____

   Psalm 49:15 _____
   _____

   (3) John 11:25 speaks of Job 14:13. Underline in your Bible.

6. **THE LESSONS YOU SHOULD LEARN FROM LAZARUS:**

   (1) Just as Lazarus was dead physically, so people around us are dead spiritually.
   (2) Lazarus was raised because Jesus called him by name. Augustine said that if Jesus had not called Lazarus by name, all the dead in the vicinity would have come forth at His voice.
   (3) Jesus never changed His method of raising the dead. *He spoke.* Life still comes through His Word.
   (4) Lazarus was a witness to the power of Christ and what Christ had done for him. Everytime a person is raised to spiritual life, they should witness of His power.
   (5) The news of Lazarus caused the enemies of Jesus to seek to put Him to death. When the Lord is magnified, expect Satan to be near by.
   (6) Lazarus never spoke a word recorded in Scripture. He served in silent obedience to the Master. One does not have to be "center stage" to make an impact for Jesus.

DO YOU REMEMBER?

1. Only one wrote of Lazarus. Who was he?
2. Why do you think Lazarus is recorded in only one Gospel?
3. Why did Jesus delay going to help Martha and Mary?
4. Can sickness be used for the glory of God?
5. Why was the resurrection of Lazarus so special to Jesus?
6. What happened among the Jews when they saw Lazarus?

YOUR NEXT ASSIGNMENT:
1. Read Matthew 10:2-6; John 6:70-71; John 12:3-8; John 13:21-35; Matthew 26:14-25; Matthew 26:47-50; Matthew 27:3-10; Acts 1:16-19.
2. The next lesson will be a study of Judas Iscariot.
3. Review your lesson on Lazarus.
4. Mark your Bible where new truths are learned.

182

Lesson 42
"Judas Iscariot"

(Where lines are provided, look up the Scripture and write it or its meaning in the space provided.)

1. **THE MEANING OF THE NAME:**

   Judas means "praise of God"
   Iscariot means "citizen of Kerioth"

2. **BASIC SCRIPTURES:**

   Matthew 10:2-6; John 6:70-71; 12:3-8; 13:21-35; Matthew 26:14-25; Matthew 26:47-50; Matthew 27:3-10; Acts 1:16-19.

3. **FAMILY BACKGROUND:**

   Judas was a popular name and had significant meaning until this Judas ruined the name. The name which means "praise of God" became a name associated with betrayal, treachery. Judas is the Greek form of the Hebrew proper name, Judah.

   Judas was the son of Simon Iscariot (John 6:71). Iscariot was his surname and it distinguished him from another of the twelve who was named Judas.

   Iscariot simply means "son of Kerioth" or "citizen of Kerioth." This tells us that he came from a small village south of Jerusalem in the same area where the prophet Amos was born. Amos came from Tekoa and Kerioth was in the extreme southern part of Judah. It is mentioned in Joshua 15:25.

   Judas Iscariot came from a totally different background than did the other eleven. The eleven were all from Galilee while Judas was from Judea. He was a man with some education and we would call him a "city man." The others were farmers, fishermen and laborers with little or no formal education.

4. **WHAT THE NEW TESTAMENT SAYS ABOUT JUDAS ISCARIOT:**

   (1) He Was Listed Last Among The Twelve In The Gospels (Matthew 10:4; Mark 3:19; Luke 6:15).

   In all three references, Judas is named last. He was placed in the proper position by each writer.

   (2) Jesus Referred to Judas as a Devil (John 6:70).

   (a) Jesus knew that Judas Iscariot was the one who would betray Him. Notice John 6:70 and underline in your Bible. Write in the next verse, 71 _____

   _____

   (b) The declaration by Jesus that Judas was the devil literally came to pass. Satan actually entered Judas. Look up John 13:27 _____

   _____

   Also John 13:2 _____

   _____

   Luke 22:3 _____

   _____

NOTES

(3) Luke Called Judas the Traitor (Luke 6:16).

In listing the twelve, Judas is named last by Luke and also called a traitor. Underline this verse in your Bible.

(4) John Called Judas A Thief (John 12:6).

Judas was the one appointed to care for the money bag for the twelve and Jesus. He was a thief, according to John 12:6 _____

_____

Also refer to John 13:29 and underline in your Bible.

(5) Jesus Also Called Judas The Son of Perdition (John 17:12).

In our Lord's prayer for us, he referred to all that God the Father had given Him and none were lost but one. Write in the verse: __

_____

The "son of perdition" was Judas Iscariot. The same name was used by Paul for the "man of sin." (II Thessalonians 2:3).

(6) Judas Iscariot Made A "Deal" With the Chief Priests (Matthew 26:14-16).

After Jesus rebuked Judas for his denouncing Mary of Bethany, Judas resented Jesus. Mary had only anointed Jesus with expensive ointment. Judas preferred to sell the ointment "to help the poor." Jesus told Judas that she was preparing Him for burial (Matthew 26:6-13).

Judas had wanted a Messiah who would conquer the Romans, crush all the enemies of Israel, restore national independence and become the King Messiah. He could not understand the ideas Jesus had about being the Messiah. Jesus had never said He was the Messiah, but He never denied it either (Mark 8:29-30). Judas knew that Jesus had unusual powers. Why didn't He use them to rule the nation? Judas wanted dominion; Jesus spoke of suffering. Judas wanted a sword and a crown to rule while Jesus spoke of thorns and a cross.

Judas couldn't take it anymore. He decided to talk to the chief priests and offered to "deliver" Jesus into their hands. The traitor had begun to work.

Judas, thinking of what he could get out of it, asked for a price. Write in Matthew 26:14-15 _____

_____

"And from that time he sought opportunity to betray Him" (verse 16).

(7) Jesus Foretold His Betrayal (John 13:21-27).

(a) All four Gospels record this event. They are found in:
- Matthew 26:20-25
- Mark 14:17-21
- Luke 22:21-22
- John 13:21-27

All four writers reveal the same truth. All four use different wording. Compare all four.

(b) At the last Passover, Jesus told the twelve that one of them would betray Him. He knew who it was and Matthew and Mark record the words of Jesus which were most severe. Look at Matthew 26:24 and Mark 14:21. In both, Jesus said, "it had been good for that man if he had not been born."

(c) Jesus identified the betrayer in John 13:26-27 _____

_____

(d) In Matthew 26:25, Judas asked, "Master, is it I?" Jesus said, "Thou hast said," which was the same as "yes."

(e) When Jesus told Judas to do quickly what he was going to do (John 13:27), the eleven thought Jesus had told Judas to go buy the things needed, or to help the poor (John 13:28-29).

(f) Judas *immediately* left them (John 13:30). Write in the verse:

_____

Note the fact that he left at night.

(8) Jesus In the garden of Gethsemane (Matthew 26:36-46).

(a) After the institution of the Last Supper, Jesus departed with the eleven and went to the Mount of Olives and to the place called Gethsemane. On the way from the Upper Room to the garden, Jesus did some of His most profound teaching. All of John 14 through 17 were spoken just before, and during, the walk to the place of prayer.

(b) In John 14 through 17, Jesus taught them that He would come again. He told them of the coming of the Holy Spirit to indwell believers, the new privilege of prayer, the Vine and branches, the work of the Holy Spirit, His death, resurrection, second coming, and the great prayer of intercession for us. All of this in a short time in these four chapters. (Read all four chapters.)

(c) When Jesus arrived at the garden, he took Peter, James and John while the others were to sit outside the garden. He left the three and went farther and began to pray. Three times He returned to find the three sleeping. The third time he told them (verse 45): _____

_____

Underline verse 46.

(9) Judas Iscariot Betrayed Jesus (Matthew 26:47-50).

(a) Judas stood with a great multitude of people with swords and staves. They were there for blood. Judas stood there in front with them. Judas, who had been with Christ three years, was ready to betray Him.

(b) The sign Judas had given the multitude was a kiss.
Matthew 26:48 _____

_____

Judas stepped toward Jesus and said, "Hail, Master; and kissed Him" (verse 49).

The response of Jesus was just like the Master. Look at verse 50: "Friend, wherefore art thou come?"

(c) Then the crowd took Jesus. He was then on His way to the cross.

(10) The Remorse of Judas (Matthew 27:3-10).

(a) The next morning when Judas saw that Jesus was condemned, he had a great sense of quiet. He tried to undo what had been done. Notice in Matthew 27:3: ". . . repented himself, and brought again the thirty pieces of silver to the chief priests."

(b) Notice what he said, Matthew 27:4 _____

_____

(c) Judas threw the thirty pieces of silver down in the temple and went and hanged himself (verse 5).

The chief priests took the silver and, since they could not put it into their treasury, they bought a potter's field to bury the strangers and those without means (verses 6-8). The allusion in verse 9 to Jeremiah 18:1-4 and 19:1-3 was more distinctly to Zechariah, as we shall see.

The gory details of the death of Judas is given in Acts 1:18.

(11) Why Was Judas Chosen As One of the Twelve?

There is only one answer. That answer is found in Matthew 26:56

_____

To go a step farther, why were we chosen? All who are believers in Jesus, of our own free will and choice, were chosen before the foundation of the world (Ephesians 1:4).

5. **THE USE OF THE OLD TESTAMENT IN REFERENCE TO JUDAS ISCARIOT:**
   (1) Psalm 109:5-8, directed at a contemporary of David, found its fulfillment in Acts 1:16 and 20. Compare the two Scriptures.
   (2) Matthew 26:23 is a fulfillment of Psalm 41:9 _____

   _____

   (3) Matthew 26:15 is a fulfillment of Zechariah 11:12 _____

   _____

   (4) Matthew 26:31 is a fulfillment of Zechariah 13:7. Underline in your Bible.
   (5) Matthew 26:45 is a direct reference to Psalm 69:20. Compare the two Scriptures.
   (6) Matthew 26:39 is a reference to Psalm 40:8 _____

   _____

   (7) Matthew 27:5, 9, and 10 is a direct reference to Zechariah 11:13

   _____

   (Jeremiah is mentioned in Matthew 27:9. The reference is to Jeremiah 18:1-4. The King James marginal reference in Jeremiah leads you to Zechariah 11:13.)

6. **THE LESSONS YOU SHOULD LEARN FROM JUDAS ISCARIOT:**
   (1) There is no sin worse than denying Christ because you cannot accept His way above your own.
   (2) Betrayal still takes place, not only in Judas. How often have we witnessed "followers of Christ" show bitter, cruel and impatient pride.
   (3) Judas became a devil incarnate. Jesus said, "one of you is a devil." Satan works in orthodox ways.
   (4) Judas went to his own place (Acts 1:25). Judas did what he did because of sin. It was Judas' choice. To the end Christ gave Judas a chance to change, even called him "friend" before the kiss of death.
   (5) The path of sin always goes from bad to worse. The speed picks up and goes down, down.
   (6) It is possible to hear the Word, witness His power in many lives, yet refuse to accept Him and give Him our lives and thus be lost.

DO YOU REMEMBER?

1. What was the difference between Judas and the eleven?
2. Where did Judas Iscariot rank among the twelve?
3. What did Jesus call Judas Iscariot? (two names)
4. When did Jesus do some of His greatest teaching?
5. What was Jesus' response to the kiss of Judas? What did Jesus then call him?
6. The paramount question: was Judas Iscariot lost?

YOUR NEXT ASSIGNMENT:
1. Read Matthew 10:1-6; John 11:1-16; John 14:1-6; John 20:19-31; John 21:1-2; Acts 1:13.

2. The next lesson will be a study of Thomas, a little known character, except the fact that he was "doubting Thomas."
3. Review your lesson on Judas Iscariot.
4. Mark your Bible where new truths are learned.

Lesson 43
"Thomas, the Doubting Apostle"

(Where lines are provided, look up the Scripture and write it or its meaning in the space provided.)

1. **THE MEANING OF THE NAME:**

   Thomas, also called Didymus, means "twin." Didymus is a Greek name meaning, like Thomas, "twin."

2. **BASIC SCRIPTURES:**

   Matthew 10:1-6; John 11:1-16; John 14:1-6; John 20:19-31; John 21:1-2; Acts 1:13.

3. **FAMILY BACKGROUND:**

   Thomas, in Hebrew, and Didymus, in Greek, means "twin." In Genesis 25:24, it is said of Rebekah that there were twins in her womb; the Hebrew word being "thomin." Probably Thomas was a twin but we know nothing about the brother or sister who was the twin.

   Thomas was a native of Galilee and by trade, a fisherman. Nothing is recorded in Scripture of his parents nor his early years.

   Had the fourth Gospel never been written, Thomas would have only been a name. The first three Gospels give nothing in detail about him. What we know of him is in the Gospel of John. His name appears with the apostles in Matthew 10:3; Mark 3:18; Luke 6:15 and Acts 1:13.

4. **WHAT THE NEW TESTAMENT SAYS ABOUT THOMAS:**

   (1) Thomas Was Driven By Emotion (John 11:16).

   (a) When Jesus announced His intention of going to Bethany again to raise Lazarus from the dead, Thomas immediately knew what it was going to mean for Christ. Thomas knew that the hostile Jews would be there and the imminent danger Jesus would have to face.

   (b) Thomas alone opposed the other disciples who sought to persuade Jesus not to go to Bethany, in Judea. Look at John 11:8 _____

   _____

   (c) Thomas gave an emotional appeal to his fellow disciples. Look at John 11:16 _____

   _____

   Some Bible commentaries indicate that Thomas meant that they should go and die with Lazarus. In its context, that meaning is just not indicated. Thomas, knowing the danger expressed by the disciples, meant a willingness to die with Christ.

   Matthew Henry paraphrases the words of Thomas as, "Let us go and die with our Master who is now exposing Himself to death by venturing into Judea."

   Thomas manifested a willingness and readiness to die with Christ. From a heart of affection, Thomas gave the emotional statement to the others.

(2) Thomas Was Inquisitive (John 14:5).

(a) Without apology, Thomas contradicted the Lord Jesus.

The Master had just stated that great comfort section in John 14:1-4, wherein He told them: "Let not your heart be troubled; ye believe in God, believe also in me. I go to prepare a place for you. I will come again, and receive you unto myself; where I go ye know, and the way ye know."

(b) Thomas, hearing that he should know the way, said to Jesus, John 14:5 _____

_____

(c) Had he not heard the teachings of Jesus to His own chosen twelve? Had he been deaf? Had he forgotten His teachings about betrayal, death, resurrection?

Thomas, like the others, dreamed of a temporal kingdom. When Jesus spoke of going away, and their being with Him, they really turned on their Hebrew imaginations. They could just see Jesus going to some city, there to be anointed King and restore the kingdom of Israel. That is what they wanted to believe.

(d) Jesus answered both questions as a good teacher.

Thomas had asked, "we know not where Thou goest." That is the first question. Then the second: "how can we know the way?"

The answer you probably know from memory. Look at John 14:6 _____

_____

(3) Thomas Was A Doubting, Skeptical Person (John 20:24-25).

(a) Thomas is known as "doubting Thomas," but he had to be more than a man of doubt, or his name would not be listed among the original twelve disciples. Jesus included him to share His ministry and carry it on after His death.

(b) For three years he had lived close to Jesus. He had felt the impact of the personality of Jesus, and had heard His teachings. Thomas had been present at the Last Supper (Matthew 26:26-29). He had been nearby in the Garden of Gethsemane (Matthew 26:36). It would be unfair to remember Thomas as that one who only doubted. The Holy Spirit had some special reason for such teaching.

(c) Thomas was absent the first time Jesus appeared to the disciples, after His resurrection. Look up John 20:24 _____

_____

Scripture does not give a reason for his absence. We can surmise how we would have felt had we been in the shoes of Thomas.

He had seen the body of Jesus laid in the tomb. He was miserable with sorrow. He just wanted to be alone with his grief. With the loss of the Master and his own skeptical attitude about a resurrection, Thomas was steeped in self pity.

(d) When the disciples said to Thomas, "we have seen the Lord," notice what he said to them. Write in the rest of John 12:25 _____

_____

This was the statement which has given him the name through the ages as "doubting Thomas." Thomas had to see and feel the Resurrected One before he would believe the resurrection testimony.

(e) Some skeptics don't want to believe. Thomas was seemingly sincere. He really wanted to see Jesus again and know that He was not dead.

190

(4) Thomas Had His Doubt Removed (John 20:26-29).

(a) From a doubt of deep despair, Thomas stayed with the disciples seven days waiting to see if what they had said was really true. For one week, Jesus delayed His meeting with them again. It was a week of joy for the others but a week of anxiety for Thomas.

(b) He had rejoined the group, indicating that he needed to be with them. It was no time to pull away from all that Jesus had taught.

Jesus did not appear to Thomas until he was with the rest of the disciples. Jesus had taught them Matthew 18:20 _____

_____

(c) "Then came Jesus." Jesus graciously returned to that place in Jerusalem. The doors were shut for fear of the Jews. Jesus appeared and said, "Peace be unto you." Write here John 20:26 _____

_____

(d) Jesus addressed Thomas in particular. Notice John 20:27 __

_____

Jesus knew what Thomas had said, what he was thinking; yet He condescended to Thomas, *one man*. Jesus could have returned to the Father and there be in the midst of the throne of God. For our benefit, as well as Thomas's, He lingered and visited with His select group. Jesus valued *one* soul, one man.

(e) Thomas declared his faith, John 20:28 _____

_____

Thomas was fully satisfied of the truth of Christ's resurrection. His human skepticism and slowness to believe should help us understand two truths. First, the carnal, doubting attitude of most people; and secondly, the grace of the Lord Jesus in continually inviting us to "come unto Him."

Thomas had seen the risen Lord and believed!

(5) Jesus Rebuked Thomas (John 20:29).

Jesus graciously reminded Thomas of a fundamental truth of Christianity. That truth was FAITH. Notice verse 29 _____

_____

Jesus wanted Thomas to learn that real faith does not require visible proof. True faith believes what it can not see or touch. Jesus loved Thomas and had come back so Thomas could see Him. In the process, Jesus left the truth of faith without the necessity of evidence.

The same Thomas who had said, "Let us also go, that we may die with Him," was the Thomas who had to see the risen Christ to believe He had come out of the grave.

Don't be critical of Thomas. He pictures most of us.

5. THE USE OF THE OLD TESTAMENT IN REFERENCE TO THOMAS:

(1) John 20:25 is a reference to Zechariah 12:10 _____

_____

(2) John 20:28, "My Lord and my God," expressly declares the deity of Christ.

His deity is expressed in:

- Psalm 2:2-9

191

- Isaiah 7:13-14
- Isaiah 9:6-7

6. **THE LESSONS WE SHOULD LEARN FROM THOMAS:**
   (1) We should learn to identify with the disciples who rejoiced rather than with one who had to see to believe.
   (2) Many people inside and outside churches, identify with Thomas because skeptics look for other skeptics.
   (3) Doubt of the real resurrection of Jesus Christ causes doubt about most of the great doctrines of the faith.
   (4) The world says, "see and believe." Jesus says, "believe and see."
   (5) Depression, self pity, anxiety, grief were the marks of Thomas, causing emotional doubts. All of us have gone through the same condition, but we should never remain in that condition.
   (6) Hebrews 11:1 should become a reality to us.
   (7) I Peter 1:8 is precious to all who believe. It says, "Whom having not seen, ye love; in whom, though now ye see Him not, yet believing, ye rejoice with joy unspeakable and full of glory."

DO YOU REMEMBER?

1. What does Thomas mean?
2. What brave appeal did Thomas make to his fellow disciples?
3. What were the two questions Thomas asked of Jesus as Jesus talked of going to prepare a place for us?
4. Why wasn't Thomas present when Jesus appeared to the disciples the first time?
5. What does real faith require?
6. Do you identify with Thomas?

(**For your own information:** Tradition and documentation of facts reveal that Thomas was used mightily by the Lord in establishing churches in Persia (Iran today), and did his greatest work in India in establishing "The Church of the East." "The Church of the East" is also referred to as the Assyrian Church, Nestorian Church, Chaldean Syrian Church. Thomas died a martyr's death in India. He was buried in Mylapore, India. His influence in that part of the world has been documented in many books. One work is "The Traditions of the St. Thomas Christians," by A.M. Mundadan, who wrote this as his doctoral dissertation in 1960 at a German University.)

YOUR NEXT ASSIGNMENT:
1. Read John 1:40-42; Matthew 4:18-25; Matthew 16:13-23; Matthew 26:69-75; John 20:1-8; John 21:1-22; Matthew 28:16-20; Acts 1 through 12 and 15; I and II Peter.
2. The next lesson will be a study of the Apostle Peter.
3. Review your lesson on Thomas.
4. Mark your Bible where new truths are learned.

Lesson 44
"Simon Peter"

GREAT
CHARACTERS
OF THE
BIBLE

(Where lines are provided, look up the Scripture and write it or its meaning in the space provided.)

NOTES

1. **THE MEANING OF THE NAME:**

   Simon, his natural name, means "hearing."

   Peter, his new name given by Christ, meaning "stone," which is the Greek form of the Aramaic name,

   Cephas, Cephas is the Hebrew word for "stone." The Greek equivalent is "Petros," translated Peter in our Bible.

2. **BASIC SCRIPTURES:**

   John 1:40-42; Matthew 4:18-31; Matthew 16:13-23; Matthew 26:69-75; John 20:1-8; John 21:1-22; Matthew 28:16-20; Acts 1 through 12 and 15; I and II Peter.

3. **FAMILY BACKGROUND:**

   Simon was the son of Jona (John). He and his brother, Andrew, were fishermen on the Sea of Galilee (Matthew 4:18). They were in partnership with James and John, the sons of Zebedee (Luke 5:10). He was a native of Bethsaida, which means "the house of fishing" (John 1:44). Later he lived in his own house at Capernaum (Matthew 8:5 and 14). From verse 14, you know that Simon Peter was married. One can see the site of Peter's house in Capernaum even today. Jesus frequently stayed with Simon Peter during His Galilean ministry.

4. **WHAT THE NEW TESTAMENT SAYS ABOUT SIMON PETER:**

   (1) Simon Peter Was Won To Christ By His Brother, Andrew (John 1:40-42).

   (a) Andrew and another disciple of John the Baptist, who is not named, heard John the Baptist declare, "Behold the Lamb of God." They were looking upon Jesus at the time and heard Jesus speak and they followed Jesus. John had prepared them for the Messiah. They went with Jesus, at His invitation, and spent time with Him where He dwelled (John 1:35-39).

   (b) Andrew went to find his brother, Simon (John 1:41).

   After spending six to eight hours with Jesus, Andrew had to tell the good news. Note John 1:41 _____

   _____

   In the next verse, the first sentence is a lesson for all. In verse 42, "And he brought him to Jesus."

   These were Jesus' first followers.

   (2) Jesus Gave Simon Another Name (John 1:42).

   (a) At the first meeting of Jesus and Simon, Jesus looked at him and saw in Simon something only He could see. Jesus called Simon by name, then gave him another name. Notice verse 42, "Thou art Simon, thou shalt be called *Cephas* (Peter)."

   (b) Why did Jesus give him another name? Simon was his name by his first birth. It was his first name. He was Simon, a son of a man, with his father's nature, carnal, sinful.

   Jesus said, "Thou shall be called Cephas (Peter)." This was the new name for a new man. It was a promise, but *not* until the public declaration of faith in Matthew 16 do we see the promise come to pass.

(3) Simon Peter's Confession (Matthew 16:16-18).

    (a)   Simon Peter confessed Christ in Matthew 16:16 _____

    _____

    (b)   Jesus then stated, in the present tense, "Blessed art thou, Simon Barjona (son of John): for flesh and blood hath not revealed it unto thee, but my Father which is in heaven. And I say also unto thee, That *thou art* Peter." (Matthew 16:17-18a). (Notice, present tense.)

    (c)   Jesus reminded him that he was still Simon. His confession of Jesus was not a result of his own reasoning as Simon, but was a revelation of the Father in heaven. "Flesh and blood" revealed nothing. In other words, the old nature — Simon — had nothing to do with his confession but was a supernatural gift of God.

    (d)   Applying this in a practical way, Jesus said to Simon, in essence, "by your first birth, you were flesh and blood, a son of Adam. Now, by faith in Me, you have become a son of God, a child of my Father. While your name is still Simon, your new name is now Peter and now you are two men, Simon, the natural and sinful man, and Peter, the spiritual man. Now, Simon Peter you have two natures, the old and the new. The battle is on between the flesh and the spirit and there can be no compromise."

    (e)   Peter never got rid of the old Simon, but thank God, Simon never ceased to be Peter, the new man. Throughout the record, his name remains Simon Peter. Sometimes we see the old nature, Simon; and then again, we see the new nature, Peter, most evident.

    (**Note:** We have placed the confession of Simon Peter here so one can see the importance and meaning of the names.)

(4) Simon Peter Called To Be A Disciple and Apostle (Matthew 4:18-20; Matthew 10:2).

    (a)   Simon Peter became a disciple (learner, follower) of Jesus. Notice Matthew 4:18 and underline. Write in verse 19 _____

    _____

    (b)   He was one of the twelve apostles. Look at Matthew 10:2 and underline the verse in your Bible.

        Remember an apostle was "one sent forth" and chosen by the Lord. An apostle was one who saw Jesus and was an eye witness of the resurrection.

    (c)   He is always named first in the lists of the apostles (Matthew 10:2; Mark 3:16; Luke 6:14).

    (d)   In the more intimate circle of the three most favored disciples, he is also named first. It is always Peter, James and John (Matthew 17:1; Mark 5:37; Mark 9:2; Mark 13:3; Mark 14:33; Luke 8:51; Luke 9:28). Look up these Scriptures in your Bible.

(5) The First Mention of the Church Was To Simon Peter (Matthew 16:18).

    (a)   After Jesus said, "Thou art Peter" (present tense), He then said, "and upon this rock I will build my church." This is the first mention of the church in all Scripture.

    (b)   Jesus did not mean that the church was to be built on Simon Peter. His name, given to him by Jesus, was Peter. The name in the Greek is "Petros," and means a "little rock or stone." The word "rock," in verse 18, is "Petra" in the Greek and means "a mighty rock." Jesus founded the Church, the "ecclesia," "the called out ones," on Himself, the Rock of our salvation.

(c) The church was established on Christ and verse 18 should read, when translated: "Thou are Petros (a little stone) and upon this Petra (a mighty rock, i.e. Christ), I will build my church."

There are many Scriptures to confirm the truth of that verse. In I Corinthians 10:4 Paul says, "That Rock was Christ." In I Corinthians 3:9-11 Paul affirms that Jesus is the foundation. Write in verse 11 _____

_____

Ephesians 2:20 _____

_____

Peter knew very well that he was not the rock upon which the Church was to be built. In I Peter 2:1-6, he said the church was to be built on Jesus Christ. Underline I Peter 2:5-6.

(6) Jesus Gave To Simon Peter The Keys of the Kingdom (Matthew 16:19).

(a) There were at least three keys committed to Peter. (These were not the keys of the church but of the Kingdom of Heaven.)

(b) First, the key that opened the door to the Jew (Acts 2).

The first use of the keys was at Pentecost. Peter was God's vessel to present the Gospel first to the Jewish nation. This was according to God's divine order, which was "beginning at Jerusalem" (Acts 1:8; Luke 24:47).

(c) The second use of the keys was to open the door to Samaria (Acts 8:4-25). Following the death of Stephen and the persecution which followed, Philip, the preaching deacon, went to Samaria and witnessed a great revival. In Acts 8:14 note ___

_____

Peter had the key to open the door as he had at Pentecost. The believers were indwelt with the Holy Spirit. Underline Acts 8:25.

(d) The third use of the keys of the Kingdom was to open the door of the Gospel to the Gentiles (Acts 10).

In Acts 7, Israel rejected the final message of Christ through Stephen. In Acts 8, the message went to Samaria. In Acts 9, Saul (Paul), was converted to prepare him for his ministry unto the "uttermost part of the earth."

In Acts 10, Peter was a Jew and made a strong objection to the Lord concerning going to "the unclean" Gentiles. Read Acts 10:14-15.

A Gentile, Cornelius, sent for Peter to come to Caesarea and present the Gospel to them. Peter was addressed by the Holy Spirit in Acts 10:20 _____

_____

The results of Peter's preaching is found in Acts 10:44-45.

(e) Peter had fulfilled his mission in opening the doors to Jerusalem, Samaria, and Caesarea. The message changed. No longer was the message only to the Jew, "repent ye for the kingdom of heaven is at hand." The new message was a message of grace and of the Holy Spirit indwelling all who believe. The new message said, and still says, "believe on the Lord Jesus Christ and thou shalt be saved."

(7) **Simon Peter's Last Acts (Acts 15:7-10; I and II Peter).**

    (a) Simon Peter will always be known as the "big fisherman." Neither time nor space will allow all about this man; but for excitement, turn to Luke 5:1-11. In this passage we see the natural man, Simon. Jesus was with him. Notice Jesus was on "Simon's ship," verse 3; "said unto Simon," verse 4; "Simon answering," verse 5. Luke called him Simon Peter, in verse 8, upon his confession. Jesus said, "Fear not; from henceforth thou shalt catch men" (verse 10). Jesus called him Simon, his natural name, because he was acting as a natural man.

    (b) After the Gospel was opened to the Gentiles, Peter spoke one more time in Jerusalem, at the famous Jerusalem Council (Acts 15:7-10). Underline verses 7 and 10.

    (c) Peter wrote his two epistles from Gentile territory. They were written after Peter's great ministry in opening the Gospel to all people.

    I Peter was written to comfort and to build up the saints during a time of suffering and persecution. It is a jewel for us to read for endurance and patience.

    II Peter was Peter's "swan song." It was written to warn against apostasy, false teachers.

    Peter is known as the "apostle of hope." In his two small books he gives foundational truths for the Christian life. Read both I and II Peter.

    (d) Peter died as Jesus had indicated in John 21:19. Where or when is not stated. Jesus had indicated he would be crucified. Legend tells us that he did not feel worthy to die as Jesus, and so begged his crucifiers to crucify him head down.

6. **THE USE OF THE OLD TESTAMENT IN REFERENCE TO SIMON PETER:**

(1) John 1:39 is a reference to Psalm 27:8 _____

_____

(2) Matthew 16:19 is a reference to Isaiah 22:22 _____

_____

(3) Acts 2:16-18 is a part of Peter's sermon on the day of Pentecost and refers to Joel 2:28-29. Look up and underline.

(4) Acts 2:25 is a reference to Psalm 16:8 _____

_____

(5) Acts 10:14 is a reference to Ezekiel 4:14 _____

_____

(6) Acts 10:34 is a reference to Deuteronomy 10:17. Underline in your Bible.

(7) Acts 10:44-45 is a reference to Psalm 68:18 _____

_____

(8) I Peter 2:4 is a reference to Psalm 118:22 _____

_____

(9) I Peter 2:6 is a reference to Isaiah 28:16. Underline, please.

(10) II Peter 2:15 is a reference to Numbers 22:5. Underline, please.

    All of the teaching of Simon Peter had its root in the Old Testament, and what Jesus taught him. The references are innumerable.

6. *THE LESSONS WE SHOULD LEARN FROM SIMON PETER:*

(1) All of us can simply tell others that we have met the Lord Jesus Christ and have accepted Him. Simon Peter was won to Christ by

his brother Andrew.

(2) When we accept Jesus Christ, we become "new creatures in Christ." Simon, the natural man, became Peter, the spiritual man.

(3) Simon Peter teaches us that we have two natures if we are Christians: the natural, sinful, Adamic nature and the spiritual, regenerated nature.

(4) The church is not built upon Peter or any other apostle. The Rock, Jesus, is the foundation of the church. Peter was a small stone (as he said in his own writing) among the "living stones being built up a spiritual house."

(5) Simon Peter had the keys of the kingdom and opened the Gospel to all, even to us in our generation. The Jew, the Samaritan, and the Gentile received the Word, in that order.

(6) The new message of hope, which we accept casually, was a remarkable revelation. The new message caused phenominal growth in the church at Jerusalem. The same message still causes people to accept Christ if we faithfully teach, preach and live accordingly.

DO YOU REMEMBER?

1. What is the significance of the following: Simon? Cephas? Peter?
2. Who was Simon Peter associated with in the fishing business?
3. Simon Peter presents two sides of a man. Name them.
4. When did Jesus apply the name, Peter?
5. Simon Peter was a disciple and an apostle. What is the difference?
6. What impression did Simon Peter make on you?

YOUR NEXT ASSIGNMENT:

1. Read Acts 6:5; Acts 8; Acts 21:8.
2. The next lesson will be on the *layman,* Philip, one of the seven Deacons; not the *apostle* Philip.
3. Review your lesson on Simon Peter.
4. Mark your Bible where new truths are learned.

Note: The lesson on Simon Peter did not, and could not, cover all areas of his life. The denial of Christ was left out because he is best remembered for his bad traits. Uniquely his ministry of opening the doors of the Gospel was his, yet this is seldom covered in a Bible lesson.)

Lesson 45
"Philip, the Layman, Deacon, Evangelist"

(Where lines are provided, look up the Scripture and write it or its meaning in the space provided.)

1. **THE MEANING OF THE NAME:**

   Philip means "warrior" or "lover of horses."

2. **BASIC SCRIPTURES:**

   Acts 6:5; Acts 8; Acts 21:8.

3. **FAMILY BACKGROUND:**

   Philip, the layman, deacon and evangelist was named one of the seven to help the apostles in the administration of the church. Nothing is written in Scripture about his background or family. The Scriptural account does give the qualities of the seven selected. He, therefore, had a good reputation among the people. The seven men selected were all Grecian, or Hellenistic Jews, Greek speaking Jews. The reason for the selection was the trouble in the church between the Greek-speaking Jews and the Aramaic-speaking Jews. To solve the problem, the twelve apostles let the people select the men. In nearly every commentary, these seven are called "deacons" which means "a servant, a messenger." Philip was named second, the first was Stephen.

4. **WHAT THE NEW TESTAMENT SAYS ABOUT PHILIP:**

   (1) Philip Was Named As One of the Seven Deacons (Acts 6:1-7).

   (a) Because of the trouble in the church, the apostles needed help. There arose a murmuring of the Grecian Jewish believers who were born outside of Palestine, and the Hebrews, the Aramaic speaking Jewish believers of Palestine (Acts 6:1).

   (b) The apostles saw the potential harm in such division. They called together the multitude of believers and placed the problem before them. Notice Acts 6:2 _____

   _____

   The calling of the apostles was to preach the Word of God and pray. They were not to leave the Word and "serve tables." Matthew Henry says, "the seven, whose business it should be to serve tables" (in the original, "to be deacons to the tables").

   (c) The apostles stated the qualifications of the seven to be selected by the people (Acts 6:3).

   The people were to nominate the seven, "look ye out among you seven men." The seven were to possess three qualities:

   1. *"of honest report,"* men free from scandal.
   2. *"full of the Holy Ghost,"* filled with the Holy Spirit.
   3. *"full of wisdom,"* have the wisdom of the Spirit.

   The apostles were to appoint the seven selected, to care for the problems of the church. They would then be free to give themselves to what God had called them to do as apostles.

Write in Acts 6:4 _____

_____

    (d) The seven were selected by the people, all seven being Hellenists, Greek-speaking Jewish believers. The seven were named and Philip was placed second. Notice verse 5.

        The people presented the seven to the apostles. Look at verse 6: _____

_____

        The apostles prayed and ordained the seven. The principle here is a good one for the church today. The first contention in the Christian church was about a money matter. One group was receiving more than another group. The problem, placed before the people, was solved with the selection of Godly men to assist the apostles. The twelve could then pray and study the Word and proclaim the truths of God. The pastors today need the same assistance.

    (e) Look at the result of the action in verse 7: _____

_____

(2) Philip Was One In The Church That Was Scattered Abroad (Acts 8:1-4).

    (a) Because of the death, martyrdom, of Stephen, the church at Jerusalem was scattered abroad. Look up Acts 11:19 and underline the first part of the verse.

    (b) Great persecution against the church scattered the believers throughout Judea and Samaria, *except the apostles* (Acts 8:1).

        Write in Acts 8:4 _____

_____

        The apostles continued to stay in Jerusalem that they might be ready to help where they were needed, as in Acts 10:23-35.

(3) Philip Went To Samaria and Preached Christ (Acts 8:5).

    (a) All that were scattered preached the Word and Philip went down to the Samaritans to preach Christ (verse 5). Out of martyrdom, trouble and persecution the Gospel began to spread. The Samaritans were of mixed blood, half-Jewish.

    (b) The Greek-speaking Jews were the ones scattered. The Samaritans looked with contempt and hatred on the Jew. The high priest in Jerusalem had no jurisdiction in Samaria. When Philip went to Samaria, he had an opportunity to preach Christ to them. He was an Hellenistic Jew and more acceptable to the Samaritans.

    (c) Philip was successful, too, because of the previous ministry of Jesus in Samaria. Look up John 4:4 _____

_____

        There, Jesus spoke to the Samaritan woman at Jacob's well. As a result, many heard her testimony and believed. Read John 4:39.

(4) Signs of God Confirmed the Truth of the Word (Acts 8:6-8).

    (a) In verse 6, the word "miracle" should be "signs." There were signs of God confirming the truth Philip preached.

    (b) Philip was there to break the power of Satan. Look at verse 6:

_____

        Look at that verse. It says, "seeing and hearing the signs which he did." One does not hear a sign. In verse 7, "For unclean spirits, crying with a loud voice, came out of many."

The word for crying, "boao," can mean "a cry of agony," but the first meaning is "a shout of joy and deliverance." "With a loud voice" in Greek is "megale," "a great, intense" voice. So Philip was preaching Christ to those who were possessed with unclean spirits, such as lust, hatred, idolatry; and as they were delivered they shouted their joy of salvation. That is why the phrase was written "the people *heard* the signs." They were saved, delivered from old habits and Satan's hold was broken.

(c) Physical healings authenticated Philip's ministry. He was probably more popular for healing the lame and palsied than for healing the sin sick souls of the multitude. God always authenticated His work during the days of the apostles. All healing was, and is, divine healing, whether it be through prayer, medicine, proper care, doctors or any other method. All of these are only "helps" to the body because God ultimately does the healing.

(d) "And there was great joy in that city" (verse 8).

Dr. W.A. Criswell says in his book *Sermons on Acts*, "There is a little family of words in the Greek New Testament that are similar: kara meaning "Joy;" karis, "grace;" karisma, "a grace gift;" "karismata," the plural form. One of the meanings of *kara* is "an exalted gladness in the Lord." One of the meanings of *karis*, "grace," is "a beautiful spirit and attitude," or "a marvelous overflowing heart." And there was *megale*, "intense joy (gladness of deliverance and salvation) in that city" (verse 8). The whole story is one of heavenly intervention and revival."

(5) Philip's Ministry Paved the Way for the Apostles (Acts 8:14-17).

(a) If you recall the lesson on Simon Peter, this will reaffirm the teaching on the use of the keys of the kingdom. God always does His work according to a purpose and plan. The Book of Acts is an introduction to a new era. It is an account of transition from the Jew to the Gentile, from Judaism to Christianity, from Judea to the uttermost parts of the earth, from law to grace.

In Matthew 16:18-19; you find the pattern of God. In Matthew 18:18 the apostles were told the same thing about "binding and loosing." (See note at the end of this lesson.)

In Acts 1:8, the Lord gave direction on the progression of their work. He said, "You are to be witnesses unto me *both* in Jerusalem and Judea, and in Samaria." The "both" refers to the ethnic group of the Jew. Jerusalem and Judea are as one. The Jew was to be first, then Samaria.

(b) When Philip preached, he preached Christ and the people believed. It was only when Simon Peter and John went down to Samaria, sent by the apostles, that the Samaritans received the Holy Spirit. This was the second use of the keys of the kingdom. Underline Acts 8:15-16 and write in verse 17: ___

_____

Then write in verse 25: _____

_____

(6) Philip Preached Jesus to the Ethiopian (Acts 8:26-40).

(a) Philip was directed by an angel of the Lord. He was to leave Jerusalem and go to Gaza, in the desert. Notice the call in verse 26.

(b) "He arose and went." Philip obeyed the call of God. Write in verse 27: _____

201

The man was an Ethiopian eunuch with great authority, a Chancellor, a treasurer in the government of Candice, the queen.

(c) He had been to Jerusalem to worship. On his return home, he read from Isaiah 53. Philip was there to interpret the Scripture. Write in verse 35: _____

_____

(d) Philip baptized the Ethiopian which indicated complete obedience and a public profession of faith in Christ. Read verse 36. Now, underline verse 37. The prerequisite for baptism is faith, trust and belief on the Lord Jesus Christ. Verse 37 says exactly that in reference to baptism.

(e) The Lord caught away Philip and there remained the new Christian, holding the Old Testament in his hands. The miraculous taking of Philip was a confirmation of the power of God to the eunuch. "the eunuch saw him no more: and he went on his way rejoicing" (verse 39).

(7) Philip Preached In All the Cities Until He Reached Caesarea (Acts 8:40).

(a) Philip was at Azotus, which is "Ashdod" in our day. This was about thirty miles from where he had left the eunuch.

(b) He preached all the way home. In every city he told them about Jesus. Finally, he reached Caesarea.

(c) Paul visited in Philip's home (Acts 21:8). Look up Acts 21:8-9 and underline. The place was Caesarea by the Sea and not Caesarea Philippi.

(d) This is the last reference to the faithful deacon, evangelist, Philip. What a testimony of a layman.

5. **THE USE OF THE OLD TESTAMENT IN REFERENCE TO PHILIP:**
   (1) Acts 6:3 is the teaching of Exodus 18:21. Underline verse 21.
   (2) Acts 8:27 — compare with Psalm 68:31.
   (3) Acts 8:32-33 is a reference to Isaiah 53:7-8. Write in Isaiah 53:7

   _____

   (4) Acts 8:39 compare — with II Kings 2:11 and underline in your Bible.
   (5) Also compare Acts 8:39 to Ezekiel 8:3.

6. **THE LESSONS YOU SHOULD LEARN FROM PHILIP:**
   (1) God can use a person who yields his life and will to the Lord.
   (2) The pastor of a church should not be involved in mundane things. Protect him, in order that he may study, pray and preach.
   (3) We should never select church leaders because of *who* they are but because of *what* they are, in their heart and soul.
   (4) A deacon, or officer of the church, can preach and should be "apt to teach." Philip was a good lay evangelist.
   (5) When the Holy Spirit guides us, as with Philip, do we respond to such instructions as "Arise, go?" We seldom see that response. The mission field suffers because we do not respond.
   (6) The Gospel can be shared anywhere, anytime, even in a desert. Satan makes sure that we just *delay* telling someone about Christ.

DO YOU REMEMBER?

1. What were the three qualifications for the seven?
2. Why did the apostles let the people select the seven?
3. When persecution came to the church, did it help or hurt the work of the Lord?

4. What made Philip acceptable to the Samaritans?
5. How did Philip leave the Ethiopian?
6. Did Philip have a family? How do you know?

YOUR NEXT ASSIGNMENT:
1. Read Acts 6:5-15; Acts 7; Acts 8:1-3; Acts 11:19; Acts 20:20.
2. Our next study will be the first Christian martyr, one of the seven, Stephen.
3. Review your study of Philip.
4. Mark your Bible where new truths are learned.

(**Note:** The subject of "binding and loosing" found in Matthew 16:18-19 and in Matthew 18:18 is very confusing to some students. To shed some light, read John 20:21-23. The exhortation was not given to Peter alone but to the apostles and to the church. The context of Matthew 18:15-18 shows the church involvement.

What does the "binding and loosing" mean? When the apostles or pastors of today preach the Gospel, they become the means for the remission of sins to those who believe, and the retaining of sins to those who reject the message of Jesus. Paul clarifies the matter in II Corinthians 2:15-16. Look up this passage and understand it.)

Lesson 46
"Stephen, the First Christian Martyr"

(Where lines are provided, look up the Scripture and write it or its meaning in the space provided.)

1. **THE MEANING OF THE NAME:**

   Stephen means "a crown."

2. **BASIC SCRIPTURES:**

   Acts 6:5-15; Acts 7; Acts 8:1-3; Acts 11:19; Acts 20:20.

3. **FAMILY BACKGROUND:**

   Stephen was one of the seven selected by the people to assist the apostles. The Scriptures give nothing concerning his family background, but we can be assured of his character from the Biblical account given in the Book of Acts.

   Stephen was a *Hellenist,* a Greek-speaking Jew. He was a different type of man. The apostles were Galileans, and were crude, uneducated men. Stephen was a man of culture and great reputation. Stephen was not an apostle: he was not a pastor, nor an ordained minister. He was a layman and a deacon, or "servant." The account of his defense of the Gospel shows the power of a layman used of God. He was responsible in his testimony and death for the spreading of the Gospel to the Samaritans and the Gentiles.

4. **WHAT THE NEW TESTAMENT SAYS ABOUT STEPHEN:**

   (1) He Was a Man Full of Faith and the Holy Spirit and Power (Acts 6:5; Acts 6:8).

   Stephen was the first of the seven selected. The Bible says, "Stephen, a man full of faith and of the Holy Ghost." He was a man of strong faith and such faith produced power. Notice Acts 6:8 and you see, "full of faith *and* power." By his faith, the power of God was given to him and he did great wonders and miracles just as Philip had done. This caused a great disturbance among the Greek-speaking Jews in Jerusalem.

   (2) Stephen Before the Sanhedrin (Acts 6:9-14).

   (a) Stephen spoke to his opponents in the synagogue of the Cilicians. (Saul (Paul) was from Tarsus, the capital city of the Roman province of Cilicia. The Jews from other countries had their own synagogues in Jerusalem.) In the synagogue of the Cilicians, Stephen stood and proclaimed the message of Jesus Christ. The teachers and leaders of the synagogue disputed with Stephen (verse 9).

   (b) Stephen was a scholar and the Jewish leaders could not support their own argument nor answer him because of his wisdom and spirit. Look at verse 10: _____

   _____

   (c) Those disputing Stephen and his message could not match the power of God in him. They hired witnesses to swear that Stephen had spoken against Moses and God (verse 11).

   (d) The hired witnesses and the ones disputing Stephen stirred up

205

the people, the elders, the scribes; and they took him before the council, which is the Sanhedrin (verse 12).

The charges were false, as you read in verses 13 and 14.

(3) Stephen's Countenance and His Defense of the Gospel (Acts 6:15-7:50).

(a) The false accusations against Stephen brought the power and presence of God to him. Write in Acts 6:15 _____

_____

They said he had spoken blasphemous words against Moses, but God intervened and made Stephen's face appear as the face of an angel, as the face of Moses as he came out of the holy mount. With this startling sight to behold, the Sanhedrin had to ask Stephen about the charges (Acts 7:1).

(b) One question of the high priest, "Are these things so?," brought a masterpiece from the lips of Stephen. He had not *created* the confrontation between Judaism and Christianity. But the conflict was inevitable. Stephen sounded the keynote of foundational Christian freedom.

(c) Stephen's defense covered the entire history of God's dealings with the Jewish race. Notice the broad outline:

- God's early choice and guidance of the patriarchs (Acts 7:2-22). Stephen brought that out from the beginning. God had been leading Israel to a definite goal which would come from the seed of Abraham.

- He spoke of the repeated resistance of Israel toward God and His purpose from the days of Moses. (Acts 7:23-43).

Notice verse 37: _____

_____

That verse refers to Jesus Christ!

- **Israel failed to see the temporary and typical character of both the tabernacle and the temple (Acts 7:44-50).**

Write in verse 49: _____

_____

This is a quote from Isaiah 66:1-2.

(4) Stephen's Allegation and Accusation (Acts 7:51-53).

(a) What courage! Stephen said (and I paraphrase), "You make much of the rite of circumcision given to Abraham, but you are uncircumcised in heart and soul and you resist the Holy Spirit: as your fathers did, so you do the same" (verse 51).

(b) "You have slain the Just One, Jesus, as your fathers have slain the prophets" (verse 52).

(c) "Your fathers received the law, ordained by angels (Galatians 3:19), and you have not kept, nor do you intend to keep, the law" (verse 53).

(d) The rebuke was sharp and cutting. He had testified as a Christian should testify, fearlessly, boldly, courageously.

(e) Stephen spoke in his sermon of the temporary character of all Jewish worship. The Jew, who refused the Messiah, believed that the institutions and rituals given to them by Moses were eternal — nothing would change. Stephen preached that all are in need of forgiveness in Jesus Christ, Jew and Gentile. Jesus once addressed the same people in Matthew 23:27 ___

_____

(5) Stephen Was Martyred Because of His Faith (Acts 7:54-60).

(a) The anger of the audience was bitter and they appeared outra-

206

geous. They looked as a group of mad dogs, showing their teeth in anger (verse 54).

(b) Stephen saw something altogether different (verse 55). As he stood in front of that mad crowd, Stephen looked up toward heaven and he saw heaven open. Write in verse 55: _____

_____

This is the only place in the Bible where the Ascended Lord stands. Everywhere else in Scripture He is seated at the right hand of God. The Lord Jesus stood to receive His first martyr. He stood in honor of a layman, not an apostle, or some notable person; just a layman filled with the Spirit.

(c) Stephen told the Sanhedrin what he saw in glory (verse 56). He voiced, so that all could hear, what he saw (verse 55).

(d) The crowd reaction was total anger. They could not bear to hear more from the Christian layman. Notice verse 57-58 __

_____

So great was their anger, they did not consult any authority, not even the Roman governor. They seized Stephen, took him out of the city, and as was the custom in Jewish executions, went through what is *now* called St. Stephen's Gate on the east side to the Kidron Valley. There, they hurled him down from the height of about twelve feet, casting two great stones upon him. Then the crowd had their chance to pick up rocks and stone the criminal. That was custom, and it was the way Stephen died.

(e) Criminals were given a chance to confess their crime before being cast down in the Kidron Valley. As they paused for Stephen's confession, they heard his statement in verse 59 _

_____

The witnesses, the ones who had lied and accused him, placed their garments at the feet of a young man, Saul. **Don't forget this fact.**

(f) Stephen's last words were words of testimony and conviction. Look at verse 60 _____

_____

He prayed for his killers and "fell asleep." To "fall asleep" is the Christian way of describing the physical death of a Christian. We fall asleep in Jesus, as did Stephen.

(6) Stephen's Influence Will Never Die (Acts 8:1, 3; 22:19-20).

(a) Attending the murder of Stephen was a young man named Saul. Look back at Acts 7:58. Now look at Acts 8:1 _____

_____

(Write in only the first part of the verse.)

(b) Acts 8:3 indicates that this Saul was the leader in the persecution of the church. But a strange thing happened as a result of Stephen's death. Saul had consented to his death and the Holy Spirit convicted him. Everytime he was alone the appeal of Stephen was in his thoughts. In the very next Chapter, Acts 9, Jesus said to Saul in verse 5: "It is hard for you to get rid of your conscience, your conviction."

(c) Saul never saw a man die as Stephen died. In Acts 22:19-20, Paul recounted his conversion. Notice his words about Stephen. Underline verses 19-20.

(d) Stephen was buried and great sorrow came upon those who loved him. Look at Acts 8:2 _____

From his life and testimony, the Gospel was preached to the Samaritans and the Gentiles. Because of Stephen's death and his testimony, Saul (Paul) believed and became an apostle, the great preacher and writer of the Pauline epistles of the New Testament.

5. **THE USE OF THE OLD TESTAMENT IN REFERENCE TO STEPHEN:**

   (1) Compare Acts 6:8 with Micah 3:8.

   (2) Acts 6:15 looks back to Exodus 34:30 _____

   (3) Acts 7:3 refers back to Genesis 12:1 _____

   _____

   (4) Acts 7:2-50 can be traced back to the Old Testament.

   (5) Acts 7:33 refers back to Exodus 3:5 and Joshua 5:15. Write in Joshua 5:15 _____

   _____

   (6) Acts 7:37 refers to Deuteronomy 18:15 _____

   _____

   and also Deuteronomy 8:18. Underline in your Bible.

   (7) Acts 7:49 refers to Isaiah 66:1-2. Write in the main thought in Isaiah: _____

   _____

6. **THE LESSONS YOU SHOULD LEARN FROM STEPHEN:**

   (1) A man full of faith has power with God and people. Stephen was a perfect example.

   (2) To know the Word of God brings conviction to even the "religious." Stephen knew the Word well, as indicated in Acts 7.

   (3) A layman martyred caused the Gospel to spread. We have Paul's writings today because of the faithful testimony of Stephen.

   (4) We should never fear criticism or even persecution for Christ. Criticism is a sure sign of success in the work of the Lord.

   (5) A person does not die when he dies. The influence lives on. Stephen is still living today in us, in the Word, in millions who have read the account of his faith in the Word of God.

   (6) A layman — not an apostle, nor pope, nor preacher — but a layman was the first Christian martyr. Jesus stood to receive him. What a great honor. Jesus placed importance upon the work of the lay people.

DO YOU REMEMBER?

1. What is a Hellenist?
2. What was unique about Stephen?
3. What made the leaders of the synagogue so mad?
4. Was Stephen like the apostles?
5. How did the Lord show His approval of Stephen?
6. What is your impression of Stephen now? Write your own impressions.

YOUR NEXT ASSIGNMENT:

1. Read Acts 9 through 28; Romans 7:15-25; II Corinthians 4; Galatians 1:10-24; Galatians 3; Ephesians 4. If you have limited reading time, by all means read the assignment in the Acts.

2. The next study will be on Paul, the apostle.

3. Review your notes on Stephen.

4. Mark your Bible where new truths are learned.

Lesson 47
"Paul, the Apostle"

Apostle"

(Where lines are provided, look up the Scripture and write it or the main truth of the Scripture.)

GREAT CHARACTERS OF THE BIBLE

NOTES

1   **THE MEANING OF THE NAME:**

Paul means "little," "small" (his Gentile name).

Saul means "asked for," "demanded" (his Jewish name).

2. **BASIC SCRIPTURES:**

Acts 9 through 28; Romans 7:15-25; II Corinthians 4; Galatians 1:10-24; Galatians 3; Ephesians 4; II Timothy 4.

3. **FAMILY BACKGROUND:**

Saul was his Jewish name. He went by that name until Acts 13:9; and there he is called Paul. Some think it was because of the conversion of Sergius Paulus, the Roman Proconsul of the Roman province of Cyprus. It is more probable that he had both names all along, like most Jews. Luke introduced his Gentile name, Paul, when his work among the Gentiles began and this is the important fact to remember about the name change.

Paul was a Hellenist, a Greek-speaking Jew. He was born in Tarsus, the capital city of Cilicia (Acts 21:39). He was of the tribe of Benjamin (Philippians 3:5). He was brought up in the strict observance of the Hebrew faith. He was a Pharisee and the son of a Pharisee (Acts 23:6). He was born a Roman citizen, and this became important in the work of the Lord (Acts 22:25-30).

Paul was sent to Jerusalem at an early age and went to school there under one of the most learned and distinguished teachers, *Gamaliel*. He was taught according to the strict manner of the law of the fathers (Acts 22:3). Gamaliel was famous for his rabbinical learning. He was a Pharisee, who understood some of the Greek culture and was ideal as the teacher of young Paul. He grew up as an ardent Pharisee who believed in the resurrection, angels, and other fundamentals of the faith. Pharisaism became something altogether different over the years. It became a religion which was external. The Pharisees made changes and added to what Moses had written and the changes became "tradition," which our Lord rebuked (Matthew 15:1-7).

Young Saul had an unusual background. He was a Roman citizen, a Jew, of the tribe of Benjamin, a Pharisee. He had strict religious training in Jerusalem and was circumcised as a part of the covenant relation. He was a tentmaker by trade. His background had a profound influence upon his later life.

4. **WHAT THE NEW TESTAMENT SAYS ABOUT PAUL:**

(Author's note: To cover such a vast subject in one lesson would be like pouring an ocean into a glass. We shall cover the highpoints in Paul's life, with the hope that you will make a personal in-depth study of Paul.)

(1) Paul First Appears in Scripture at Stephen's Death (Acts 7:58; 8:1-3).

(a) He was present at the stoning of Stephen (Acts 7:58). He consented to his death and watched Stephen die (Acts 7:59 through 8:1). To him, Stephen was a bitter enemy of the Judaistic faith. Paul, in his mind, thought the martyrdom of Stephen was right. In his heart, he knew that he had never seen a man die like Stephen had died. He had died praying for God to forgive the ones who killed him. That stayed in Paul's mind and conscience.

(b) He was the chief persecutor of the church (Acts 8:1, 3).

Paul thought it his duty to persecute the Christians. Write in Acts 8:3 _____

_____

Now, underline Acts 26:9-11. Paul's own words.

(2) The Conversion of Paul, A Believer in Jesus (Acts 9:3-19).

(a) Paul, on his way to Damascus to punish Christians, saw a great light from heaven and he fell to the ground. Then he heard a voice calling him by name, "Saul, Saul, why persecutest thou me" (verse 4).

Jesus identified Himself in verse 5 and said, "I am Jesus whom you persecute: it is hard for you to kick against your conscience." The thing Paul had seen in the death of Stephen and other Christians got into his soul, and he was convicted by *their* faith in death. That was what Jesus referred to in verse 5.

(b) The turning point in his life is found in Acts 9:6. "Lord, what wilt Thou have me to do?" He finally broke. He became a different man. He actually trembled. His helpers were there.

The Lord told him to go to Damascus and there he would receive instructions.

(c) He was blinded for three days. Neither did he eat (verse 9).

(d) The Lord sent Ananias to Paul. He obeyed and Paul was healed, baptized and filled with the Spirit of God (verses 10-19). Note especially verse 15: _____

_____

Paul restated his conversion experience in Acts 22:1-16 and in Acts 26:9-18. Read all three accounts.

(3) Paul Began His Ministry as an Apostle (Acts 9:15; I Corinthians 15:8-9).

(a) He immediately started to preach in Damascus. He was so successful, the Jews tried to kill him but his followers let him down a wall in a basket and he escaped (Acts 9:20-25).

Notice Acts 9:20 _____

_____

(b) He was an apostle because he had seen Christ (I Corinthians 15:8-9). Paul was an apostle "born out of due time." Write in verse 9 _____

_____

(c) Instead of going to Jerusalem, he went to Arabia and back to Damascus (Galatians 1:17).

After his return to Damascus, he went up to Jerusalem to see Peter and stayed fifteen days (Galatians 1:18; Acts 9:26-29). The Christians in Jerusalem were afraid of him because of his former life. Barnabas believed Paul and took him to the apostles, Peter and James, and told them of Paul's conversion. Paul then preached to his old friends, the Greek-speaking Jews in Jerusalem. The account in Galatians 1 and Acts 9 must be compared to see the events in order.

(4) The Purpose of God was Revealed to Paul (Acts 22:17-21; Acts 11:19-26).

(a) Paul, while in Jerusalem, had a vision from the Lord, telling him that his mission would be to the Gentiles (Acts 22:17-21). Notice, he refers to the death of Stephen in verse 20.

210

Then in verse 21, his mission: _____

_____

(b) That mission began when the Jerusalem church sent Barnabas to Antioch. Those that had been scattered, after the death of Stephen, began to preach. Help was needed in Antioch. Barnabas left and went to Tarsus to find Paul. They went to Antioch and preached and taught one year (Acts 11:19-26). Notice the last sentence of verse 26: "And the disciples ____

_____

(Note: This Antioch was in Syria. Another Antioch was in Pisidia.)

(c) God's purpose for Paul, as indicated, was to preach to the Gentiles and to spread the Gospel to the uttermost part of the world.

(d) The greatest departure in the Christian faith happened at Antioch. For the first time, the Gospel was preached directly to Greek idol worshippers and they were saved.

(5) Paul's Call and His First Missionary Journey (Acts 13:2 to Acts 14:28).

(a) The call by the Holy Spirit is found in Acts 13:2 _____

_____

(b) The first missionary journey was to reach people and to establish churches. A quick glance is all that can be covered. Barnabas and Paul went from Antioch, in Syria to:

Selucia (port city of Antioch, Acts 13:4), and sailed to

Cyprus (on Cyprus they preached at Salamis and Paphos, Acts 13:5-6), to

Perga in Pamphylia (Acts 13:13): John Mark left them there, to

Antioch, in Pisidia, where they preached much (Acts 13:14-50), to

Iconium (Acts 13:51), a divided multitude (Acts 14:4), to

Derbe (Acts 14:6), to

Lystra (Acts 14:8-19), and then retraced to Derbe, Lystra and Iconium (Acts 14:20-21), back to Pisidia, Perga and ordained men in all the churches (Acts 14:23-25). Then they sailed to

Antioch, in Syria, their starting point (Acts 14:26-28).

(c) The Jerusalem Council (Acts 15:1-35).

The Council was called in Jerusalem to answer the question, "Can a man become a Christian by trusting Jesus, or must he also keep the law of Moses, such as circumcision?" (Acts 15:1, 5). Peter knew the will of God and defended Paul and Barnabas. He spoke for Christian liberty (Acts 15:7-11). James, presiding over the conference declared the decision (Acts 15:19-27). The decision was that the Gentiles were not under the law. Gentiles were to show grace by not offending a Godly Jew (Acts 15:28-35). *The decision is spelled out in Galatians 2:7-9.* Peter, James and John were to preach to the Jew. Paul and Barnabas were to preach to the Gentiles. Look at Galatians 2:9 _____

_____

(6) Paul's Second Missionary Journey (Acts 15:36 to 18:22).

(a) Paul and Barnabas disagreed over taking John Mark on the second journey. Barnabas took Mark and went to Cyprus. Paul took Silas (Acts 15:36-41).

211

(b) The journey to establish churches and preach took them:

Through **Syria** and **Cilicia** (Acts 15:41), then back to **Derbe** and **Lystra** (there he found Timothy, Acts 16:1), then to **Phrygia** and **Galatia** down to **Troas** (Acts 16:6-8). At **Troas,** a man in a vision called them to **Macedonia** (Acts 16:9), Luke joins them in verse 10, with the use of "we." They landed at **Neapolis,** (now in Europe, acts 16:11), then went to **Philippi**, founded a church, were persecuted (Acts 16;11-40), then on to **Thessalonica** (Acts 17:1-9). Luke remained at Philippi. Notice *"they."* Then they journeyed to **Berea** (Acts 17:10-14), then Paul went alone to **Athens** (Acts 17:15-34), then on to **Corinth** (Acts 18:1-22), where he founded a church and was judged. (He wrote I and II Thessalonians from Corinth.)

(c) The result of this journey was the establishment of Christianity in Europe. This was a giant step in fulfilling the Lord's outline in Acts 1:8.

(7) Paul's Third Missionary Journey (Acts 18:23 to 21:14).

(a) Paul visited the churches of Galatia and then went to Ephesus. There he spent three years. The entire Roman province of Asia heard the Word of God from his journey to Ephesus (Acts 19). The riot in Ephesus sent him on his way and he revisited the churches of his second journey. When he arrived at Miletus, the port south of Ephesus, he called for the elders of the church and spoke to them great doctrinal truths (Acts 20:17-38). Note especially verses 21, 27, 28, 31, and 32.

(b) The Holy Spirit warned Paul not to go to Jerusalem, so he tarried at Philip's house (Acts 21:4-9). He was told a second time not to go to Jerusalem (Acts 21:10-13), but he went anyway (Acts 21:14-17). This concluded his missionary journeys.

Why go through all that material: *Because had Paul not taken those journeys and opened the Gospel to Europe and Asia, we would not have churches, as we know them, in the western world.*

(8) Paul's Suffering Gave us Doctrine (Acts 21:27 to 28:31).

(a) Even in Jerusalem he had to defend the faith (Acts 21:27 to 23:11).

Notice he gave a strong testimony of his conversion (Acts 22:1-21).

He has taken to the Sanhedrin, for preaching the Gospel, and there he caused the Pharisees and Sadducees to argue among themselves (Acts 23:1-9).

Write in the verse of grace in Acts 23:11 _____

_____

(b) Paul was sent to Caesarea to appear before Felix (Acts 23:23 to 24:27).

Two years he was imprisoned and then Festus succeeded Felix as the procurator, or governor, for Rome.

(c) Paul appeared before Festus, Herod Agrippa II and Bernice (Acts 25:6 to 26:32).

Paul had to plead his case before Festus, then King Agrippa II (the first Agrippa in Acts 12 beheaded James). He again preached by using his testimony. Notice Acts 26:28 _____

_____

(d) He was sent to Rome (Acts 27 through 28).

The Lord had told him he would bear witness of Him in Rome (Acts 23:11). Christians already in Rome met him on the Appian Way (Acts 28:15).

During this imprisonment, Paul wrote the Philippian Letter. He also wrote Philemon and Colossians and Ephesians.

(e) After two years, it is certain he was freed. One cannot place the Pastoral epistles, I and II Timothy and Titus, in the book of Acts. After Paul's liberation in Rome, he went back to Ephesus and left Timothy there (I Timothy 1:3). He went to Crete and left Titus (Titus 3:12). After this, he was arrested again, in or near Dalmatia, and taken back to Rome.

Nero was then in power and his pleasure was killing Christians. Someone informed against Paul and he was placed in the Mamertine prison in Rome.

We do know that Paul wrote II Timothy in Rome shortly before his death. Tradition states that he was beheaded.

(f) The writings of Paul give us the doctrinal interpretation of the work and Word of our Lord. He sets forth fundamental doctrines of Scripture such as salvation is in justification of the sinner, by the Father, on the ground of Christ's atonement. The saved then, are partakers of all spiritual blessings.

His is emphatically the theology of grace. He interpreted the Hebrew Messiah to the Gentile world.

He wrote:

- Romans — from Corinth. **Theme:** In Christ, justification.
- I Corinthians — from Ephesus. **Theme:** In Christ, sanctification.
- II Corinthians — from Philippi. **Theme:** In Christ, consolation.
- Galatians — from Corinth. **Theme:** In Christ, liberation.
- Ephesians — from Rome. **Theme:** In Christ, exaltation.
- Philippians — from Rome. **Theme:** In Christ, jubilation.
- Colossians — from Rome. **Theme:** In Christ, completion.
- I Thessalonians — from Corinth. **Theme:** In Christ, translation.
- II Thessalonians - from Corinth. **Theme:** In Christ, exhortation.

In the church epistles, he tells us how to organize and conduct our churches.

The book of Hebrews is exactly that, a letter to the Hebrews. The authorship is always questioned, but from the evidence in Scripture, and from just reading the epistle, a layman can see the influence and authorship of Paul. Look at Hebrews 10:34; Hebrews 13:24; Hebrews 13:18-19.

(9) The Incomparable Ministry of Paul (II Timothy 4).

How do you explain the marvelous ministry of Paul. Was it all just a lot of travel and geography? He would go, preach a few days or months, and leave a vigorous church there, such as Phillipi and Thessalonica. How does one explain that? All of our churches of all faiths have missionaries and they labor for years, even a lifetime in one place. They may win one or a thousand, build a church or a school. It is so difficult to explain the difference?

There is a sovereign, elective purpose of God that cannot be explained in words. God does things in His way with His servants when He decides. So He took Paul and the only explanation is found in Acts 9:15.

Paul summed up his life in II Timothy 4.

5. THE USE OF THE OLD TESTAMENT BY PAUL:

(1) Every epistle is filled with Old Testament references. Paul had studied under Gamaliel. He was a Hebrew of the tribe of Benjamin. He knew the Old Testament and used it well to interpret Jesus Christ and the grace of God.

(2) Only one of Paul's letters is needed to see the depth and the way he used the Old Testament. Just read through the book of Galatians. What depth, what treasures, what truths are found in this epistle.

(We shall not give specific references.)

6. **THE LESSONS YOU SHOULD LEARN FROM PAUL:**

(1) Paul had been a Hebrew of Hebrews. The Lord changed Paul into a chosen vessel. All of us who are believers were chosen, just like Paul. The fact that we are chosen is based upon our freewill to accept Jesus in our hearts.

(2) A testimony of courage, like Stephen's death, makes an impression upon one who does not believe.

(3) Paul immediately started preaching. We often delay our service and testimony. Satan's greatest tool in the church is "delay, put off, wait."

(4) Paul traveled and started churches in Europe and Asia. He was the apostle to the Gentiles. America should honor his name for the way he was used of God to go to the Gentiles.

(5) Paul's teaching and doctrine of the grace of God is found in the epistles he wrote.

(6) The sovereign will and purpose of God is hard to explain in human terms but easy in spiritual terms.

DO YOU REMEMBER?

1. What was Paul's background?
2. What made Paul such a special chosen vessel for God?
3. What made Paul an apostle?
4. Who was Paul's first cohort and companion?
5. What was the great decision of the Jerusalem Council?
6. Where did Paul spend his last days and what did he do?

YOUR NEXT ASSIGNMENT:
1. Read Acts 4:32-37; Acts 11 through 15; Galatians 2:1-18.
2. The next study will be Barnabas, a great influence in the life of Paul.
3. Review your study on Paul.
4. Mark your Bible where new truths are learned.

(Note: Teachers will need a map for class study. Pupils will find a map of Paul's ministry in the back of most Bibles.

For the doctrines and teachings of Paul, study "Through the Bible In One Year," Volume 1, Lessons 34 through 46.)

Lesson 48
"Barnabas"

(Where lines are provided, look up the Scripture and write it or the main truth of the Scripture.)

1. **THE MEANING OF THE NAME:**

    Barnabas means "son of prophecy or exhortation."

2. **BASIC SCRIPTURES:**

    Acts 4:32-37; Acts 11 through 15; Galatians 2:1-18.

3. **FAMILY BACKGROUND:**

    Barnabas was a Levite of the land or island of Cyprus. He possessed land in Cyprus; in those days, he would have been a rich and influential man. Cyprus was a rich area, producing wine, oils, figs, honey and wheat. The Scripture does not give a reference to his background or family other than the fact that he was a Levite.

4. **WHAT THE NEW TESTAMENT SAYS ABOUT BARNABAS:**

    (1) The Great Generosity of Barnabas (Acts 4:32-37).

    (a) Influenced by the thrill and happiness of becoming Christians, and the afterglow of Pentecost, many men gave up their possessions and gave them to the apostles (verses 34-35).

    (b) Barnabas, so named by the apostles, was above all because of his great wealth. Underline Acts 4:36 and write in verse 37:

    _____

    His great generosity toward the spreading of the Gospel speaks of his Christian character. He was willing to give all that he possessed to help the apostles in their ministry.

    (2) Barnabas Believed Paul and Defended His Conversion (Acts 9:26-29).

    (a) The disciples in Jerusalem were afraid of Paul and would not believe that this man, of all men, had received Jesus in his heart. Write in Acts 9:26 _____

    _____

    They just could not believe that Saul of Tarsus was a disciple of Jesus Christ. His past was so fresh in their memories. He had persecuted the believers and had become the most feared and hated man in all Jerusalem.

    (b) Barnabas alone held out his hand to help Paul. Among all the believers, Barnabas was the only one who believed Paul's testimony of conversion on the road to Damascus. He rejoiced in the fact that such a man as Paul had found the same saving grace as he and other believers. One of the most important verses of Scripture in reference to Barnabas is found in Acts 9:27 _____

    _____

    (c) Barnabas took Paul to the apostles and told them about Paul's conversion. If Barnabas had done nothing else, he would deserve our thanks and admiration. He used his influence with the disciples and apostles because he believed in Paul and befriended him. As a result, Paul was to become an honored guest at any function or at any home. But it was Barnabas who first opened his heart and hand to Paul.

(3) Paul Visited In Peter's Home (Galatians 1:18-19).

(a) Barnabas had done good work for Paul. He took Paul to see the apostles, and he stayed with Paul until he was accepted. Barnabas was a big man, spiritually. He stepped aside and Peter, a pillar in the church, received Paul.

(b) Paul recorded the event in Galatians 1:18 _____

_____

Paul stayed with Peter for fifteen days. He also saw James, another pillar of the church, who would play a great part in the ministry of Paul. Underline Galatians 1:19.

(4) Barnabas Sent to the Church in Antioch (Acts 11:19-23).

(a) The scene now moves to Antioch, in Syria. Some of the believers who were scattered because of Stephen's martyrdom, left Jerusalem to bear witness. They had arrived in Antioch, the third largest city of the Roman Empire and the residence of the Roman governor of Syria.

(b) In Acts 11:19, some going to Phoenicia (modern Lebanon), and Cyprus and Antioch, preached *only* to the Jew. Underline verse 19.

(c) But those who were from Cyprus and Cyrene spoke to the Grecians or Greeks (this context refers to pure Greeks, rather than Greek-speaking Jews). In Antioch there existed a large Jewish colony. The city was , however, primarily Gentile and Greek, and those new arrivals preached the Gospel directly to the Gentiles. They believed and were converted. Write in Acts 11:20-21 _____

_____

(For further edification, see the "Wycliffe Bible Commentary" and "Acts, an Exposition," by W.A. Criswell.)

Those new converts had never been Jews; they were Gentiles who had come out of Greek idol worship and had been saved.

(d) This new venture was so successful that the church at Jerusalem selected Barnabas to go to Antioch and examine the conditions there. Their selection of Barnabas was another example of their high regard for this good man. Underline or mark Acts 11:22.

He was to look over and confirm the work as Peter and John had superintended the new work in Samaria (Acts :14-17).

(e) Barnabas gave encouragement and exhorted the new Christians to be faithful (Acts 11:23). His name indicates his gift of exhortation.

(5) Barnabas Had a Great Ministry at Antioch (Acts 11:24-30).

(a) The three graces given to Barnabas also give the key to his insight and spiritual wisdom. Notice Acts 11:24 _____

_____

After the graces of God are mentioned, then "much people were added to the Lord."

(b) Barnabas was so spiritually in tune with the workings of the Holy Spirit in Antioch that he knew he needed help. To cope with all of the questions of doctrine from so many people who had accepted Christ was too much for one man. Barnabas knew that only one man was equal to the great challenge in Antioch, and that man was Paul. So he went to Tarsus to find him. Notice Acts 11:25 _____

_____

Notice, "And the disciples were called Christians *first* at Antioch."

(c) Barnabas found Paul and took him to Antioch. There they spent one year working in the church and teaching the new Christians the Word of God. Write in Acts 11:26 _____

_____

(d) The church at Antioch sent help to the church at Jerusalem which was suffering from a famine. Paul and Barnabas were sent to take the offering (Acts 11:27-30).

The two returned to Antioch with John Mark (Acts 12:25).

(6) Barnabas and Paul Were Separated by the Holy Spirit (Acts 13:1-3).

(a) The church at Antioch was instructed by the Holy Spirit to separate Barnabas and Paul to a special work. Note Acts 13:2

_____

(b) The church recognized the call and they prayed and set the two apart and sent them on what is known as "the first missionary journey" (Acts 13:3). Read all of Acts 13. Note especially verses 46-52.

(7) Barnabas and Paul Sent to the Jerusalem Council (Acts 15:1-34).

(a) The church at Jerusalem heard about the message of Paul and Barnabas. The message was direct to the Gentiles and it was a message of grace. Some in the church at Jerusalem argued the fact that "circumcision and the keeping of the law" was necessary for admission into the church. They did not believe people could be saved out of the Gentiles by trusting Christ. Thus the council at Jerusalem was called to settle the question (Acts 15:1-5).

(b) The apostle Peter defended the Gospel of grace (Acts 15:7-11). Notice Peter's statement in verse 7, and underline.

(c) Barnabas and Paul spoke of work of the Holy Spirit among the Gentiles (Acts 15:12).

(d) James, the presiding officer at the council, gave the verdict of the Council (Acts 15:13-35). The verdict by James declared that the Gentiles were free. Write in Acts 15:19 _____

_____

Underline Acts 15:24 in your Bible.

The account given by Paul in Galatians 2 is an inside story of the results at Jerusalem. The key verse is Galatians 2:9 _____

_____

From Jerusalem, Barnabas and Paul returned to Antioch.

(8) The Contention Between Barnabas and Paul (Acts 15:36-41).

(a) Paul proposed a second missionary journey (Acts 15:36). Barnabas wanted to take John Mark, who had left them on their first journey when they had reached the mainland of Asia Minor. He had returned to Antioch. Paul did not like that instability and refused to take John Mark (Acts 15:37-38).

(b) The contention was sharp between them (Acts 15:39). Barnabas and Paul parted company and Barnabas took Mark and sailed to Cyprus. Paul selected Silas and started his second missionary journey (Acts 15:40-41). Remember that John Mark was a nephew to Barnabas (Colossians 4:10).

(9) The Affection Between Barnabas and Paul Did Not Cease.

(a) Paul spoke of Barnabas in three of his epistles. The tie that bound them together was Christ. Paul could not let a personal matter destroy his admiration of Barnabas. Notice I Corin-

217

thians 9:6 and underline in your Bible.

Now look at Galatians 2:1 _____

_____

Look again at Galatians 2:9.

(b) Paul spoke well of John Mark, the cause of the contention.
Notice II Timothy 4:11 _____

_____

How Barnabas spent the rest of his days is not revealed to us.
He does not appear in Scripture again.

5. **THE USE OF THE OLD TESTAMENT IN REFERENCE TO BARNABAS:**

(1) Acts 11:26 is a reference to Isaiah 62:1-2 _____

_____

(2) Acts 13:46-47 is a reference to Isaiah 42:6 _____

_____

(3) Acts 15:1 refers to Leviticus 12:3. Underline in your Bible.

(4) Acts 15:16-17 refers to Amos 9:11-12 _____

_____

(5) Barnabas and Paul preached the purpose of God through Israel and used Old Testament Scripture to prove their point. All of Acts 13 is a good example.

6. **THE LESSONS YOU SHOULD LEARN FROM BARNABAS:**

(1) He was generous when the Lord's work needed to go forward.

(2) He offered his heart and hand to one that was hated, even Paul. This was Christianity in action.

(3) Barnabas put his own reputation on the line by standing with Paul before the disciples and apostles. He turned the tide in favor of Paul.

(4) He had the qualities of a Christian gentleman. He was "a good man, full of the Holy Spirit, and faith."

(5) He saw the hand of God on Paul and went to seek Paul to take the lead position. Because of Barnabas doing that one thing, Paul became a giant in the faith.

(6) Barnabas was never jealous. He was absent of all envy. He stepped back and let Paul lead the way. All of these are characteristics of the real Christian life. We should learn from them.

DO YOU REMEMBER?

1. Barnabas was a _____ from _____
2. What did Barnabas do to show his devotion for the Lord?
3. When all others ran, or turned their back, what did Barnabas do for Paul?
4. What is the one great thing that makes Barnabas stand out in our minds?
5. What were some of his qualities?
6. What caused the contention between Barnabas and Paul? Did it last?

YOUR NEXT ASSIGNMENT:

1. Read Acts 16, 17, and 20; I Thessalonians 3:1-8; I Timothy 4:14; II Timothy 1, 3, and 4; I Corinthians 4:17; II Corinthians 1:19.
2. The next study will be Timothy, Paul's son in the faith.
3. Review your study of Barnabas.
4. Mark your Bible where new truths are learned.

Lesson 49
"Timothy, Paul's Son In the Faith"

(Where lines are provided, look up the Scripture and write it or the main truth of the Scripture.)

1. **THE MEANING OF THE NAME:**
   Timothy means "honored of God."

2. **BASIC SCRIPTURES:**
   Acts 16, 17, and 20; I Thessalonians 3:1-8; I Timothy 1; I Timothy 4:14; II Timothy 1, 3, and 4; I Corinthians 4:17; II Corinthians 1:19.

3. **FAMILY BACKGROUND:**
   Timothy was raised in Lystra. He was the son of Eunice, a Jewess, and a Greek father (Acts 16:1). His father probably passed away when Timothy was very young. He lived in a home he loved with his mother, Eunice, and his grandmother Lois. Both of these women were Christian Jews. Timothy had a good reputation in Lystra and was given a good report by the brethren there. Paul desired to have Timothy be a part of his ministry.

4. **WHAT THE NEW TESTAMENT SAYS ABOUT TIMOTHY:**
   (1) Timothy's Childhood Influence (II Timothy 1:5; 3:14-17).
      (a) Paul knew the background of young Timothy. We get a glimpse of his early influences in Paul's letter to his son in the faith. Look at II Timothy 1:5 _____

      _____

      (b) Timothy was taught the Scriptures from early childhood, in his home, by his mother and grandmother. Read and underline II Timothy 3:14 and write in verse 15 _____

      _____

      (c) From a child Timothy was taught the Scriptures. Paul affirms the importance of learning the Scriptures in his famous declaration to young Timothy in II Timothy 3:16 _____

      _____

   (2) Timothy Was Paul's Son In the Faith (I Timothy 1:2).
      (a) During Paul's second missionary journey, he discovered Timothy and invited him to join in the ministry. Because Timothy had a Greek father, Paul circumcised Timothy to render silent the many Jews who knew Timothy (Acts 16:1-3). From that point Timothy was Paul's faithful helper.
      (b) He was Paul's son in the faith, as indicated in I Timothy 1:2

      _____

      Also II Timothy 1:2 _____

      _____

   (3) Timothy Was Ordained to the Ministry (I Timothy 4:14).
      (a) Timothy was set apart, ordained, to the Gospel ministry.

Underline I Timothy 4:14.

Write in II Timothy 1:6 _____

_____

(b) He had, among many, the gift of evangelism. Look at II Timothy 4:5 _____

_____

(4) Timothy Accompanied Paul in His Work (Acts 17:14).

(a) Timothy undoubtedly left Lystra in Acts 16:4-5 and accompanied Paul through Galatia all the way to Berea. Look at Acts 17:14 and underline. In the next verse, Paul sent word for Silas and Timothy to follow him to Athens. Then he sent Timothy to Thessalonia.

(b) In I Thessalonians 3:1-2, Paul gives the account of Timothy being sent to that church. Look at verse 2 _____

_____

Timothy did not rejoin Paul until Paul had reached Corinth. After Paul left Athens, he went to Corinth. There Silas and Timothy joined him (Acts 18:5).

(c) Timothy remained with Paul in Corinth. Look at I Thessalonians 1:1 _____

_____

and II Thessalonians 1:1 _____

_____

But these verses were written to the church at Thessalonica, you might say. Yes, but they were written from Corinth and Paul mentions Silvanus (same as Silas) and Timothy as being with him.

(d) Timothy was sent to Corinth to handle some problems in the church. This occurred during Paul's three year ministry at Ephesus, so Timothy was sent back. His was a delicate task. Look at I Corinthians 4:17 _____

_____

If you want to know the problems facing Timothy, read on in I Corinthians 4 and 5.

(e) In Acts 20:4, Timothy is mentioned as one in the group who escorted Paul on the return from his third journey going toward Jerusalem. Scripture does not indicate that Timothy went to Jerusalem with Paul. Silence in Scripture speaks loud. It would seem that Timothy was in Jerusalem part of the time to know and understand the persecution of Paul.

(f) No mention is made of Timothy during Paul's imprisonment in Caesarea or his voyage to Rome.

(5) Timothy Was in Rome With Paul During His First Imprisonment (Philippians 1:1; Colossians 1:1).

(a) Timothy had evidently followed Paul to Rome. Since he was Paul's closest friend, Timothy got there some way. We know this fact from two of the prison epistles written by Paul.

(b) Look up Philippians 1:1 _____

_____

The letter written to Philippi, from Rome, mentions Timothy as being with Paul.

How do we know they are in Rome and imprisoned? Look at Philippians 4:22 and underline. There were some Christians even in Caesar's household. Paul and Timothy were there.

(c) Look at Philippians 2:19-22 and write in the central truth: ___

_____

(d) Turn to Colossians 1:1 _____

_____

Timothy was with Paul when he wrote this epistle. Then Paul uses "we" and "us" in his writing.

Notice Colossians 4:18 and you read, "Remember my bonds." The words tell us where Paul was as well as Colossians 4:3 _____

_____

(6) Timothy Received Two of the Pastoral Epistles (I and II Timothy).

(a) Timothy was serving the church at Ephesus when Paul wrote this first epistle to him (I Timothy 1:3). This was a post of great responsibility for one still so young. Look at I Timothy 4:12 _____

_____

(This is a good text for any youth gathering.)

(b) To Timothy, Paul wrote instructions about the order of the church. The basis of this first letter can be found in I Timothy 3:15 _____

_____

Paul warned Timothy about false teachers; gave him instructions concerning the worship in the church; the qualifications of church officers; the walk and life of a minister.

All of this was, and is, a pattern for the church of the living God.

(c) Personal exhortations instruct the church today.

Look up and underline I Timothy 4:16; 5:21. Write in I Timothy 6:11 _____

_____

(d) The charge to Timothy was great. He was to keep the order in the churches. Look at I Timothy 6:20 and underline.

This book, along with II Timothy and Titus, gives to the church today a standard, a guide. Oh, that more churches would teach these three books over and over.

(e) The second epistle to Timothy was written from Rome, just before Paul's death.

Note in II Timothy 1:2, "To Timothy, my dearly beloved son." This is a very personal book, containing some of the richest truths Paul ever wrote.

Notice II Timothy 2:1-2 and write in verse 2 _____

_____

(f) In this final epistle Paul warns again about apostasy (false teaching). In Chapter 3, Paul writes one of his greatest warnings to the church. Read verses 1 through 7 and then 11 through 17. Underline verse 16 if not already underlined.

(g) Paul's final words, ever to be penned by the great man of faith, are in II Timothy 4.

Have your class, or group, read verses 1-9 in unison and try to imagine Paul, in prison, ready to die, writing such a masterpiece.

(7) Timothy Was the Recipient of Great Church Truths.

(a) The two letters to Timothy are important to the church today.

Without them the order and organization of the church would be a constant problem.

(b) The lesson in these epistles, at first reading, should be:

— The Lord selected a "chosen vessel" named Paul.

— The Lord then placed Timothy with Paul.

— Paul taught Timothy how to care for the churches.

— Paul taught Timothy doctrine, and how to rebuke false doctrine.

— Paul taught Timothy concerning apostasy (false teaching).

The Lord used men, selected through His sovereign will, to give us the great truths of Scripture. Timothy is one of those unique characters of the Lord.

5. **THE USE OF THE OLD TESTAMENT IN REFERENCE TO TIMOTHY:**

(1) Paul and Timothy knew the Old Testament well. They were dealing with the church in the main. We will refer to only a few of the Old Testament passages used by Paul to Timothy.

(2) I Timothy 3:4 refers to Psalm 101:2 _____

_____

(3) I Timothy 3:6 refers to Proverbs 16:18 _____

_____

(4) I Timothy 4:14 refers to Deuteronomy 34:9 _____

_____

(5) I Timothy 5:18 refers to Deuteronomy 25:4 _____

_____

You will find other references as you study.

6. **THE LESSONS YOU SHOULD LEARN FROM TIMOTHY:**

(1) Every child should be taught the Word of God early in life, very early.

(2) A young person, dedicated to God, can be a great help and influence when serving in a secondary position.

(3) Timothy learned by doing, by listening, by watching and by the leadership of the Holy Spirit.

(4) Faithfulness and loyalty are hard to find in our day. Timothy was, and is, a good example.

(5) Suffering and rebuke should be anticipated by the Christian who faithfully serves the Lord. God can use those things to make us stronger in the faith.

(6) God always works through people. Timothy is another character of the Lord which speaks to young and old alike. Thank God for his life and ministry.

DO YOU REMEMBER?

1. Name the mother and grandmother of Timothy.

2. What was Timothy's nationality?

3. Why were I and II Timothy written?

4. What impression has Timothy left with you?

5. What were his apparent gifts?

6. Timothy was called Paul's _____

YOUR NEXT ASSIGNMENT:

1. Read the 25 verses of Philemon; Colossians 4.

2. Our study will be Philemon at the next session.

3. Review your study of Timothy.

4. Mark your Bible where new truths are learned.

Lesson 50
"Philemon"

(Where lines are provided, look up the Scripture and write it or the main truth of the Scripture.)

1. **THE MEANING OF THE NAME:**

   Philemon means "affectionate," "profitable."

2. **BASIC SCRIPTURES:**

   The 25 verses of Philemon; Colossians 4.

3. **FAMILY BACKGROUND:**

   Philemon was a wealthy, influential man of Colosse. He was a Christian, having been won to the Lord by Paul. The book reveals the goodness and mercy of God to a poor sinner, a slave, and the restoration of one to a place of dignity and service. The letter teaches ministers, and all Christians, not to look with disgust, nor to judge any person, regardless of their station in life.

   Philemon was written by Paul during his first imprisonment in Rome. It is a priceless page in the Scripture because it deals with practical righteousness, Christian brotherhood, Christian courtesy and love.

4. **WHAT THE NEW TESTAMENT SAYS ABOUT PHILEMON:**

   (1) Philemon, Dearly Beloved and Fellow Laborer (Philemon 1).

   (a) Paul sent the short letter to Philemon and called him "our dearly beloved and fellow laborer." The term "our" was used because Timothy was with Paul.

   (b) Paul also included the family of Philemon in his greeting (verse 2).

   Apphia was Philemon's wife. Archippus was his son and also the pastor of the church at Colosse. Look at Colossians 4:17

   _____

   (c) The church met in the home of Philemon (verse 2).

   (d) Paul extends his gracious wish for Philemon in the familiar words "grace and peace" (verse 3). These were the same endearing words the Lord used with the children of Israel in Numbers 6:24-26. This prayer is one of the great benedictions in the Bible. Write in Numbers 6:25 and 26 _____

   _____

   (2) Praise and Prayer for Philemon (verses 4—7).

   (a) Intercession was a part of Paul's prayer life. He did not make such statements as in verse 4 lightly or casually. Paul wrote to that church in Colosse the same type intercession. Look at Colossians 1:3.

   (b) Look at the words written to Philemon in verse 5 and then Colossians 1:4 _____

   _____

   Remember, Colosse was Philemon's home.

(c) Philemon's faith was a testimony of what Christ had done through him (verse 6).

(d) The hearts of the believers were refreshed because of Philemon's testimony (verse 7).

(3) Intercession Was Made for a Slave (verses 8-16).

(a) Paul was a diplomatic Christian. He had already mentioned his intercession for Philemon and his family; had complemented him on his faith and love for the Lord Jesus; had told Philemon of his testimony; had told him of the joy he and Timothy had in Philemon's love because the believers were refreshed by his devotion.

(b) Then, Paul said, "Wherefore," and began his intercession for the slave, Onesimus (verse 8). Paul mentioned his own boldness in Christ — a good characteristic for a Christian. Onesimus had stolen from Philemon and made his way to Rome. He ran from Philemon into the hands of Paul.

(c) Paul gave three reasons for his request (verse 9):

- "For love's sake" — Philemon's love for Paul.
- "Paul, the aged" — his suffering and persecution had aged Paul.
- "A prisoner of Jesus Christ" — actually in bonds in Rome.

(d) Paul's plea for Onesimus to Philemon (verse 10).

Paul called Onesimus, "my son, whom I have won to the Lord while a prisoner in Rome."

Don't forget the meaning of the name, Onesimus, "profitable."

(e) Paul knew the meaning of the name and he used the "old" and "new" man with Philemon (verse 11).

"In times past unprofitable, but now profitable to you and me." Since Onesimus had accepted Christ, he would be profitable to Philemon, to Paul and to Christ.

(f) Paul had to send Onesimus back to Philemon (verses 12-14).

Paul would have kept Onesimus, but he felt it was Philemon's place to decide. Paul said, "Receive him as you would my own heart" (verse 12).

The Scripture reveals that he was received in Colossians 4:9

_____

Onesimus had gone back to Colosse with Tychicus, who had taken the letters to Colosse and Ephesus.

(g) Paul emphasized the new relationship between Philemon and Onesimus because the slave had become a Christian (verse 15-16).

Onesimus was still a slave, according to the Roman law. The relationship was different now. Write in verse 16 _____

_____

Onesimus was "a brother beloved" since he had accepted Christ.

(4) Paul's Glorious Illustration of Imputation (verses 17-18).

(a) Paul wrote Philemon to receive Onesimus as he would receive Paul, himself. This appeal was based on the plea of Christ, to the Father, on behalf of the sinner who trusts Christ as Saviour. The sinner is received on the same standing that Christ is received.

(b) In verse 18, Paul said "If Onesimus has wronged thee or oweth thee anything, put that on my account."

This is an illustration of imputation. Impute means, "to lay

224

the responsibility or blame for one to another," "to credit by transferal." (Webster.)

In spiritual terms, *impute* or *imputation*, is the act of God whereby He accounts righteousness to the believer in Christ, who has borne the believer's sins. In other words, our sins were put on Christ who paid the penalty; therefore, because of that faith, "it is imputed to us for righteousness." Look at James 2:23 _____

_____

(5) Paul Expected Philemon to Respond as a Christian (verses 19-21).

   (a) Paul wrote with his own hand that he would repay the debt. In the same sentence he reminds Philemon of all he owed to Paul. Paul had won Philemon to the Lord during his ministry at Ephesus (Acts 19:10). Philemon owed Paul some consideration since the matter was the soul and life of a "brother beloved" (verse 19).

   (b) Paul would receive joy in the Lord if he could see the fruit of Christian love in Philemon. Paul needed the joy and refreshment from Philemon since he was in bonds in Rome (verse 20).

   (c) Paul expected and had confidence that Philemon would obey, and even do more than expected. He said so very bluntly in verse 21.

(6) Paul's Final Request of Philemon (verses 22-25).

   (a) Paul expected to be released from prison. Through the prayer of Philemon and others, Paul told his friend to prepare his home for his visit (verse 22).

   (b) The last three verses are greetings from others and a prayer for Philemon (verses 23-26).

5. **THE USE OF THE OLD TESTAMENT IN REFERENCE TO PHILEMON:**

   (1) Philemon 4 expresses praise. All praise is due to Him as in I Chronicles 29:13-14 _____

_____

   (2) Philemon 10 refers to Onesimus being found and won. Look up Isaiah 65:1 _____

_____

   (3) Philemon 15 refers back to Genesis 45:5-8. Write in Genesis 45:7

_____

   (4) Philemon 17 and 18 refers to Genesis 15:6 _____

_____

6. **THE LESSONS YOU SHOULD LEARN FROM PHILEMON:**

   (1) Since Onesimus was received so graciously (Colossians 4:9), we have every reason to believe Philemon and the church forgave him of all in the past. We should not hold ill will in our hearts regardless of a person's past life.

   (2) We see the effect of Christian love and concern toward one who might be a servant; one with little worldly goods.

   (3) The Lord allowed this little book to be in Scripture so we might learn, in a real way, the act of imputation.

   (4) This letter teaches the vital lesson that social issues are corrected when the heart is corrected.

   (5) We should learn the value of one person, a slave, who ran because he had done wrong. He was led providentially to Paul. His value was restored in Christ.

(6) This little book teaches the effect of Christianity on labor, management, business relationships generally, and the spirit of love and justice toward all.

DO YOU REMEMBER?

1. What does the book of Philemon teach, practically?

2. What was Philemon's station in life?

3. Philemon was from Colosse and he had a church _____

4. How did Paul show diplomacy in writing to Philemon?

5. What is imputation?

6. Who was Onesimus?
    What did he do?

7. What did you learn about the Christian life from this study?

YOUR NEXT ASSIGNMENT:

1. Read Matthew 13:55; Mark 6:3; Acts 1:13-14; Acts 15:13-23; I Corinthians 15:7; Galatians 1:19; Galatians 2:9-12; James 1 through 5; Jude 1.

2. The next study will be on the Bible character, James, the Lord's brother.

3. Review your notes on Philemon.

4. Mark your Bible where new truths are learned.

Lesson 51
"James, the Lord's Brother"

(Where lines are provided, look up the Scripture and write it or the main truth of the Scripture.)

1. **THE MEANING OF THE NAME:**

   James means "supplanter," the same as Jacob.

   (James is the English equivalent for the Hebrew *Jacob*.)

2. **BASIC SCRIPTURES:**

   Matthew 13:55-57; Mark 6:1-6; Acts 1:13-14; Acts 15:13-23; I Corinthians 15:7; Galatians 1:19; Galatians 2:9-12; James 1 through 5; Jude 1.

3. **FAMILY BACKGROUND:**

   James was the son of Joseph and Mary. The name appears approximately forty times in the New Testament and refers to three different men. This lesson shall deal with that James who was mentioned as one of the "brethren" of Jesus. Arguments rage over this James. Some scholars think he is the James who was a cousin of Jesus, known as the son of Alphaeus. This, in most cases, is an argument in favor of the perpetual virginity of Mary. The New Testament teaches that Jesus grew up among a family of four brothers named James, Joses, Juda and Simon; and several sisters. (Naturally, these were half brothers and sisters, *in the flesh*.) This James, of the family of our Lord, is the James for our study in this lesson.

4. **WHAT THE NEW TESTAMENT SAYS ABOUT JAMES:**

   (1) James Was Among the Brothers of Jesus (Matthew 13:55).

   (a) When Jesus went back to His hometown of Nazareth, He taught them in the synagogue as He had in other places. But in "His own country," He was doubted. The crowd referred to Jesus: "Is not this the carpenter's Son? Is not His mother called Mary?"

   (b) Then you read Matthew 13:55-56 _____

   _____

   His brothers are named and His sisters mentioned. *The James of this passage was not the son of Zebedee or Alphaeus, but the son of Mary and the carpenter, Joseph.*

   (c) Mark also recorded the same truths about the family of Jesus. For Mark to write about the brothers and sisters of Jesus makes it very important. Mark wrote brief, factual material. He had no time to write details, only the necessary facts. Look at Mark 6:1-6 and read the passage. Now write in verse 3 _____

   _____

   (2) James Was Not a Believer During the Life of Jesus (Matthew 13:57-58).

   (a) It seems strange that the "brethren" (a name signifying the four brothers of Jesus), did not believe in the Messiahship of our Lord during His life. Notice Matthew 13:57 and note that Jesus said, "A prophet is not without honor, save in his own country, *and in his own house*."

Write in the next verse, 58 _____

_____

    (b)   Look at John 7:5 _____

_____

Read the entire context of John 7:1-10. The emphasis of unbelief is found in the entire passage.

    (c)   James was an eyewitness of the goodness and the character of Jesus. He lived with Jesus in the same house. The impact of Jesus upon James was not revealed until after James believed in Jesus as the Messiah.

(3) James Was a Witness of the Resurrection of Christ (I Corinthians 15:7).

    (a)   It was a special manifestation of the risen Lord that changed James. Look at I Corinthians 15:7 _____

_____

In verse 5, of the same Chapter, Jesus had been seen by the twelve, then of five hundred at once (verse 6), then "seen of James," then "he was seen by Paul, as one born out of due season" (verse 8).

Paul would only know of one James whom he loved and admired. That was the James so prevalent in the Acts of the apostles, the same James Paul saw in Jerusalem after his conversion. Look up Galatians 1:19 _____

_____

In that verse, Paul calls James "the Lord's brother."

    (b)   When James saw Jesus, after His resurrection, he was transformed into a disciple and a believer.

    (c)   James, the Lord's brother, was *not* an apostle.

(4) The Brethren and Mary Were With the Apostles in the Upper Room (Acts 1:13-14).

    (a)   From the passage, we know the brethren (brothers) of Jesus were in the Upper Room with their mother, Mary. Write in Acts 1:14 _____

_____

Note: "Mary, the mother of Jesus, and with *His* brethren." These are the same "brethren" as you will find in Matthew 12:46-50; Mark 3:31-35; Luke 8:19-20; John 2:12; John 7:3-10.

    (b)   James had seen the resurrected Lord, and then the "brethren" are among the believers, with Mary, waiting in the Upper Room. James had gone rapidly and told them about the Lord Jesus.

(5) James Became the Head of the Church at Jerusalem (Acts 12:17; Acts 15:13-34; Acts 21:18; Galatians 2:9-12).

    (a)   From the first organization of the church at Jerusalem, James appeared to be the head, the leader, the chief elder, the pastor. Look at Acts 12:17 and underline.

    (b)   James presided over the famous Jerusalem council. Look at Acts 15:13 _____

_____

He declared the final result of the council in Acts 15:19-34. Write in verse 19 _____

(c) James was the head of the elders (Acts 21:18). Write in: ___

___

(d) James, along with Peter and John, were pillars in the church at Jerusalem. Notice Galatians 2:9 and 12. Write in verse 12

___

(e) In his position, James' lifework was to smooth the passing of Jews over to Christianity. He stood on the same foundation of faith as Paul, as was mentioned in Acts 15:13. Just as Paul became all things to all men because he was sent to all, James became a Jewish Christian to the Jews. He did not think it wise for Gentile believers to offend the Jews. Read Acts 15:19-21 again.

(6) James Was the Author of the Epistle of James (James 1:1).

(a) James wrote his epistle to Hebrew Christians. Look at James 1:1 _____ _____

___

In this verse, James called himself a servant, not a brother of the Lord Jesus. He wrote to the "twelve tribes scattered abroad." In becoming Christians, they had not ceased to be Jews.

(b) James was probably the first epistle of the New Testament, written about A.D. 45.

(7) James, a Pastor, Wrote as a Pastor (James 1 through 5).

(a) James wrote practically and experientially. He started the writing of this epistle by telling the Hebrew Christians to "count it all joy when ye fall into testings" (James 1:2).

"The trying of faith worketh patience (James 1:3). Through tests we are brought to the point of asking for wisdom and "God giveth liberally to all who ask of God" (James 1:5-6).

(b) James wrote, "Be ye doers of the Word and not hearers only" (James 1:22). This gives to each individual a mirror, which is the Word of God, and the Word gives liberty (James 1:23-25).

(c) James 2:1-13 deals with attitudes toward people. We are not to discriminate between the rich and poor in the house of God.

(d) James declared that faith is tested by works (James 2:14-26). He used Abraham as an illustration. The reference should guard against misunderstanding. Abraham's justification by faith (Genesis 15:6) was before the seal of the covenant, circumcision (Genesis 17:10). His offering of Isaac was twenty years later (Genesis 22). The man who was justified by works had already been justified by faith for twenty years. So *faith* justifies the person and *works* justifies the faith.

(e) Again, practical James dealt with the tongue (James 3:5-10). The tongue should be controlled by faith and used to praise God, not curse Him.

(f) James spoke of the Christian attitude toward the world (James 4:1-10). The theme of James, "Submit yourselves therefore to God. Resist the devil and he will flee from you" (verse 7). This is one of the most practical chapters in the Word.

(g) James' teaching on prayer (James 5:13-16) is practical fundamental teaching. (See *Through the Bible In One Year,* Volume 1 p. 211, for thorough study.)

(**Note:** the purpose of these points in the book of James is to make the pupil read the book and see what a giant pastor and preacher James was. His writings reveal his character and personality.)

229

(8) Secular References to James, the Lord's Brother.

  (a) Josephus wrote about James and said that when Annas, the high priest and ruler of Jerusalem, slew this godly man, it so infuriated the people of Jerusalem that they deposed Annas and the governor after a reign of only three months. James was martyred for the cause of Christ.

  (b) James was the great personality of the first Christian century. The apostles John, Peter and Paul showed respect and deference to James.

5. THE USE OF THE OLD TESTAMENT IN REFERENCE TO JAMES:

  (1) John 7:2-3 is a reference to Leviticus 23:34 and Nehemiah 8:14 and 18: _____

  _____

  (2) John 7:3-5 is a fulfillment of Psalm 69:8 _____

  _____

  (3) Acts 15:5 refers to Leviticus 12:3 _____

  _____

  (4) Acts 15:29 refers to Genesis 9:4 _____

  _____

  (5) James 1:10-11 refers to Isaiah 40:8 _____

  _____

  From these few examples one can see how the Old explains the New.

6. THE LESSONS YOU SHOULD LEARN FROM JAMES:

  (1) Jesus grew up in a normal atmosphere of a home. He had a family of brothers, sisters, mother, and foster father. He was human, yet God in the flesh.

  (2) If you had been in James' position, would you have reacted any differently to Jesus? Brothers often disagree.

  (3) The influence of a person is often more effective with casual acquaintances. Yes, some people are without honor in their own hometown. Why? The people always look upon the person as "that mean kid" or some other remembrance.

  (4) All the family of Jesus believed when James testified of the risen Christ. It would be psychologically difficult to accept an older brother as the Messiah, the Son of God.

  (5) James became the leader of the Jerusalem church, a "bridge," for the passing over of Jews to Christianity. He was a vital part of the first Christian church.

  (6) James was a practical preacher and writer. The book of James is the Proverbs of the New Testament, a practical learning experience for the believer.

DO YOU REMEMBER?

1. Who was this James, the one in our study?
2. When did James finally believe in his brother as the Messiah?
3. This James became _____
4. James presided over the _____
5. What kind of a preacher was James?
6. Was this James an apostle?

YOUR NEXT ASSIGNMENT:

1. Your assignment for the next study is different. Read twenty Chapters; all of Galatians, Ephesians, Philippians, and Colossians.

2. The study at the next session will be "Jesus Christ, the Name Above Every Name." What do those twenty Chapters have to do with Jesus? Read them and find out for yourself.

3. Review your notes on James.

4. Mark your Bible where new truths are learned.

Lesson 52
"Jesus Christ, the Name Above All Names"

(Where lines are provided, look up the Scripture and write it or the main truth of the Scripture.)

This lesson shall be different. There will be no standard outline form as in other lessons. Jesus is the subject of both Old and New Testaments.

The lesson is *not* meant to be a complete theological study of Jesus. It is rather a simple, down to earth study for laypeople and young people. A lot of Scripture searching will be necessary so you will remember the main truths of this lesson.

1. **HIS NAMES:**

   There are more than 200 names attributed to Jesus. The three most used are:

   Jesus, His personal name, "He shall save His people from their sins" (Matthew 1:21).

   Christ, His title, meaning "anointed," corresponding to the Hebrew Mashiah, "anointed, Messiah" (Luke 2:11).

   Lord, His sovereignty and majesty and power. No one can own Him as Lord until they receive Him into their heart and life (Luke 2:11). Look at Acts 2:36 _____

   _____

2. **HIS PRE-EXISTENCE:**

   (1) Jesus existed before He came in human form as a babe in Bethlehem. A few Bible truths will be sufficient.

   (2) "In the beginning was the Word (Jesus), and the Word (Jesus) was with God, and the Word (Jesus) was God." (John 1:1).
   Look at John 1:2 _____

   _____

   Now, John 1:3 _____

   _____

   (3) Jesus declared His glory with the Father. Look up John 17:5 ___

   _____

   (4) Jesus humbled Himself for us. Look at Philippians 2:5-8 and underline the seven steps down from glory for Jesus:

   - "being in the form of God, thought it not robbery to be equal with God."
   - "but made Himself of no reputation."
   - "took upon Him the form of a servant."
   - "and was made in the likeness of men."
   - "He humbled Himself."
   - "became obedient unto death."

- "even the death of the cross."

From these verses, Paul speaks of the pre-existence of Jesus and why He came to the earth made in the likeness of man. He came to take upon Himself our sins.

(5) Jesus was before all things. He was creator with God, the Father. Turn to Colossians 1:15-19 and underline verse 16. Write in verse 17 _____

_____

3. **PROPHECIES OF HIS FIRST COMING:**

(1) The first direct prophecy of Christ is in Genesis 3:15. **This becomes one of the most important verses in Scripture.** God said to Satan (in the form of a serpent), *The seed of this woman, whom you have deceived, will crush your head, Satan, and you will only bruise His heel.* That is one of the most unusual things in the Bible because a *woman does not have seed. Seed is masculine.* The term is only used in reference to Jesus Christ and not to any other person ever born. Jesus was to be the seed of the woman and He would finally defeat Satan. You are the seed of your father. His seed started your life, your blood stream and gave you your name.

Jesus, and only Jesus, was the seed of woman.

(2) God selected a nation who would produce that Seed. Genesis 9:26 and 11:10 gives the first clue. He would be a descendant of Shem. Notice Genesis 11:16, then verses 24, 25, and 26. The nation was to be the Hebrew nation, later named Israel.

Notice Genesis 12:3; 14:13. He would be the seed of Abraham, the first Hebrew.

(3) He, the Seed, Jesus, would come through Isaac (Genesis 17:19).

(4) He was to be a descendant of Jacob (Israel) (Genesis 28:10-15). Look at Numbers 24:17 _____

_____

(5) He was to come through the tribe of Judah (Genesis 49:10).

(6) He was to be born of the house of David and be heir to David's throne (II Samuel 7:12-15). Look up Isaiah 9:7 and underline in your Bible.

(7) Micah 5:2 predicted His birth in Bethlehem.

(8) Isaiah 7:14; Micah 5:3 foretold His virgin birth.

(9) Isaiah 53:3 predicted His rejection by His own people.

(10) Psalm 22:1-21; Isaiah 50:6; 53:1-12; Zechariah 13:7; are all prophecies of His suffering and death on the cross.

(11) Isaiah 53:9. His burial.

(12) Psalm 16:9-10; Jonah 1:17 prophesied His resurrection.

(13) Psalm 8:5-6; 110:1 describes His ascension into heaven.

These are only a few of the prophecies of His coming, His death and resurrection. These are pure prophecies from Old Testament men of God.

4. **HIS INCARNATION, THE VIRGIN BIRTH**

(1) The word "incarnation" means "in the flesh" or "in bodily form." Jesus came from glory and took upon Himself the flesh of humanity. He came as the Son of God, the Seed of woman.

(2) He became man and God. In becoming flesh, He laid aside His glory but in no sense did He lay aside His deity. He was God-Man.

(3) Jesus was born of a virgin, Luke 1:30-31; Matthew 1:18, 25.

(4) The Word, Jesus, became flesh, incarnate. Look at John 1:14 __

_____

(5) Jesus came to the earth exactly as the Old Testament prophets had proclaimed. Galatians 4:4 is one of the great Scriptures (along

with John 1:14) about His incarnation. Please write in Galatians 4:4 _____

_____

(6) Jesus declared His incarnation in John 16:28. Underline in your Bible.

(7) The incarnation was "God manifest in the flesh" (I Timothy 3:16).

(8) Jesus, the full revelation of God's glory, was the exact image of His person (Hebrews 1:3).

(9) His incarnation fulfilled the prophecies of the Old Testament prophets. The prophecies noted in a previous section of this lesson, section 3, numbers (1) through (8), have been answered.

Notice:

- Genesis 3:15 fulfilled in Galatians 4:4
- Genesis 9:26; 11:10 fulfilled in Luke 3:36
- Genesis 12:3; 14:13 fulfilled in Matthew 1:1
- Genesis 17:19 fulfilled in Luke 3:34
- Genesis 28:10-15 fulfilled in Matthew 1:2
- Genesis 49:10 fulfilled in Matthew 1:2
- Isaiah 9:7 fulfilled in Luke 1:32
- Micah 5:2 fulfilled inLuke 2:4-7
- Isaiah 7:14 fulfilled in Luke 1:30-31.

These Scriptures verify the fact that *"Prophecy came not in old time by the will of man: but holy men of God spake as they were moved by the Holy Spirit" (II Peter 1:21).*

5. HIS BODY, THE CHURCH

(1) Before He died on the cross, Jesus prophesied that He would build His church (Matthew 16:18). The church in Greek is the "ecclesia," meaning "the called out ones."

(2) Paul said, "the household of God, built upon the foundation of the apostles and prophets, Jesus Christ Himself being the chief corner stone" (Ephesians 2:19-20). Now underline Ephesians 2:21-22.

(3) The church was a mystery, hidden from the prophets of old and Paul describes the mystery in Ephesians 3:1-10. Read and underline verses 5, 9, and 10.

(4) The church is the body of Christ. The church is the bride and Jesus is the groom. Paul compared the wife-husband relationship to that of the church and Christ. Read Ephesians 5:21-33. Write in verse 33 _____

_____

(5) Every believer is a priest unto God (I Peter 2:5, 9, and 10).

Every member of His body is a living stone, Jesus being the chief corner stone. Look at I Peter 2:6 and underline. Write in verse 10

_____

_____

The main privilege of a priest is access to God, through one Mediator, Jesus Christ (I Timothy 2:5).

Jesus is our Great High Priest (Hebrews 4:14).

6. HIS DEATH ON THE CROSS

(1) Jesus died as a sacrifice for the sins of the world. He became our Redeemer (redemption means "to deliver, or save, by paying a price"). Look at Mark 10:45; I Corinthians 6:20; Ephesians 1:7. Underline in your Bible I Peter 1:18-19 and Galatians 3:13.

(2) Jesus, in His death, took our sins and paid the price for sin (I Peter 3:18; 2:24-25; II Corinthians 5:21).

Write in Romans 5:6 _____

_____

Also Romans 5:8 _____

_____

(3) By accepting Christ, and His death on the cross, one is justified. "Justification" is God declaring a sinner righteous on the basis of his faith in Jesus Christ. Look at Romans 3:24, 26, and 28 and write in verse 24 _____

_____

7. HIS RESURRECTION

(1) The resurrection of Jesus Christ is the cornerstone of the Christian faith and it proves His deity, who He is (Acts 2:24).

(2) The resurrection was victory over sin and death (I Corinthians 15:54-57).

(3) Christ arose to be the head of the church (Ephesians 1:20-23).

(4) He was raised for our justification. Look at Romans 4:24-25 and write in verse 25 _____

_____

(5) The resurrection assures our faith and our ultimate victory in Him (I Corinthians 15:14, 17, 25, 26). Write in only verse 17 _____

_____

(6) Jesus always spoke of resurrection when He spoke of His death. Notice this in Matthew 16:21 _____

_____

Also Matthew 17:22-23 _____

_____

Also Luke 9:22; Mark 9:30; Matthew 20:19.

(7) Proof of His resurrection (I Corinthians 15:6).

There are at least seventeen appearances of Christ after His resurrection recorded in Scripture. He was seen, recognized and conversed with many people. Just a few of the Scriptures are given.

John 20:11-17; Matthew 28:9-10; Luke 24:34; Mark 6:12-13; Mark 16:14; Luke 24:36-43; John 20:26-29; John 21:1-23; I Corinthians 15:5-7.

8. HIS ASCENSION

(1) Jesus told of His Ascension (John 14:2-3).

Jesus, talking with the eleven, said, "I go and prepare a place for you. And if I go and prepare a place for you, I will come again, and receive you unto myself; that where I am, there ye may be also."

In that same chapter, Jesus told them He would not leave them comfortless. The Holy Spirit would be sent by the Father, in the name of Jesus. He would come to teach all truth (John 14:16, 17, 26).

Again in John 14:28, Jesus said He was going away.

(2) The Ascension marked the end of His earthly ministry (Mark 16:19; Luke 24:50-51; Acts 1:9-11).

Look at Acts 1:9; "He was taken up"

"A cloud received Him out of their sight"

verse 10: "He went up"

verse 11: "is taken up (received up) into heaven."

He had promised them, in verse 8, the power of the Holy Spirit.

(3) Jesus is at the right hand of God, a place of universal Lordship (Acts 7:55-56).

Turn to Ephesians 1:20 _____

Also Colossians 3:1 and underline.

Other references as to His position in glory are: Hebrews 1:3; Hebrews 10:12, I Peter 3:22.

(4) His present work on the right hand of the Father (Romans 8:34). He is our High Priest (Hebrews 8:1). He is there for believers. "He ever liveth to make intercession for us" (Hebrews 7:25).

Look at Hebrews 2:17 _____

_____

We pray "in the name of Jesus." He intercedes for us with the Father. He is our Advocate. Look at Romans 8:34 _____

_____

(5) His present work on the earth is indicated in many Scriptures. He is at work in His church and is with His church "always, even to the end of the earth." Look at Matthew 28:19-20; John 14:18, 20; John 10:10.

His present work is the formation, calling out a people, to form His body, the church.

9. **HIS SECOND COMING (John 14:3).**

(1) The same Jesus shall come again just as He ascended into Heaven. Look at Acts 1:11 _____

_____

(2) Jesus did go away and He said He would come again (John 14:3).

(3) Jesus shall come for His bride (I Thessalonians 4:13-18). Look at that Scripture and write in verse 16 _____

_____

Notice, "the Lord *Himself.*" He is coming, literally.

(4) He is coming in the clouds, just as He ascended in the clouds. Look at Revelation 1:7 _____

_____

Also I Thessalonians 4:17 and underline. He shall be clothed in God's garments.

(5) He will come as King (Matthew 25:31, 34).

He shall sit upon the throne of His glory as indicated in verse 31.

_____

(6) He will come in power and glory (Matthew 24:27-31).

The entire Chapter of Matthew 24 should be read and studied. The coming of Jesus will be literal; as literal as His ascension, His resurrection, His death.

(7) We should look for His appearing (II Timothy 4:8). Look at Titus 2:13 _____

_____

(8) Then shall be fulfilled Revelation 22:20 _____

_____

"Even so, come Lord Jesus."

10. **OTHER NAMES OF JESUS**
  - *Emmanuel* Isaiah 7:14
  - *Wonderful* — Isaiah 9:6
  - *Counselor* —Isaiah 9:6
  - *The Mighty* God — Isaiah 9:6
  - *The Prince* of Peace — Isaiah 9:6

- *The Branch* — Zechariah 6:12
- *The Last* Adam — I Corinthians 15:45

There are so many names for Jesus. These are the most familiar to most people.

As we close this study of Bible Characters, your knowledge of Jesus Christ should swell in your heart. From the first prophecy of Jesus in Genesis 3:15 to Revelation 22:20, the paramount purpose has been to reveal how God uses people to bring about His will and His purpose.

We started the study with the first Adam and have concluded with the Second Adam, the only two men created without sin. The first was "earthly" and the second was "heavenly." Between these two we find God's record of the sin of man and His plan of salvation offered to all through His Son, the Second Adam.

In all 52 lessons, covering 61 characters, you have witnessed God working in mysterious ways in lives and nations. He is still the same. If you are one of His body, you should now be ready for service. If you are not a Christian, redemption is dependent on personal acceptance of the Redeemer.

"Eye hath not seen, nor ear heard, neither have entered into the heart of man, the things which God hath prepared for them that love Him" (I Corinthians 2:9). Amen!

Declaration of Christ's Lineage

"IN THE BEGINNING GOD CREATED THE HEAVEN AND THE EARTH" GEN. 1:1

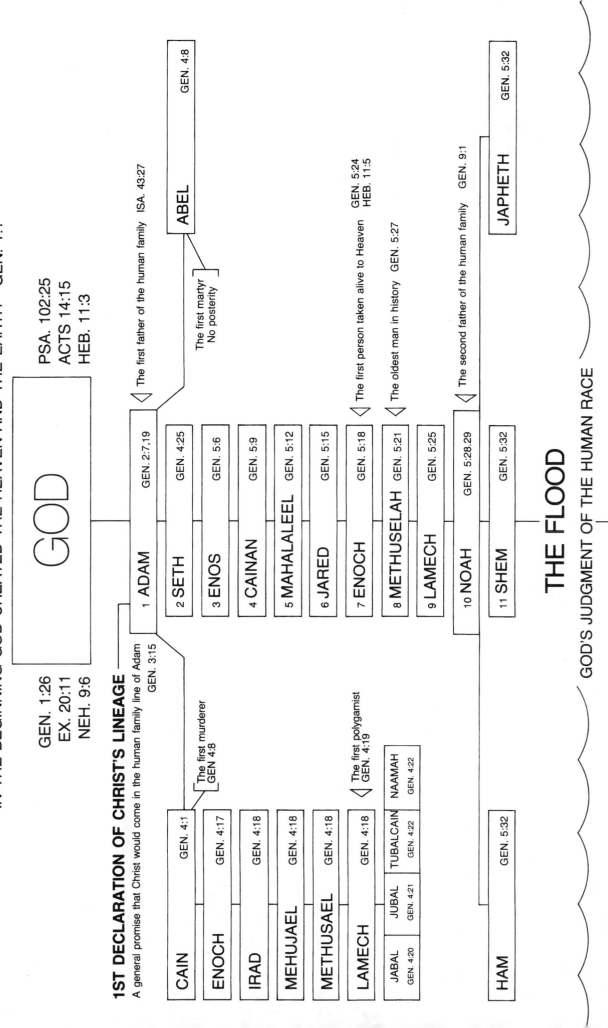

GEN. 1:26
EX. 20:11
NEH. 9:6

PSA. 102:25
ACTS 14:15
HEB. 11:3

GOD

1ST DECLARATION OF CHRIST'S LINEAGE
A general promise that Christ would come in the human family line of Adam
GEN. 3:15

The first father of the human family ISA. 43:27

ABEL GEN. 4:8

The first martyr
No posterity

1 ADAM GEN. 2:7,19

2 SETH GEN. 4:25

3 ENOS GEN. 5:6

4 CAINAN GEN. 5:9

5 MAHALALEEL GEN. 5:12

6 JARED GEN. 5:15

7 ENOCH GEN. 5:18

The first person taken alive to Heaven GEN. 5:24 HEB. 11:5

8 METHUSELAH GEN. 5:21

The oldest man in history GEN. 5:27

9 LAMECH GEN. 5:25

The second father of the human family GEN. 9:1

10 NOAH GEN. 5:28,29

JAPHETH GEN. 9:1 GEN. 5:32

11 SHEM GEN. 5:32

THE FLOOD
GOD'S JUDGMENT OF THE HUMAN RACE

CAIN GEN. 4:1

The first murderer
GEN 4:8

ENOCH GEN. 4:17

IRAD GEN. 4:18

MEHUJAEL GEN. 4:18

METHUSAEL GEN. 4:18

LAMECH GEN. 4:18

The first polygamist
GEN. 4:19

JABAL GEN. 4:20

JUBAL GEN. 4:21

TUBALCAIN GEN. 4:22

NAAMAH GEN. 4:22

HAM GEN. 5:32

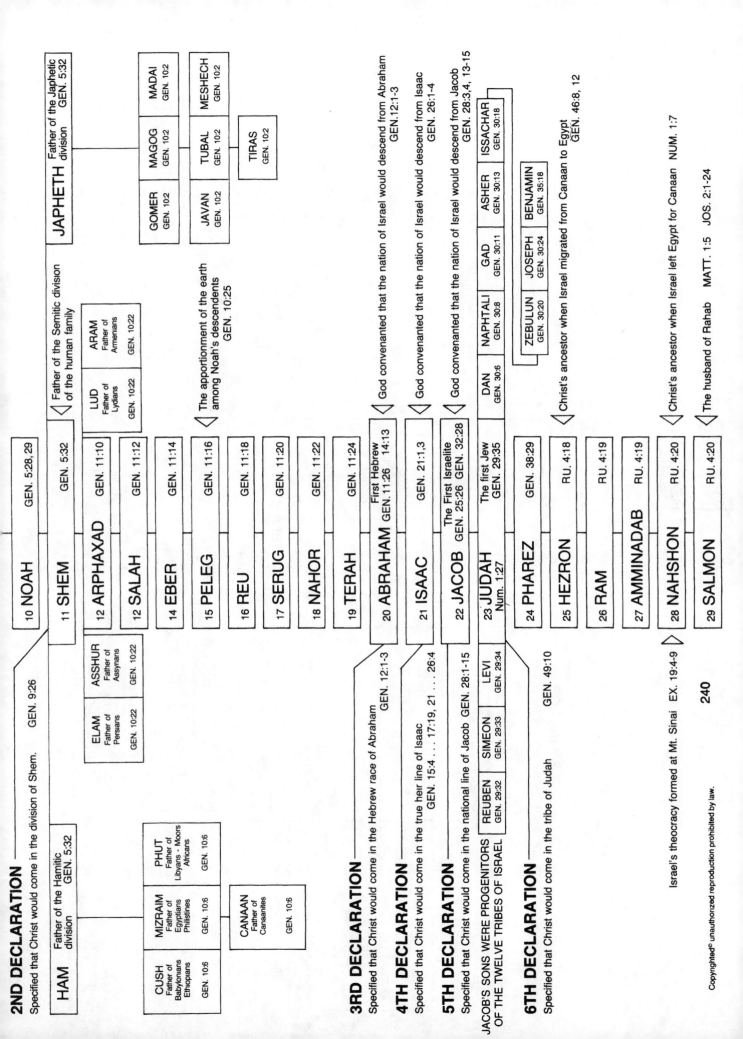

2ND DECLARATION

Specified that Christ would come in the division of Shem. GEN. 9:26

HAM — Father of the Hamitic division GEN. 5:32

- CUSH — Father of Babylonians, Ethiopians GEN. 10:6
- MIZRAIM — Father of Egyptians, Philistines GEN. 10:6
- PHUT — Father of Libyans - Moors, Africans GEN. 10:6
- CANAAN — Father of Canaanites GEN. 10:6

JAPHETH — Father of the Japhetic division GEN. 5:32

- GOMER GEN. 10:2
- MAGOG GEN. 10:2
- MADAI GEN. 10:2
- JAVAN GEN. 10:2
- TUBAL GEN. 10:2
- MESHECH GEN. 10:2
- TIRAS GEN. 10:2

SHEM — Father of the Semitic division of the human family GEN. 5:32

- ELAM — Father of Persians GEN. 10:22
- ASSHUR — Father of Assyrians GEN. 10:22
- LUD — Father of Lydians GEN. 10:22
- ARAM — Father of Armenians GEN. 10:22

Line of descent:

- 10 NOAH — GEN. 5:28, 29
- 11 SHEM — GEN. 5:32
- 12 ARPHAXAD — GEN. 11:10
- 12 SALAH — GEN. 11:12
- 14 EBER — GEN. 11:14
- 15 PELEG — GEN. 11:16 (The apportionment of the earth among Noah's descendents GEN. 10:25)
- 16 REU — GEN. 11:18
- 17 SERUG — GEN. 11:20
- 18 NAHOR — GEN. 11:22
- 19 TERAH — GEN. 11:24
- 20 ABRAHAM — First Hebrew GEN. 11:26 14:13
- 21 ISAAC — GEN. 21:1,3
- 22 JACOB — The First Israelite GEN. 25:26 GEN. 32:28
- 23 JUDAH — The first Jew GEN. 29:35 Num. 1:27
- 24 PHAREZ — GEN. 38:29
- 25 HEZRON — RU. 4:18
- 26 RAM — RU. 4:19
- 27 AMMINADAB — RU. 4:19
- 28 NAHSHON — RU. 4:20
- 29 SALMON — RU. 4:20

God convenanted that the nation of Israel would descend from Abraham GEN.12:1-3

God convenanted that the nation of Israel would descend from Isaac GEN. 26:1-4

God convenanted that the nation of Israel would descend from Jacob GEN. 28:3,4, 13-15

Twelve tribes:

- REUBEN GEN. 29:32
- SIMEON GEN. 29:33
- LEVI GEN. 29:34
- DAN GEN. 30:6
- NAPHTALI GEN. 30:8
- GAD GEN. 30:11
- ASHER GEN. 30:13
- ISSACHAR GEN. 30:18
- ZEBULUN GEN. 30:20
- JOSEPH GEN. 30:24
- BENJAMIN GEN. 35:18

Christ's ancestor when Israel migrated from Canaan to Egypt GEN. 46:8, 12

Christ's ancestor when Israel left Egypt for Canaan NUM. 1:7

The husband of Rahab MATT. 1:5 JOS. 2:1-24

3RD DECLARATION

Specified that Christ would come in the Hebrew race of Abraham GEN. 12:1-3

4TH DECLARATION

Specified that Christ would come in the true heir line of Isaac GEN. 15:4 ... 17:19, 21 ... 26:4

5TH DECLARATION

Specified that Christ would come in the national line of Jacob GEN. 28:1-15

JACOB'S SONS WERE PROGENITORS OF THE TWELVE TRIBES OF ISRAEL

6TH DECLARATION

Specified that Christ would come in the tribe of Judah GEN. 49:10

Israel's theocracy formed at Mt. Sinai EX. 19:4-9

240

7TH DECLARATION

Specified that Christ would come in the kingly line of David
2 SAM. 7:12-15 . . . PSA. 89:3, 4, 28-37;132:11

THE KINGLY LINE OF THE "KING OF KINGS"
ISA. 9:6-7   REV. 19:16

THE "SEED OF THE WOMAN" LINE OF
THE SUFFERING MESSIAH   GEN. 3:15   ISA. 53:1-12

30 BOAZ	RU. 4:21
31 OBED	RU. 4:21
32 JESSE	RU. 4:22

The husband of Ruth   RU. 4:13

| 33 DAVID | RU. 4:22 |

Kingly line (left column):

The builder of the Jews' first great Temple 1 KI. 5:5; 6:38; 8:1-66

| 34 SOLOMON | 2 SAM. 12:24, 1 CHR. 3:5 |

The Kingdom of Israel was divided, and never again was a nation of power 1 KI. 12:1

35 REHOBOAM	1 CHR. 3:10
36 ABIA	1 CHR. 3:10
37 ASA	1 CHR. 3:10
38 JEHOSHAPHAT	1 CHR. 3:10
39 JORAM	1 CHR. 3:11
40 AHAZIAH	1 CHR. 3:11

The only member of the royal line not destroyed by wicked Queen Athaliah 2KI. 11:1-3

41 JOASH	1 CHR. 3:11
42 AMAZIAH	1 CHR. 3:12
43 AZARIAH	1 CHR. 3:12
44 JOTHAM	1 CHR. 3:12
45 AHAZ	1 CHR. 3:13
46 HEZEKIAH	1 CHR. 3:13

In 721 B.C. Israel was taken captive by the king of Assyria, and became known as the "Ten Lost Tribes" 2 KI. 17:1-6 18:9,10 1 CHR. 5:26

| 47 MANASSEH | 1 CHR. 3:13 |
| 48 AMON | 1 CHR. 3:14 |

Seed of the woman line (right column):

34 NATHAN	LU. 3:31
35 MATTATHA	LU. 3:31
36 MENAN	LU. 3:31
37 MELEA	LU. 3:31
38 ELIAKIM	LU. 3:30
39 JONAN	LU. 3:30
40 JOSEPH	LU. 3:30
41 JUDAH	LU. 3:30
42 SIMEON	LU. 3:30
43 LEVI	LU. 3:29
44 MATTHAT	LU. 3:29
45 JORIM	LU. 3:29
46 ELIEZER	LU. 3:29
47 JOSE	LU. 3:29
48 ER	LU. 3:28

241

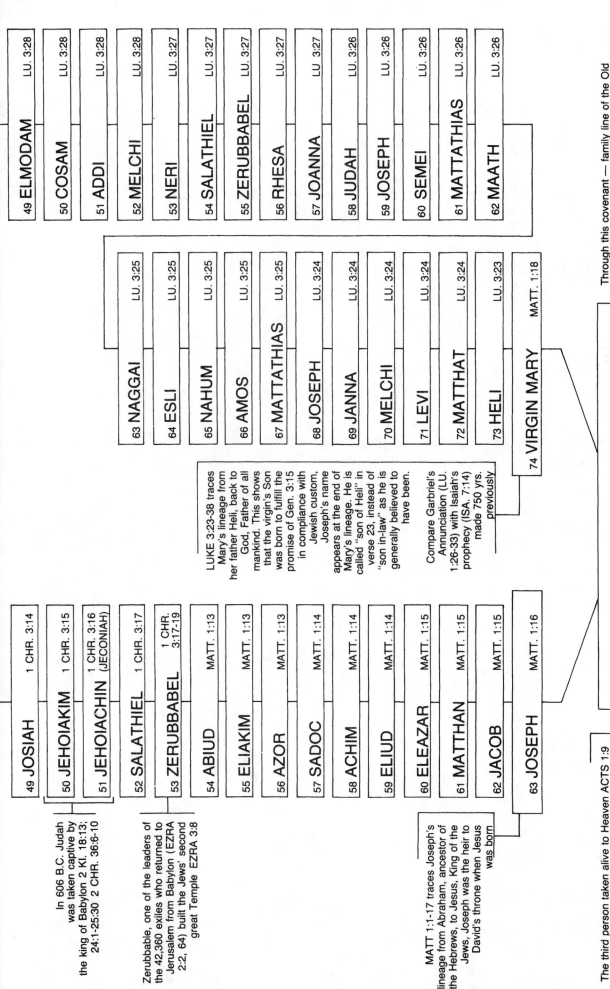

49 ELMODAM	LU. 3:28
50 COSAM	LU. 3:28
51 ADDI	LU. 3:28
52 MELCHI	LU. 3:28
53 NERI	LU. 3:27
54 SALATHIEL	LU. 3:27
55 ZERUBBABEL	LU. 3:27
56 RHESA	LU. 3:27
57 JOANNA	LU. 3:27
58 JUDAH	LU. 3:26
59 JOSEPH	LU. 3:26
60 SEMEI	LU. 3:26
61 MATTATHIAS	LU. 3:26
62 MAATH	LU. 3:26

63 NAGGAI	LU. 3:25
64 ESLI	LU. 3:25
65 NAHUM	LU. 3:25
66 AMOS	LU. 3:25
67 MATTATHIAS	LU. 3:25
68 JOSEPH	LU. 3:24
69 JANNA	LU. 3:24
70 MELCHI	LU. 3:24
71 LEVI	LU. 3:24
72 MATTHAT	LU. 3:24
73 HELI	LU. 3:23
74 VIRGIN MARY	MATT. 1:18

LUKE 3:23-38 traces Mary's lineage from her father Heli, back to God, Father of all mankind. This shows that the virgin's Son was born to fulfill the promise of Gen. 3:15 in compliance with Jewish custom, Joseph's name appears at the end of Mary's lineage. He is called "son of Heli" in verse 23, instead of "son in-law," as he is generally believed to have been.

Compare Garbriel's Annunciation (LU. 1:26-33) with Isaiah's prophecy (ISA. 7:14) made 750 yrs. previously

49 JOSIAH	1 CHR. 3:14
50 JEHOIAKIM	1 CHR. 3:15
51 JEHOIACHIN	1 CHR. 3:16 (JECONIAH)
52 SALATHIEL	1 CHR. 3:17
53 ZERUBBABEL	1 CHR. 3:17-19
54 ABIUD	MATT. 1:13
55 ELIAKIM	MATT. 1:13
56 AZOR	MATT. 1:13
57 SADOC	MATT. 1:14
58 ACHIM	MATT. 1:14
59 ELIUD	MATT. 1:14
60 ELEAZAR	MATT. 1:15
61 MATTHAN	MATT. 1:15
62 JACOB	MATT. 1:15
63 JOSEPH	MATT. 1:16

In 606 B.C. Judah was taken captive by the king of Babylon 2 KI. 18:13; 24:1-25:30 2 CHR. 36:6-10

Zerubbable, one of the leaders of the 42,360 exiles who returned to Jerusalem from Babylon (EZRA 2:2, 64) built the Jews' second great Temple EZRA 3:8

MATT 1:1-17 traces Joseph's lineage from Abraham, ancestor of the Hebrews, to Jesus, King of the Jews, Joseph was the heir to David's throne when Jesus was born

JESUS THE CHRIST

Through this covenant — family line of the Old Testament, God revealed himself as the Christ, and established the church of the New Testament, MATT. 16:13-9.

JN. 12:45	COL. 2:9	JN. 8:58
JN. 17:5	1 TIM. 3:16	JN. 1:1-14
		JN. 3:16
		JN. 10:30

The third person taken alive to Heaven ACTS 1:9

Christ was of the fruit of David's body. God was His real Father, Mary, his mother, and Joseph, his legal father. God gave Him His Spirit, Mary gave Him His body, and Joseph gave Him His throne
REV. 22:13, 16.

242

ENERGIZE, REVITALIZE, REVOLUTIONIZE

Your Bible Study With Another Selection
From Hensley Publishing

Through the Bible in One Year
Alan B. Stringfellow • ISBN 1-56322-014-8

God's Great & Precious Promises
Connie Witter • ISBN 1-56322-063-6

Preparing for Marriage God's Way
Wayne Mack • ISBN 1-56322-019-9

Becoming the Noble Woman
Anita Young • ISBN 1-56322-020-2

Women in the Bible — Examples To Live By
Sylvia Charles • ISBN 1-56322-021-0

Pathways to Spiritual Understanding
Richard Powers • ISBN 1-56322-023-7

Christian Discipleship
Steven Collins • ISBN 1-56322-022-9

Couples in the Bible — Examples To Live By
Sylvia Charles • ISBN 1-56322-062-8

Men in the Bible — Examples To Live By
Don Charles • ISBN 1-56322-067-9

7 Steps to Bible Skills
Dorothy Hellstern • ISBN 1-56322-029-6

Great Characters of the Bible
Alan B. Stringfellow • ISBN 1-56322-046-6

Great Truths of the Bible
Alan B. Stringfellow • ISBN 1-56322-047-4

The Trust
Steve Roll • ISBN 1-65322-075-X

Inspirational Study Journals

A Fresh Approach
to Individual and Small-Group Study

In His Hand
Patti Becklund • ISBN 1-56322-068-7

In Everything You Do
Sheri Stout • ISBN 1-56322-069-5

Rare & Beautiful Treasures
Nolene Niles • ISBN 1-56322-071-7

Love's Got Everything To Do With It
Rosemarie Karlebach • ISBN 1-56322-070-9

AÑADE ENERGIA, REVITALIZA Y REVOLUCIONA

Tu Estudio Biblico Con Otras Selecciones
De Publicaciones Hensley

A Traves De La Biblia En Un Año
Alan B. Stringfellow • ISBN 1-56322-061-X

*Preparando El Matrimonio
En El Camino De Dios*
Wayne Mack • ISBN 1-56322-066-0

Mujers En La Biblia
Sylvia Charles • ISBN 1-56322-072-5

Parejas En La Biblia
Sylvia Charles • ISBN 1-56322-073-3

Decisión Difícil
Dr. Jesús Cruz Correa & Dra. Doris Colón Santiago
ISBN 1-56322-074-1